Bulbs

The TIME LIFE
Complete Gardener

Bulbs

By the Editors of Time-Life Books
ALEXANDRIA, VIRGINIA

The Consultants

Brent Cartmell Heath is a third-generation bulb grower who owns and operates Heath Enterprises Limited in Gloucester, Virginia, with his wife, Becky. Their businesses include the internationally known wholesale and retail mail-order bulb outlet called the Daffodil Mart, a landscaping concern specializing in plantings for estates and businesses, a nature study enterprise, and a consulting firm specializing in the effective use of bulbs in today's landscapes. Heath has spent most of his life in rural Gloucester County and now devotes a considerable portion of his time to traveling around the country lecturing and consulting.

Michael A. Ruggiero has been on the staff of the New York Botanical Garden for 25 years and is currently senior curator in the horticulture department, where he oversees the Peggy Rockefeller Rose Garden, extensive bulb collections, and the work practicum for the School of Professional Horticulture. He is the author of *The Spotter's Guide to Wildflowers* (1975) and *Perennial Gardening* (1994), the latter one of the Pantheon "American Garden Guides" series. He teaches or lectures on more than 30 horticultural subjects, including a course on woody plants for the University of Connecticut at Bartlett Arboretum. He also serves as a garden judge for the American Hemerocallis Society and is active in daylily hybridization.

Library of Congress Cataloging in Publication Data
Bulbs/by the editors of Time-Life Books.
p. cm.—(The Time-Life complete gardener)
Includes bibliographical references (p.) and index.
ISBN 0-7835-4112-0
1.Bulbs. 2.Bulbs—Pictorial works. I. Time-Life Books. II. Series
SB425.B86 1995 635.9'44—dc20   95-9168   CIP

This volume is one of a series of comprehensive gardening books that cover garden design, choosing plants for the garden, planting and propagating, and planting diagrams.

Time-Life Books is a division of **TIME LIFE INC.**

PRESIDENT AND CEO: John M. Fahey Jr.

TIME-LIFE BOOKS

MANAGING EDITOR: Roberta Conlan

Director of Design: Michael Hentges
Director of Editorial Operations: Ellen Robling
Director of Photography and Research:
John Conrad Weiser
Senior Editors: Russell B. Adams Jr., Dale M. Brown,
Janet Cave, Lee Hassig, Robert Somerville,
Henry Woodhead
Special Projects Editor: Rita Thievon Mullin
Director of Technology: Eileen Bradley
Library: Louise D. Forstall

PRESIDENT: John D. Hall

Vice President, Director of Marketing:
Nancy K. Jones
Vice President, Director of New Product Development:
Neil Kagan
Associate Director, New Product Development:
Quentin S. McAndrew
Marketing Director, New Product Development:
Wendy A. Foster
Vice President, Book Production: Marjann Caldwell
Production Manager: Marlene Zack
Quality Assurance Manager: Miriam Newton

THE TIME-LIFE COMPLETE GARDENER

Editorial Staff for *Bulbs*

SERIES EDITOR: Janet Cave
Deputy Editors: Sarah Brash, Jane Jordan
Administrative Editor: Roxie France-Nuriddin
Art Director: Alan Pitts
Picture Editor: Jane Jordan
Text Editors: Paul Mathless (principal),
Darcie Conner Johnston
Associate Editors/Research-Writing: Sharon Kurtz,
Mary-Sherman Willis
Technical Art Assistant: Sue Pratt
Senior Copyeditors: Anne Farr (principal),
Donna D. Carey, Colette Stockum
Picture Coordinator: David A. Herod
Editorial Assistant: Donna Fountain
Special Contributors: Susan S. Blair, Jennifer Clark,
Marianna Tait-Durbin, Olwen Woodier (research-writing); Bonnie Kreitler, Warren Schultz (writing);
Jim Hicks (editing); John Drummond (art);
Lina B. Burton (index).

Correspondents: Christine Hinze (London),
Christina Lieberman (New York). Valuable
assistance was also provided by Liz Brown
(New York), Judy Aspinall (London).

Cover: *Hinting at the vast diversity of bulb flower shapes, 'Schoonoord' tulips, a double-flowering, early-blooming variety, front Armenian grape hyacinth spires in a Virginia garden in spring.* ***End papers:*** *A Kirkland, Washington, perennial border draws vivid color from two lily cultivars, the pink 'Malta' and the white 'Nepal'.* ***Title page:*** *Pink Cyclamen heterifolium glows in the afternoon light of autumn in a Charlottesville, Virginia, woodland setting.*

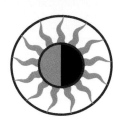

CHAPTER ONE

Gardening with Bulbs

The great and varied bulb clan holds no end of delights for gardeners. Bulbs usher in the garden's first colors in spring and see out the last blooms of fall. Ideal companions, they withdraw when their time is up, then reappear when you most appreciate them the next year.

Whether among their own kind or mixed with other types of flowers, as in the Virginia garden at left, bulbs make for a colorful scene. Here, tulips and jonquils form a pool of golden yellow with daisylike doronicums on an April morning. The rich violet-blue of grape hyacinths offers a pretty contrast to the yellow hues and picks up the lavender-pink of a nearby azalea. The emerging foliage of bee balm, a frost-tinged silver-gray, cools the scene.

Bulbs are amenable to every planting scheme from the regimental trim of a formal bed to the loose abundance of a woodland plot to the cozy confines of a window box. The following pages will show you how to cultivate, care for, and propagate all types of bulbs in all of these settings.

NOTE: *The key lists each plant type and the total quantity needed to replicate the garden shown. The diagram's letters and numbers refer to the type of plant and the number sited in an area.*

A. *Muscari armeniacum 'Blue Spike' (grape hyacinth) (many)* **B.** *Narcissus jonquilla 'Pipit' (jonquil) (30)* **C.** *Narcissus jonquilla 'Baby Moon' (jonquil) (24)* **D.** *Monarda didyma 'Violet Queen' (bee balm) (2)* **E.** *Aquilegia caerulea (Rocky Mountain columbine) (3)* **F.** *Doronicum caucasicum x 'Miss Mason' (Caucasian leopard's-bane) (5)* **G.** *Monarda didyma 'Cambridge Scarlet' (bee balm) (3)* **H.** *Rhododendron 'Girard's Pleasant White' (azalea) (1)* **I.** *Vinca minor (periwinkle) (24)* **J.** *Tulipa 'Sweet Harmony' (single late tulip) (12)* **K.** *Rhododendron hybrid (azalea) (1)*

Bulbs in the Flower Garden

A POCKET OF HARDY IRIS BULBS
Flourishing at the base of a tree in the Pacific Northwest, a patch of Iris reticulata emerges in early spring. This hardy species returns year after year if given the right conditions.

Flowering bulbs were probably the earliest ornamental plants to be grown. More than 3,500 years ago the Minoans on Crete cultivated *Lilium candidum* (Madonna lily) as a garden flower, and valued *Crocus sativus* (saffron) for its yellow pistil used in cooking. Today, many bulbous plants are grown for the distinctive shape, color, and scent of their flowers. Others, such as onions, garlic, carrots, potatoes, and celery, are more appreciated as edibles.

Bulb flowers have evolved to accommodate the insects and birds that pollinate them. They have assumed myriad forms and colors, and they range vastly in size, from a crocus less than 4 inches tall to *Dahlia imperialis* at a towering 20 feet.

Ninety percent of the bulbs we grow for flowers belong to just six genera: *Lilium, Iris, Tulipa, Hyacinthus, Narcissus,* and *Gladiolus.* But within these six are hundreds of species and thousands of varieties. And gardeners also have an array of other bulb genera from which to choose. In nursery catalogs these plants are often called miscellaneous or specialty bulbs. Regardless of their disparate physical characteristics, however, all bulbs have one thing in common—ingenious food-storage systems that ensure their survival and distinguish them from all other plants.

Understanding Bulb Botany

Garden bulbs are descendants of tough perennials that grew in areas with long periods of drought or cold. They adapted by evolving underground repositories to conserve food and moisture for hard times.

This makes bulbs particularly useful as garden plants, because they come with a ready-made food supply. When conditions become favorable, bulbs grow rapidly. As the plants expand to full size and come into bloom, they deplete those food and moisture reserves. But for the rest of their time in leaf they are busy building up the next year's provisions, using photosynthesis to convert water and nutrients into stored energy for growth and other life processes.

Among the broad category of plants known as bulbs, four distinct types of storage systems evolved: true bulbs, corms, tubers, and rhizomes *(right)*. Each type has a characteristic appearance and growth cycle *(pages 10-11)*, and understanding the way they function is essential to cultivating these plants successfully. Equally important is a knowledge of where given varieties of bulbs originated.

TUBERS

The potato-like begonia tuber (near right) produces shoots from eyes at the top and projects thin roots from its bottom surface. The dahlia's tuberous roots (far right) store food, while its smaller roots take up water and nutrients. Growth buds will cluster on the old stem, called the crown.

Four Types of Bulbs

The four types of bulbs—tubers, corms, true bulbs, and rhizomes—all consist of fleshy tissue where nutrients and moisture are stored. But each bulb type has a unique structure for housing these essentials. Even within a single type, the tubers, differences exist: Dahlias, for example, are thickened roots, whereas the swollen part of a begonia tuber is a stem. Corms, too, are modified stems, but in a corm the swollen base becomes the storage tissue. True bulbs have a modified stem, but they also contain an embryonic flower attached to a basal plate. This is surrounded by fleshy scales that hold nutrients. A rhizome is a thickened stem growing horizontally and functioning as the food reserve.

CORMS

Corms like crocus (upper left) and freesia (lower left) are actually stems packed with nutrients. Shoots emerge from the bud at the top. The corm itself is protected by a layer of dried leaf bases.

TRUE BULBS

Among true bulbs, a daffodil (left) is known as tunicate, because it has a papery protective outer cover, or tunic. Inside are fleshy leaves called scales. Shoots will emerge from the top, and roots from the basal plate. The lily bulb below is called imbricate; its scales are loosely arranged and have no tunic.

RHIZOMES

This piece of a canna rhizome consists of fleshy rootstock growing horizontally. The dried, flaky vertical tip is the remains of last season's stalk and leaves. The next season's plant will grow from the eye at the side of the rhizome, with new roots emerging around and beneath the eye.

9

Native Habitats of Bulbs

A key to raising bulbs is understanding the growing conditions that drove their evolutionary development. Most of the winter-hardy bulbs we grow today, for example, come from regions having hot, dry summers and cool, wet winters, such as California and the Mediterranean. Crocus, tulip, daffodil, hyacinth, and iris thrive in these conditions.

Another group comes from areas of steamy summers and dry winters, such as are found in areas of South America and Africa. These plants make up a group called tender bulbs—canna, freesia, amaryllis, agapanthus, dahlia, hippeastrum, and the showier gladiolus—which cannot tolerate freezing temperatures.

A third type comes from temperate areas of northern Asia and North America, where there is periodic rainfall. The tender bulb lycoris and some hardy lilies are of Asian origin. Some fritillaries, lilies, and anemones—all hardy bulbs—are natives of the United States.

Despite having come from such diverse parts of the world, many bulbs have proved able to perennialize—to grow year after year—in the United States. Even frost-tender bulbs such as agapanthus, canna, and dahlia have managed to make themselves at home in the warmer areas of the country. And where

The Growth Cycles of Bulbs

The roots and shoots of true bulbs, such as this narcissus, start to grow in autumn, slow down in winter, and lengthen rapidly in the spring when the soil warms up. As buds emerge and the blooms open, the bulb begins to divide. Though the flowers soon fade, the foliage persists, capturing light for photosynthesis. Before the foliage dies and the plant goes dormant, seed pods develop at the base of the flower where it meets the stem (far right). The narcissus's primary means of reproduction, however, are daughter bulbs that develop from the original. Lilies grow daughter bulbs too, as well as tiny bulblets, which emerge around the base of the bulb and the crown of the plant, and even smaller bulbils, found in the axils of the plant's leaves.

TRUE BULB: NARCISSUS

A corm, such as this crocus, begins its growth cycle in early spring, as soon as the ground thaws. It sends down roots, and shoots emerge from the apical bud at its top. As it grows and flowers, the corm is depleted. Then, as the plant gathers nourishment for the next season, a new corm develops on the top of the dying original (third from left). But before the plant goes dormant, additional reproductive units—miniature corms called cormels—form between the old corm and the new one (far right).

CORM: CROCUS

summers are warm but winters are frosty, a gardener can still enjoy tender bulbs from one year to the next. You simply have to lift the bulbs from the ground when they go dormant and overwinter them indoors *(pages 64-65)*— or grow the tender beauties in pots indoors or in a greenhouse.

Creating the Right Conditions

To encourage your bulbs to perennialize, it is important to approximate their native habitat. Almost all bulbs need well-drained soil; they are susceptible to rot if wet, especially during dormant periods. *Galanthus* (snowdrop), narcissus, scilla, lily, and *Trillium* (wake-robin)

tolerate summer rains; crocus, tulip, iris, colchicum, and some fritillaries prefer it dry.

Gardeners in the Deep South (Zones 9 and 10) who wish to grow such hardy bulbs as crocus, hyacinth, snowdrop, scilla, tulip, and narcissus face a challenge: Hardy bulbs require a period of chilling before they can bloom in the spring. In the warm zones this must be accomplished artificially, by taking the bulbs up and refrigerating them over the winter. Check the Plant Selection Guide *(pages 98-103)* and the encyclopedia *(pages 106-151)* for the cultural needs of your bulbs.

RHIZOME: CANNA

Rhizomes, such as this canna, send new roots downward in the summer and produce leafy flower stalks from growth buds that emerged the previous year. At the same time, new growth buds emerge on the fleshy rootstock, which grows continuously as its older portions become increasingly tough and fibrous and lose their ability to produce new buds. By the time the foliage has died back (far right), the new growth buds are poised to produce flowers once the next growing season comes around.

TUBER: BEGONIA

Unlike other bulbs, a begonia tuber is not consumed, broken up, or worn out by the effort of producing flowers and foliage. Sending out shoots from its growth buds and roots from its base (near right), it does become partially depleted. But then, as it takes up nutrients during the remainder of the season, it is replenished and develops new buds. The tuberous roots of a dahlia, on the other hand, are completely spent in the work of producing a flowering stem. Its reproductive strategy, aside from making seeds, is to grow new tuberous roots alongside the old ones.

Designing with Bulbs

Gardeners today take a heterogeneous approach to using bulbs, incorporating them into traditional beds and borders *(pages 16-19)* and using them as colorful accents in combination with other plants. Bulbs shine in these settings. Yet there is something undeniably satisfying about all-bulb groupings, with their rich, simultaneous burst of color—especially in spring, when the rest of the garden is just beginning to stir. With such unlimited design choices, it's often a good idea to create a plan on paper first, to help you see how you might include bulbs in your garden *(pages 14-15)*.

The Elements of Design

The first rule of any garden design is to be sure it marries well with your house and the site. Is the architecture of your home formal or informal? A Federal-style brick house, with its elements of balance and symmetry, seems an apt setting for a formal garden. Such a garden would likely have tidy beds of uniform plantings, outlined in straight edges and simple curves. The bulbs would be closely grouped, and the effect would be a stunning carpet of color. Tulips, hyacinths, and daffodils, placed in upright, soldierly formations and edged with annuals, make good formal plantings.

To exploit the transitory nature of bulbs, highlight different parts of the garden as the seasons progress. For example, in the spring you can brighten the entrance to the front door and the path leading to it with a mass planting of early-blooming crocuses. As the weather warms up, shift attention to a pool edged with a bank of blooming lilies and allium or perhaps to a shady bench flanked by caladium and calla lilies. On a shady terrace, arrange large pots of colorful begonias.

The grounds around a frame house of less stately lines might be planted in mixed drifts of bulbs that would multiply over the years. Such an informal approach is characterized by irregular curves and asymmetrical shapes. A cluster of lilies, for example, might be balanced by a dwarf conifer on one side and low-growing blue fescue grass on the other.

An informal garden plan could also include

The Workings of the Color Wheel

A simple color wheel like this one is based on the three primary colors, yellow, red, and blue. Mixing pairs of primaries produces the secondary colors: Red and yellow make orange, yellow and blue make green, and blue and red make violet. These six hues can be further combined to produce such intermediate colors as blue-green or red-violet. Colors from opposite sides of the wheel are said to contrast; those next to each other, to be harmonious. In addition, colors on the yellow-orange-red side are considered "warm" and have the optical effect of seeming to leap forward, while those opposite them are called "cool" and seem to recede.

naturalized plantings—drifts of robust species able to spread on their own from year to year *(pages 20-23)*. Such plantings might be started at the edge of a lawn or along a woodland floor. A rock garden made of randomly spaced stones set into a hillside also expresses a natural, informal look when planted with daffodils, scillas, or alliums *(pages 24-25)*.

Of course, you may choose some combination of formal and informal elements. Deliberate contrast can be effective—a jewel-like formal bed, say, next to a naturalized woodland shade garden. But keep proportions in mind; plant large plants in large places, small plants where they can be isolated and featured.

Choosing Bulbs for Color

Deciding on a color scheme will help organize your choice of bulbs. The color wheel above is useful for combining plant colors, showing you how to achieve contrast by choosing colors from opposite sides of the wheel or harmony by pairing adjacent colors.

Two further dimensions of color to consider are shades and tints. Shades are colors darkened by the addition of black, such as deep purple from violet. Tints are colors that have been lightened by the addition of white, such as pink from red.

Bulbs can serve as accent plants or provide color in broad swaths. For example, a small group of *Allium giganteum,* with large purple globes on 4-foot stems, would accent the foliage of a nearby planting of *Heuchera* 'Palace Purple' (alumroot) and the flowers of blooming *Lavandula* (lavender). But if you plant

the allium in large bands among ornamental grasses and the rich yellow flowers of a few *Achillea* 'Coronation Gold' (yarrow), the contrast in colors and the scale of the planting will project the allium to center stage.

It is generally best to cluster like colors together and to group the clusters next to each other to make patterns. An exception might be when you combine different colors of the same type of bulb—a spring bed of *Anemone blanda* (Greek anemone) in blue, white, and pink, for example, can be quite cheery.

White-flowered bulbs are useful to break up overly dominant color patterns or subdue strident colors. Plan for about a fourth of your bulbs at any given time to be white: crocus, narcissus, or tulip in spring; lily or dahlia in summer. White and pale shades also

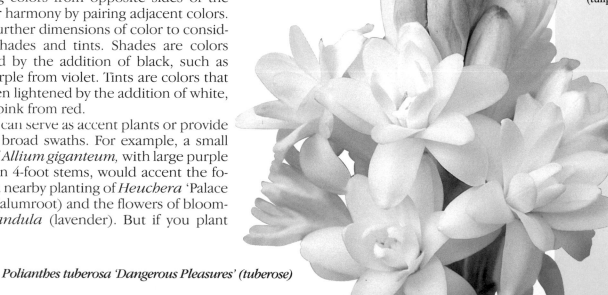

Polianthes tuberosa 'Dangerous Pleasures' (tuberose)

Scented Bulbs

Amaryllis belladonna
(belladonna lily)
Convallaria majalis
(lily of the valley)
Crinum americanum
(swamp lily)
Crocus biflorus
(Scotch crocus)
Crocus imperati
(crocus)
Cyclamen
(Persian violet)
Eucharis
(Amazon lily)
Freesia
(freesia)
Galanthus
(snowdrop)
Gladiolus calianthus
(gladiolus)
Hyacinthus
(hyacinth)
Hymenocallis
(spider lily)
Iris
(iris)
Leucojum vernum
(spring snowflake)
Lilium
(lily)
Lycoris squamigera
(magic lily)
Muscari
(grape hyacinth)
Narcissus
(daffodil)
Pancratium
(sea daffodil)
Polianthes tuberosa
(tuberose)
Puschkinia scilloides
(striped squill)
Scilla
(squill)
Sternbergia lutea
(winter daffodil)
Trillium
(wake-robin)
Tulipa
(tulip)

show up best in shady locations and at twilight.

Yellow is another color to use as an accent. A proportion of one yellow bloom to about three violet or blue ones makes a vivid combination. Green, ever present in the garden, forms a chromatic bridge between the two hues. Yellow also harmonizes with orange, a tricky hue to weave into a color scheme.

Texture and Form

Although color is a bulb's dominant attribute, the texture and overall shape of the plant can also add to the design. To begin with, there can be enormous variations in flower heads. Parrot tulips, for example, have developed ragged-edged petals that are wildly mottled in color. Lilies exhibit a wide range of trumpet shapes. Other lilylike flowers, such as the *Gloriosa superba,* have a lacy, airy quality.

Bulbs produce some of the largest and tallest of all flowers, such as the 9-inch-wide "dinner-plate" dahlia and the extraordinary *Eremurus himalaicus* (Himalayan desert-candle), with a flowering stalk reaching up to 9 feet. These giants never fail to make an impression. On the other hand, the miniature detailing of a *Cyclamen coum* or the dangling bells of a *Fritillaria meleagris* invite you to bring them up close to fully appreciate them.

Decorative Foliage

A few bulbs are grown for their interesting foliage. Notable is the caladium, whose heart-shaped leaves are speckled and striped in pink, red, lavender, and white. A common houseplant, caladium is frost-tender but will do well in a shady, moist spot in the garden. The gigantic elephant's ear, or *Colocasia esculenta,* also thrives in the shade and damp.

Many flowering bulbs have attractive foliage, which gives the plants interest after the blooms fade. Some cannas, for example, have purplish leaves, and the foliage of *Canna* x *generalis* 'Pretoria' has startling green-and-gold variegation. Several small tulip cultivars—'Red Riding Hood', 'Cape Cod', and 'Oriental Splendor', to name a few—have red-striped leaves. And *T. aucherana* has wavy-edged leaves radiating from its short stem.

The foliage of flowering bulbs such as arum, oxalis, and cyclamen, when planted in masses, makes a beautiful ground cover. And

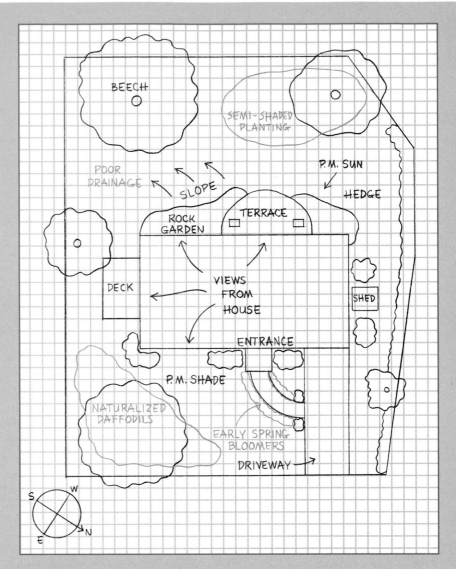

To design your own garden plan, first sketch the boundaries of your lot, house, outbuildings, trees, shrubs, and existing flower beds. Use a carpenter's tape to get field measurements, and draw the objects roughly to scale. Note where the soil stays wet or dry, and how the shadows fall during the day. Mark pockets of strong sun and warmth; note sightlines from points within the house and from porches and patios. Finally redraw the sketch on graph paper, using a scale of one square per foot. Draw the base plan in ink, but use pencil for projected new plantings and other improvements to make it easy to experiment and change.

in Zones 8 to 10, agapanthus, clivia, and canna foliage is evergreen, preserving their position in the garden through the year.

For most bulbs, however, foliage is viewed as the price a gardener must pay to enjoy the beauty of the flower. It takes some ingenuity to deal with the sprawl of daffodil foliage or the withering of allium or hyacinth leaves. With careful planning, though, you can take advantage of the emerging foliage of perennials to disguise the bulbs' progressively unsightly leaves. Ferns, for example, come into leaf just as snowdrops, crocuses, and winter

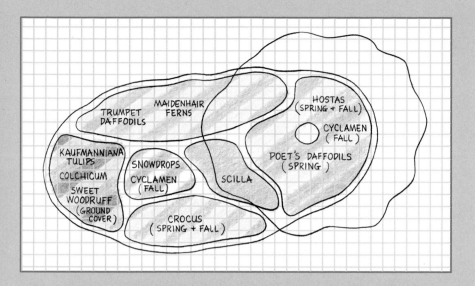

To diagram a bulb garden, measure the area for the proposed bed and make a rough sketch of it as you did for the base plan. Then draw in the areas you wish to allocate to each type of bulb, indicating the numbers of each to be planted. For a more natural look, make the areas for each bulb type asymmetrical, and allow the edges of one planting to slightly overlap those adjacent to it. Use colored pencils to develop a sense of the color combinations you will get. After the garden is in place, keep the plan as a permanent record of the bulbs and their location.

Making a Garden Layout

Assessing your property is the first step in planning a garden. The sample plan at left shows a property with a house facing northeast on land that slopes to the southwest. There is a deck and a patio, and the grounds include several large trees, a front entryway, a pathway, and a driveway. The plan notes areas that are inhospitable to bulbs—under a shallow-rooted beech tree and in wet spots—as well as areas where they will thrive, near the entryway and in sunny beds. In keeping with the hilly site, the house was designed to have an informal, asymmetrical look, creating an apt setting for naturalized and rock-garden bulb plantings that are easily seen from the house.

The diagram above presents a detailed plan for a semishaded bulb garden under the oak tree at the western corner of the property. The garden will be visible from the patio.

aconites are fading. *Astilbe* (false spirea), *Epimedium* (bishop's hat), *Paeonia* (peony), and Siberian iris are also good camouflage.

A Bulb for Every Season

Once you have settled on the bulbs and colors you like, select for bloom season. The flowering glory of most bulbs is brief—2 to 3 weeks. The Plant Selection Guide on pages 98-103 will help you pick bulbs that bloom when you want them to and in the colors and

shapes you prefer. Happily, many bulbs of the same genus bloom at different times. If you love tulips, you can extend their presence in the garden by planting early-spring-blooming species tulips, followed by Triumph and Darwin tulips, which flower in midspring, and finishing with single and double late varieties, which will carry you into summer.

The Bewitchment of Scent

The scents exuded by bulb flowers range from lemony to musky to honey-sweet. Scent evolved to attract pollinators, and the odor emitted by some lilies and narcissus may seem overpowering to human noses. By contrast, you will have to get down on hands and knees to enjoy the perfume of small spring bulbs such as crocuses and snowdrops. Most fragrant bulb flowers come in white, pale pink, mauve, or yellow, and their petals are waxy, like those of hyacinth, tuberose, and lily.

Practical Considerations

Any garden design has to take into account the growing requirements of plants. With a few exceptions, bulbs prefer soil with a more or less neutral pH and good drainage. Generally, spring bloomers such as daffodils need a dry period in the summer, when they are dormant. Cyclamen, trout lily, and other woodland bulbs need protection from hot summer sun. Plants that evolved in mountain meadows—crocuses and tulips are examples—can tolerate a good baking.

Meeting these requirements is made easier by the use of companion plants. Shrubs and perennials not only conceal the long spindly stems of tall bulb plants such as lilies—and, of course, help hide withering bulb foliage after flowering—but their roots also take up excess moisture in the soil. And later, when the bulbs are dormant, perennials shade the ground and moderate soil temperature.

To bring all these variables together into a coherent plan, make a detailed diagram of your garden *(opposite)*. It will help you analyze your property's strengths and weaknesses and decide how to exploit them. For example, a hard-to-mow slope might be just the place for a rock garden or a drift of naturalized bulbs. A diagram also helps you keep track of where your bulbs are planted.

Bulbs in the Bed and Border

Beds and borders are the most common design elements in a garden. They are self-contained plantings that give the garden its shape and character, affording the gardener an opportunity to concentrate color, form, and texture for maximum effect. The strong hues of bulbs have an immediate and vivid impact in such a setting. Indeed, many of the more formal bulbs that produce uniform shapes and colors, such as tulip and hyacinth, look most at home in a bedding display.

A bed or border will position plants where they can best be appreciated—along a walkway or near an entrance, around a pool or a garden bench. They are a versatile way of organizing your plants for viewing, presenting lovely vistas from afar or up close.

Cultivating a Bed or Border

Beds and borders also allow you to group your plants according to their growing requirements. They are the part of the garden where you can most easily focus your cultivation efforts to improve soil texture and fertility specifically for the plants you have chosen.

Bulb experts agree that the most important factor for success in growing bulbs is your soil's drainage. The soil must allow water to percolate away from the bulbs, but it also must contain enough compost or other organic matter to hold nutrients and to retain sufficient moisture to keep them from drying out completely. In a bed or border you can prepare the soil to meet those needs and thus protect your sometimes considerable investment in growing stock.

Serving a Purpose

Although they share a common purpose in the garden, beds and borders accomplish it slightly differently. A border forms the edge of a garden space and usually lies along a vertical element—a fence, a hedge, or a wall. This backdrop sets off the plants, which are laid out with the tallest at the back and the shortest in front and are generally viewed from the front only. A bed, on the other hand, is often a free-standing area visible from all sides. It can be geometric or irregular in shape and surrounded by lawn, ground cover, or even gravel.

A bed must be in proportion to the space around it—neither so small that it fades from view at a modest distance nor so large that it overpowers its surroundings. On a small lot, you can give a bed of limited size more visual weight by adding shrubs or small trees, or by mounding earth to form a raised bed *(left)*. The height of the plants should be proportional to the width of the plot. As a general guideline, no plant should be taller than one-half the width of the space.

Formal Beds and Borders

Bulbs in massed plantings make spectacular formal designs. Expect to plant the bulbs rather densely in a formal bed—inches apart—and to think of the planting as a one-season affair, good for drawing attention to an area for a time. Try, for example, a spring bed of clusters of pink, red, and yellow tulips, sur-

---

TIPS FROM THE PROS

Making a Mounded Bed

One way to make your bulb bed more visible from a distance is to create a gentle hillock or mound. The extra elevation adds dimensional interest and increases the color impact you will get from plants of similar height—for example, a grouping of tulips and daffodils. In addition, the eye will naturally be carried to the top of the mound, where you can place a special feature—a dwarf shrub with an interesting shape, perhaps, or a large ornamental rock.

Besides its decorative appeal, a mounded or raised bed is an ideal location for bulbs because you can easily mix up your own soil recipe on the site to ensure that it will have good drainage.

To make a raised bed, pile topsoil at least a foot high, so there will be enough to envelop completely the roots of your plants. A few artfully arranged rocks will help keep the soil in place until the plants can establish a root system. Depending on your preference for a formal or an informal arrangement, the raised bed can be centered within an available space on your property or given an off-center position. Orient the slope of the bed to the point from which you will view it.

rounded by an edging of vivid blue grape hyacinths. Other good edging plants include pansies, impatiens, rock cress, candytuft, primroses, coleus, or ornamental kale. Forget-me-nots are a traditional foundation plant for bulb displays, creating a misty blue haze through which the bulbs grow.

You might want to experiment with a single-color scheme. For an all-white spring garden, plant *Crocus vernus* 'Snowstorm', *Narcissus* 'Thalia' and 'Mount Hood', *Hyacinthus orientalis* 'L'innocence', *Anemone blanda* 'White Splendor', *Leucojum aestivum,* and *Tulipa* 'Ivory Floridale' and 'White Dream'.

A summer bed could have clusters of red or yellow canna with a central group of red and yellow gladiolus, surrounded by mixed dahlias. For accents, try marigold, petunia, lobelia, and alyssum.

Informal Plantings

In contrast to the uniformity of a formal bed, an informal planting should offer some surprises. Give it an irregular, asymmetrical shape, and choose a wider variety of plants.

Consider, for example, creating dramatic pairings of bulbs with trees and shrubs. Blue-flowered bulbs such as scilla, muscari, and chionodoxa can create a beautiful effect when

bunched in a ring around the base of a white-barked birch or small flowering cherry. They also combine well with spring-blooming shrubs such as witch hazel and forsythia.

Certain shrubs benefit from a screen of plants around their bare stems. For example, a hedge of lilacs, such as *Syringa* x *chinensis,* looks better with a skirt of bulbs and ferns at the beginning of the year. A succession of early-spring bulbs such as snowflakes and snowdrops, followed by crocuses and winter aconites, will finish blooming just as the dark red and pale green fronds of the maidenhair fern and the royal fern begin unfurling at the base of the lilacs. The ferns will then fill out to mask the bulbs' dying foliage.

Pastel tulips in an informal bed or border can pick up the pale blue of a *Wisteria* or lilac or the pink of spirea. Position them in front of glossy green *Ilex* (holly) or the deep maroon foliage of *Berberis thunbergii* 'Rose Glow' (barberry), and the tulips will shine. Dark purple tulips pair well with the burgundy in a cut-leaf *Acer palmatum* (Japanese maple). Their waxy blooms create a stimulating contrast with the lacy maple foliage.

Similarly, bold, waxy hyacinth flowers contrast with the fine, delicate blossoms of arabis, golden-tuft, and myosotis. While hyacinths are at their best massed in a formal bed, they can serve as a good accent dotted among other plants, and their perfume is a bonus.

A specimen tree or shrub anchoring a bed can be accented with a group of bulbs. The number of bulbs should vary with the mature size of the variety chosen—a dozen daffodils, tulips, or hyacinths, for example; half a dozen large fritillaries, lilies, or galtonias; or minor bulbs in groups of three to four dozen.

Going for a Large Effect

Whether your bedding plot is formal or informal, you can strengthen its impact by choosing bulbs for height. The white-veined green leaves of an elephant's ear, for example, would contrast dramatically with the spiky foliage of a yucca or with an upright temple juniper. Or place an immense *Dahlia imperialis* next to a mass of burgundy-leaved cannas and a vining gloriosa lily.

Lilies are generally tall plants with long, relatively bare stems. They combine well with plants that rise to conceal those stems. Low grasses work well, as do dwarf conifers. For example, plant copper-colored *Lilium* x *dalhansonii* with blue-gray *Pinus flexilis* 'Glauca Pendula' (limber pine). The purple bells of a 'Betty Corning' clematis climbing over such a pair would make a stunning display.

Other tall bulb plants include *Fritillaria imperialis, Camassia, Cardiocrinum giganteum,* the tender *Watsonia,* and the giant *Canna iridiflora*—all of which grow to more than 4 feet tall in the right conditions.

Managing Bulb Foliage

Since bulb leaves must not be cut back until they are withered and brown, you'll need various planting strategies to hide them as they decline. Daffodils, for example, develop a

GLOWING BLOOMS IN THE SUMMER SUN
Towering Lilium 'Golden Splendor' and the smaller white 'Gypsy' shine among the pastel pink of filipendula and the blue of campanula in this Oregon garden. Clipped box bushes anchor the corner of the bed.

AN ISLAND BED OF LILIES
Orange-trumpeted Asiatic hybrid lilies and purple-petaled columbine burst from a rock-edged bed in Idaho. Plum-colored oxalis climbs between the stones.

floppy habit, especially as their foliage yellows in the sun. Plant them with hostas, daylilies, peonies, astilbe, leopard's-bane, ferns, and grasses—perennials that emerge in time to hide the homely daffodil leaves. Or put them at the base of flowering shrubs or among ground covers such as ivy, vinca, or low-growing cotoneaster, allowing you to tuck the daffodil leaves out of sight.

Crocus foliage is shorter and not so troublesome, getting conveniently lost among low ground covers such as vinca, sedum, bugleweed, euonymus, ivy, and carpet junipers. Pachysandra, however, will smother crocus and cause it not to return.

Another way to hide withering bulb foliage is to plant annuals such as pansy, iberis, and *Lobularia maritima* (alyssum) among the bulbs just before the latter start to grow. Since the roots of annuals are shallow, the bulbs will find a way through them. The annuals will remain in flower through the summer, attracting attention away from the withering bulb leaves.

The foliage of certain autumn-flowering bulbs appears in the spring, long before the flowers arrive, and can be a nuisance if you have not planned for it in your design. Fall-blooming crocus and cyclamen have tidy, decorative leaves, but the foliage of the belladonna lily and colchicum is broad and floppy and should be tucked unobtrusively among other plants, such as hostas, in the spring.

Bulbs for Specific Conditions

MOIST SOIL
Caladium
(angel-wings)
Camassia quamash
(camassia)
Canna
(canna)
Convallaria majalis
(lily of the valley)
Eranthis hyemalis
(winter aconite)
Erythronium americanum
(dogtooth violet)
Fritillaria meleagris
(checkered lily)
Lilium superbum
(Turk's-cap lily)
Narcissus cyclamineus
(daffodil)

SHADE
Achimenes
(magic flower)
Anemone blanda
(Greek anemone)
Arum italicum
(painted arum)
Begonia
(begonia)
Clivia miniata
(Natal lily)
Convallaria majalis
(lily of the valley)
Crocus tomasinianus
(crocus)
Cyclamen
(Persian violet)
Erythronium americanum
(dogtooth violet)
Eucharis grandiflora
(Amazon lily)
Fritillaria
(fritillary)
Galanthus
(snowdrop)
Hyacinthoides hispanica
(Spanish bluebell)
Iris xiphioides
(English iris)
Leucojum aestivum
(summer snowflake)
Lilium candidum
(Madonna lily)
Lycoris squamigera
(magic lily)
Muscari
(grape hyacinth)
***Oxalis* spp.**
(shamrock)
Zantedeschia
(calla lily)
Zephyranthes
(zephyr lily)

Note: The abbreviation "spp." stands for the plural of "species"; where used in lists it means that many, but not all, of the species in a genus meet the criterion of the list.

Naturalized Bulb Plantings

Naturalized plantings take advantage of the ability of some bulbs to multiply and spread on their own from year to year. By integrating bulbs into an existing environment, whether woodland or meadow, you can imitate nature with a planting that appears spontaneous and unplanned. Naturalized plantings are well suited to spots that are difficult to cultivate, such as areas of dry shade under trees, hard-to-mow banks, or spots that are rocky or wet.

Most woodland bulbs that naturalize well don't require full sun, flourishing instead in the bright pale sunlight of early spring and the dappled shade of the summer woods. Many other bulbs can be naturalized in a meadow or grassy area. But, of course, because it is necessary to leave the bulb foliage in place after flowering, meadow plantings must be left unmowed for a time.

One of the charms of naturalized plantings is the reward they bring you in return for very little effort. You need only make sure the ground is well fertilized at the time of planting, especially for woodland bulbs, which must compete with shrubs and trees for water and nutrients. But after the initial work is done, these bulbs can be left alone.

Species bulbs are the best candidates for naturalizing because they spread by seed or underground by natural division, forming new plants year by year. However, some hybrid bulbs—daffodils, for example—do not self-seed. Although technically perennial, hybrid bulbs generally do not grow beyond the original clump and can only be spread by lifting and division.

To be effective, a naturalized planting should be compatible with the existing environment. In making plans for such a planting, study the landscape to determine its natural contours. Imagine water flowing across the area. This is how seeds might naturally be carried. Think of the way seeds tend to collect in pockets, such as among roots at the base of a tree. If you are planting on an embankment, take into account what the undersides of various plants look like, as these will be visible from the foot of the slope. In a meadow, imagine how the natural undulation of the ground will cause plants to spread or bunch.

In a Woodland Setting

Woodland plantings must be carried out on a fairly grand scale, or the result will look skimpy. Use trees and shrubs as the backbone of the landscape, and then put in enough of a given bulb to make a visible impact. Small woodland bulbs such as scilla, glory-of-the-snow, or snowdrops, for example need to be laid down in quantities of perhaps 100 or more bulbs per planting in order to make an effective display.

Naturalized plantings look better if different bulb varieties are not mixed. If you are planting two different species of daffodils, for example, keep them in separate clumps and

A QUIET GLADE OF NATURALIZED BULBS
Early spring brings a spectacular display to this planting of Spanish bluebells in a grove of rhododendrons. The dappled light filtering through the trees adds to the charm of this simple, naturalized woodland garden.

blend them gently, feathering the two into each other where the edges of the plantings touch. In a meadow, create broad swaths of single types of bulbs in simple curved or spiral shapes. Remember that there are few straight lines in nature.

Naturalizing in Early Spring

Among the first spring bloomers—appearing in late winter—are snowdrops and winter aconite. Spring snowflake, similar to the snowdrop but with a smaller bell-shaped flower, blooms a few weeks later and spreads freely.

Many varieties of hardy cyclamen bloom in springtime. Cyclamen is one of the few bulbs that grow well beneath evergreen trees, and the plant's delicate appearance belies its vigorous self-seeding habit. Spring-blooming *Cyclamen hederifolium* is the most free-flower-

ing species. It does well in woodlands, preferring moist, well-drained soil.

Crocus is a good candidate for naturalizing on a lawn. By the time the grass is ready for its first spring mowing, crocuses will have stored enough nutrients and moisture to meet their needs for the next year's growth, and their foliage can be cut down. *Crocus tomasinianus,* spread by seed and by cormels, multiplies easily in a naturalized setting. And unlike other crocus species, it has the added virtue of being unappealing as a food for squirrels and other animal pests such as voles.

Another spring bloomer is *Scilla siberica,* whose drooping, bright blue flowers look good under shrubs and with other bulbs, such as early daffodil cultivars. Chionodoxa is

Protecting Endangered Wild Bulbs

The destruction of habitat around the world, combined with the removal of bulbs from the wild by unscrupulous plant collectors, now threatens bulbs that were once abundant in nature, such as the trout lily above, with extinction. In an effort to reduce such depredations, an international trade convention limits the export of galanthus, cyclamen, and sternbergia bulbs from their countries of origin. You can help prevent the loss of these irreplaceable plants by insisting on knowing where the wildflower bulbs you purchase come from and buying only those labeled "nursery propagated." Finally, never dig up plants from the wild.

Interplanting Bulbs with Ground Covers

Mingling your bulbs with ground covers produces year-round benefits. First, when the bulbs are in flower, a ground cover offers contrasting color, texture, and form. An example is the *Crocus vernus* above, emerging through *Cyclamen hederifolium*. Later, the ground cover hides ripening bulb foliage. Finally, during the bulbs' dormancy, it serves as a living mulch, protecting the soil from erosion and temperature changes that can heave bulbs out of the soil.

FOR SHADE OR WOODLAND
Alchemilla
(lady's-mantle)
Ceratostigma
plumbaginoides
(leadwort)
Galium odoratum
(sweet woodruff)
Hedera
(ivy)
Lamium
(dead nettle)
Pachysandra

(pachysandra)
Phlox divaricata
(wild sweet William)
Primula x **polyantha**
(polyanthus primrose)
Vinca minor
(periwinkle)

FOR SUNNY SPOTS
Arabis
(rock cress)
Cerastium

(snow-in-summer)
Euonymus
(winter creeper)
Helianthemum
(sun rose)
Iberis
(candytuft)
Mazus
(mazus)
Phlox subulata
(moss pink)
Sedum
(stonecrop)

another early blue-flowered bulb. It needs to be planted in quantity initially in order to make a good show, but it soon spreads readily. Early-blooming *Anemone nemorosa,* with its pretty, fernlike foliage, produces 1-inch white flowers faintly tinged with pink.

Midspring Naturalizers

Among the next wave of spring bloomers is *Hyacinthoides non-scripta.* This blue-flowered bulb prefers light shade during bloom time and makes a beautiful display in wooded areas. It grows 18 to 20 inches tall and spreads rapidly by seed and bulb division. In a moist area, summer snowflake naturalizes easily. This bulb resembles spring snowflake but has larger flowers and grows to 18 inches tall.

Daffodils—which usually require full sun—nevertheless have a long tradition of being naturalized in woodland settings. Where the trees are deciduous, enough sun filters through bare branches to reach the foliage in the spring. And by the time the trees have leafed out, blocking sun and moisture, the bulbs have become dormant.

Not every daffodil cultivar fills the bill, however. Good candidates include the small cyclamineus daffodils, such as early-blooming 'February Gold', and 'Jetfire', which blooms later in spring. South of Zone 9, paper-whites multiply in shady woodland. In Zones 3 to 6, most trumpet, large-cupped, and double daffodils do well in a naturalized setting.

Another traditional use for daffodils is to plant them in orchards or unmowed meadows, where the foliage can remain undisturbed. As with other bulbs of the amaryllis family, daffodil foliage is toxic, so deer, voles, and squirrels who might be attracted by fruit trees or other plants will avoid the daffodils.

Tulips tend to be thought of as bulbs for beds and borders. But some growers are developing hybrid tulips that perennialize successfully in areas similar to the tulip's native habitat, Asia and the eastern Mediterranean. In the United States, this means roughly Zones 6 to 8, where the summers are dry and the soil drains well. Try the Darwin hybrids 'Golden Apeldorn' or 'Jewel of Spring', or the lily-flowering tulip 'West Point'. In American prairie lands of the Dakotas and eastern Colorado, species tulips such as *Tulipa tarda, T. humilis,* and *T. linifolia* can be planted in meadows and left to spread *(page 25).*

Summer and Fall Bloomers

A good summertime naturalizer is *Allium cernuum,* a member of the ornamental onion family that is native to the Allegheny Mountains and other parts of the eastern United States. It has light pink flowers and grows from 8 to 18 inches tall. This bulb also does well in rock gardens.

Two members of the lily family—*Lilium canadense* and *L. superbum*—are native to North America and naturalize well here. *L. canadense* grows wild, usually in shady areas, from Nova Scotia to Alabama, and produces yellow flowers dotted with red. It can reach a height of 6 feet. *L. superbum* has orange flowers with deep maroon centers. It too can tolerate some shade and can grow to 5 feet. Both *L. canadense* and *L. superbum* can be naturalized into a wet meadow or the edge of a woodland.

Autumn-flowering bulbs such as crocus and *Cyclamen hederifolium* tend to be small, modest bloomers that need to be planted in large groups to make a good show. Of the several autumn-flowering species crocuses, the blue-flowered *C. speciosus* is one of the easiest to grow. This crocus blooms in early fall and spreads rapidly by seed and natural division. It can be naturalized in lawns and grassy areas, where it soon runs rampant.

Colchicum autumnale is so eager to bloom that it will flower without even being planted, so put these bulbs in the ground as soon as possible. The pink, lilac, or white blooms appear on leafless stems; the foliage that grows in early spring begins to die down in summer and must be left undisturbed over the winter. Colchicum seeds are spread by ants, which are attracted to the seeds' sweet coating. The plants prefer sun and will form good-size clumps.

Native North American Bulbs

Native North American wildflower bulbs are well suited to the home garden, where they will thrive in conditions that approximate those of their natural environment. The Pacific Northwest native *Camassia quamash,* shown here blooming alongside red sorrel in an Oregon meadow, bears blue or white flowers and thrives in wet meadows and near streams. This plant was once used as a food source by native Americans, who cooked the bulbs.

Although not as large or showy as their hybridized foreign cousins, many North American woodland bulbs can make charming contributions to naturalized plantings. Bulbs such as *Arisaema triphyllum* (jack-in-the-pulpit), *Dicentra cucullaria* (Dutchman's-breeches), *Erythronium americanum* (trout lily), and *Sanguinaria canadensis* (bloodroot) have an intrinsic beauty that, paradoxically, can seem exotic when compared with the more familiar look of tulips, daffodils, and hyacinths.

Claytonia virginica (spring-beauty), with its narrow, spoon-shaped leaves and small pink flowers, seems delicate, but it has a robust habit and spreads quickly in woodlands and open thickets. *Uvularia* (great merry-bells) and *Polygonatum* (Solomon's-seal) are easy to grow.

Bulbs in the Rock Garden

A rock garden reproduces on a small scale the growing conditions of the mountain plants known as alpines. These tough little plants can thrive in pockets of gritty soil sandwiched among rocks in wind-scoured heights.

Located on a terraced slope or in a natural outcrop, a rock garden is a sheltered environment. The rocks protect the plants from wind, keep their roots cool, and channel water to them. In winter the rocks absorb the sun's heat by day and release it at night, moderating root-damaging temperature fluctuations in the soil. A coarse gravel mulch helps keep the plants' crowns and leaves from rotting.

Tailoring the Soil for Bulbs

Alpines are usually planted in a mixture of garden soil, sand or grit, and leaf mold. Additional coarse grit will create the pockets of quick-draining soil favored year-round by iris, crocus, narcissus, oxalis, and tulip. To mature well, iris, calochortus, and brodiaea plants need rapid drainage in summer. By adding more humus to the mix, you can give erythronium, cyclamen, and anemone the moisture-retentive soil they need. You can also apply water and food as needed. For example, anemone and colchicum like extra water in summer; erythronium and fritillaria need extra fertilizer.

Nestling such early-spring bloomers as *Iris reticulata,* species tulips, and crocus against rocks will give them shelter and warmth. The periods of shade the rocks provide will give cyclamen, fritillary, galanthus, oxalis, and scilla a needed respite from the summer sun.

Showcasing Smaller Bulbs

A rock garden has the right scale for smaller bulbs that might get lost at ground level among larger plants. The rocks help set off the plants. For instance, elevated in a terraced rock garden and silhouetted against dark stones, the pale blue, purple-veined petals of *Crocus speciosus* stand out. And because the plants are elevated, the scents of species tulip, crocus, narcissus, iris, and grape hyacinth more easily reach your nose. Rock gar-

Species Tulips: Tiny but Tough

Species tulips like these *Tulipa bakeri* 'Lilac Wonder' naturalize easily in a sunny spot. Natives of the Mediterranean, they bloom very early in spring in Zones 5 to 7; *T. clusiana* even grows in Zone 9. With multiple flowers on each stem, species tulips look best in an uncrowded position in a rock garden. They combine well with other bulbs that bloom at the same time—*Pulsatilla vulgaris, Adonis vernalis,* or bulbous iris. Evergreen dwarf shrubs, such as *Ilex crenata* (Japanese holly), *Chamaecyparis obtusa* (Hinoki false cypress), and *Arctostaphylos uva-ursi* (bearberry), also make good companions. Arabis and creeping phlox furnish an attractive background.

dens for hardy spring and summer bulbs like *Allium cyaneum* and *Lilium cernuum* can be as small as 3 square feet. A larger garden would be appropriate for ixia, freesia, romulea, brodiaea, babiana, or bletilla. They generally grow from 12 to 18 inches high.

In the Mixed Rock Garden

Bulbs combine handily in rock gardens with dwarf shrubs and perennials, which discreetly cover the spots left bare when the bulbs go dormant. Low-growing, mat-forming herbs such as thyme, mint, and oregano protect the bulbs from splashing mud. They also provide ground-covering greenery for colchicum or *Cyclamen hederifolium,* which bloom without foliage in the fall.

Look for drought-tolerant plants that like good drainage. Dwarf evergreens and other small shrubs such as heather, daphne, dwarf cotoneaster, ground-cover azalea, and blue spruce offer excellent possibilities for combinations with bulbs. The bulbs' upright form rising through these sprawling plants makes an interesting contrast.

Finally, choose companion perennials for color: pinks and white from saxifrage, arabis, phlox, primula, and pink; blues and lavender from bellflower, gentian, and mint; yellow and orange from dwarf aster and chrysanthemum in the fall. The silver-blue foliage of blue fescue is a good foil for brightly colored bulbs. In a shady, damp spot, plant small astilbe, fern, and hosta.

A ROCKY BED OF SPANISH BLUEBELLS
The nodding bells of Hyacinthoides hispanica seem to splash their way gaily past the mossy rocks in an Oregon garden in April. Bright pink arabis flows through a crevice alongside.

Bulbs in Containers

Growing bulbs outdoors in pots offers advantages over growing the same plants in the ground and also allows you to raise varieties you otherwise couldn't consider. In containers, you can control the exposure, soil mix, and drainage. You can move pots to give bulbs optimal growing conditions, site them to brighten balconies or patios, and bring them up close so you can enjoy their blooms.

You can grow tender bulbs in the warm months and keep them going through the winter by bringing them indoors. Shade lovers can come out of the summer sun, and bulbs that like quick drainage and extra-gritty soil can be satisfied. And potted up they are protected from rodents and other pests.

To avoid unsightly bulb foliage, you can pot-hole bulbs in the garden, digging them into the ground, container and all. When the bulbs go dormant, remove them to a discreet location to complete their growth cycle.

Choosing the Container

Certain plants seem especially suited to particular pots. Narcissus are at home in a wooden box or woven basket. Formal-looking *Lilium regale* belongs in a glazed Chinese pot or stone urn. Diminutive snowdrops or crocuses are the right size for a bonsai pot. Be sure the pot has at least one drainage hole and that you can plant the bulb at the proper depth. There should be as much space under the bulb as the depth of soil above it.

All pots have pros and cons. Plastic and glazed pots retain moisture well but heat up in warm weather, possibly damaging fragile roots. Clay pots "breathe," allowing for good air circulation and good drainage, but they require more frequent watering. Large wooden tubs are superior insulators against heat and cold, but they are cumbersome to move and will eventually rot.

Combining Plants

Bulbs don't take up much space and combine well in pots with each other and with other container plants. Annuals, with their shallow roots, are especially good companions for bulbs. In spring, try tiny hoop-petticoat daffodils with the taller scented jonquils. Rim the pot or window box with trailing variegated ivy, periwinkle, or sweet alyssum. Or pair blue scilla or grape hyacinth with white pansies in a hanging basket. In summer, smaller cultivars of lilies or cannas in a pot create a tropical atmosphere. Gladiolus, dahlia, agapanthus, allium, and calla lily all come in dwarf sizes. For colorful foliage, mix them with caladium or fern. Begonias make superb hanging-pot plants under the shade of a porch. Or try oxalis in a hanging pot or sunny window box.

POTTED LILIES IN AN OUTDOOR ARRANGEMENT
Asiatic hybrid lilies in white, yellow, and pink have been positioned in this Connecticut garden to pick up the white of potted pansies at their feet and the pink of nearby digitalis.

Coping with Cold Weather

Few bulbs, no matter how hardy, can survive a very cold winter in an outdoor container. The pot may freeze through before the bulb has established a root system, or a shallowly planted bulb may be heaved clear of the soil by repeated freezing and thawing.

To avoid these hazards, you can plant small pots in the fall, moisten them, and set them in a protected place so they remain cool and grow roots but do not freeze. For large planters or window boxes that can't be moved into shelter, start the bulbs in cell packs—small plastic starter pots—in late fall, as shown on page 87. Cover them with 8 inches of pine needles or leaves in a cool mulch pile in a north-facing location. Here they can stay evenly cold without freezing for up to 16 weeks. As soon as the danger of hard frost has passed, you can pot them up, mixing them with small perennials or half-hardy annuals.

To make an outdoor container of summer bloomers, use one of two methods, depending on the types of bulbs chosen. Achimenes, begonia, caladium, calla lily, and canna need a warm (70° F) start indoors before they go outside. Plant them in cell packs indoors in early spring, about 30 days before the spring frost-free date. Then plant them in pots when the danger of frost has passed. Acidanthera, dahlia, and gladiolus can be planted directly into pots outdoors after the last frost.

To make an irrigation tube, use duct tape to close off one end of a length of 1½-inch PVC pipe, and drill ¼-inch holes randomly at 1-inch intervals from top to bottom. Fill in soil around the tube and even with its top edge. Plant two or three bulbs about 3 inches deep in each opening of the pot, grouping them more thickly at the top so their foliage will conceal the tube's opening.

Planting a Pot of Spring Bloomers

Tiny Tulipa bakeri and 'Little Gem' daffodils are ideal for planting in a tall strawberry pot. Prepare the pot in the fall, using growing mix (page 82) and an irrigation tube to evenly distribute water through the pot. Then submerge the entire pot in a cool mulch pile until after the last hard frost, when it can be put in a sunny spot to begin growing.

CHAPTER TWO

Planting Your Garden

Beyond the familiar spring favorites of tulips, daffodils, snowdrops, and crocuses are a bounty of lesser-known but equally beautiful bulbs that flower in the summer and through the fall. By choosing and planting a wide selection in the right settings, it's possible to enjoy months of colorful bells, cups, trumpets, and pompoms. Many bulbs, hardy enough to brave the coldest winters, should be planted in the fall. Others are tender—such as the low-growing, pinky peach alstroemeria and tall, lilac-colored Tulbaghia violacea growing in this sunny California border—and must be planted after the soil warms up in spring. No matter where you live, you'll find enough variety suited to your conditions to provide a dazzling display through the seasons.

Planted properly, your bulbs will maintain themselves with a minimum of care. This chapter will tell you all you need to know about buying bulbs, preparing the site—whether it's a lawn, a rock garden, or a standard bed—and caring for your plants so they deliver years of pleasure.

A. *Bougainvillea 'San Diego Red' (bougainvillea) (1)*
B. *Tulbaghia violacea (variegated society garlic) (2)*
C. *Hemerocallis (daylily) (2)*
D. *Chrysanthemum maximum (Leucanthemum maximum) (shasta daisy) (3)*
E. *Alstroemeria (Peruvian lily) (1)*
F. *Dianthus barbatus (sweet William) (2)*
G. *Citrus limon 'Eureka' (lemon tree) (1)*
H. *Bougainvillea 'James Walker' (bougainvillea) (1)*

NOTE: The key lists each plant type and the total quantity needed to replicate the garden shown. The diagram's letters and numbers refer to the type of plant and the number sited in an area.

Choosing Your Bulbs

When you shop for bulbs, you'll find them available everywhere, from local hardware stores to garden centers and nurseries. You can also order them from one of the many catalogs that feature a range of beautiful and often unusual specimens. But because quality is key to any plant's performance, you should shop where the healthiest bulbs are sold.

You'll find a better selection of bulbs if you buy them as soon as they arrive in the stores. Hardy spring- and summer-flowering bulbs are sold in late summer, tender summer-flowering bulbs in spring, and fall-flowering bulbs in mid- to late summer. If you order from catalogs, the bulbs will be shipped to you at the best planting times for your area.

What to Look For

Bulbs are sold by size, which is measured in centimeters of circumference. "Topsize" bulbs are generally the biggest of a species or class and are the most expensive. The larger the bulb, the more reserve food energy it contains, enabling it to produce more and bigger flowers. "Midsize" bulbs, also called premium, are considered a better buy for some bulbs; they cost less than topsize, and though they produce only one flower the first year, they'll send up multiple flowers the next year. Small bulbs (or planting stock) are at the lowest end of the scale. Their performance will be spotty, and they may have a short life span.

Narcissus bulbs are measured according to the number of growing points, or noses, that they have. The largest bulbs, called DN-1, have three to five noses, DN-2 bulbs have two noses, and healthy DN-3s—also called rounds—have one nose *(right)*. Size is also a factor when selecting tuber varieties such as caladiums and dahlias. The largest tubers have been maturing for a number of years and have several eyes. For this reason, they cost significantly more than small and midsize tubers, which have one or two eyes. Topsize caladium tubers will produce more than 20 leaves—even more if you break off the biggest eye with a gentle push of the thumb. The tuber then sends up leaves from other growing points.

But for some bulbs, bigger does not always mean better. Tulip bulbs larger than 14 centimeters often produce deformed flowers. And oversize bulbs may have been treated with nitrogen, which can weaken their cellular structure, making them more vulnerable to disease.

In addition to size, consider these factors when making your selections:

• A healthy bulb is plump and firm; the bottom should be hard. A soft, withered bulb has been in storage too long and has dried out, or it is diseased.

• The bulb should be dormant and show no premature growth of roots and shoots.

• There should be no damage to the base or the growth tips and minimal scars and bruises on the rest of the bulb. However, a split or flaking brown tunic—the bulb's skin—is normal. If a bulb has lost most of its tunic but shows no sign of disease or damage, it will likely perform well.

• When buying from garden centers, look for bulbs that are sold in mesh bags or boxes;

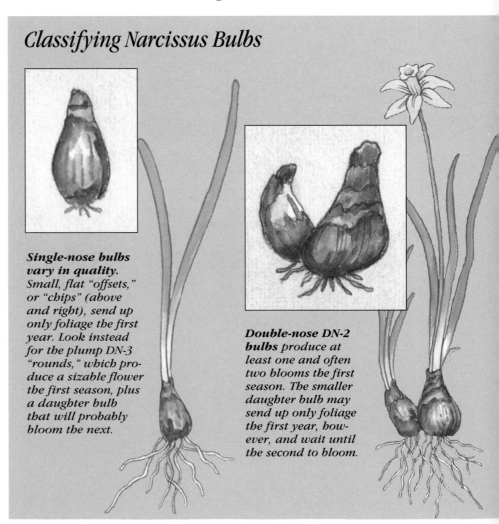

Classifying Narcissus Bulbs

Single-nose bulbs vary in quality. *Small, flat "offsets," or "chips" (above and right), send up only foliage the first year. Look instead for the plump DN-3 "rounds," which produce a sizable flower the first season, plus a daughter bulb that will probably bloom the next.*

Double-nose DN-2 bulbs *produce at least one and often two blooms the first season. The smaller daughter bulb may send up only foliage the first year, however, and wait until the second to bloom.*

30

loose bulbs in open bins may be damaged by excessive handling and jostling.

• Most reliable bulb specialists offer large to medium sizes only, depending on the bulb variety. When many bulbs are offered for a low price, expect to receive very small, immature bulbs that may not bloom for years.

• Select a suitable bulb species for your climate. The encyclopedia *(pages 106-151)* or the Plant Selection Guide *(pages 98-103)* will show which bulbs do best in your region.

Holding Bulbs for Planting

If you aren't planting your bulbs as soon as you get them home, hardy spring bloomers can be kept in any place where the temperature doesn't rise above 60° F. Place them in open trays or loosely folded paper bags. Summer- and fall-blooming bulbs can be stored in a closed plastic bag with wood shavings, peat, vermiculite, or a combination of these; place the bulbs in a cool, dry, well-ventilated area. Try to get your bulbs in the ground as soon as planting conditions are right, to avoid tissue deterioration and dehydration.

A PAIRING OF SPRING BLOOMERS
Delicate blue bells of Muscari (grape hyacinth) and roselike Ranunculus asiaticus (Persian buttercup) make ideal early spring companions in a warm climate, where the ranunculus can stay in the ground all year. Hardy only to Zone 7, ranunculus tubers are available from garden centers and specialty catalogs in spring, while the more cold-tolerant muscari bulbs appear in stores in time for fall planting.

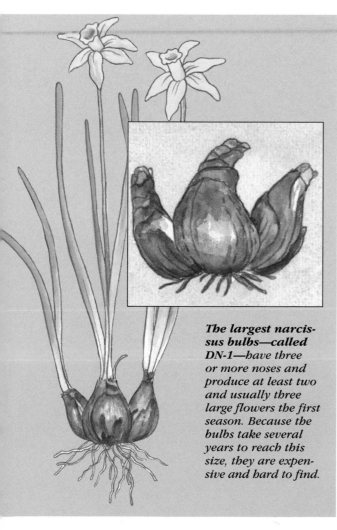

The largest narcissus bulbs—called DN-1—have three or more noses and produce at least two and usually three large flowers the first season. Because the bulbs take several years to reach this size, they are expensive and hard to find.

Planting Your Bulb Garden

When choosing a site for your bulbs, you first need to consider the area's light and temperature. Early-flowering bulbs such as snowdrop, winter aconite, spring snowflake, endymion, spring cyclamen, and crocus can be planted beneath deciduous trees and shrubs, whose bare branches in the first weeks of spring do not block the sun's rays. Areas that receive partial shade (3 to 4 hours of full sun) work well for wild and dwarf daffodils, snowflake, windflower, winter aconite,

meadow saffron, and trout lily. The bulbs of late-flowering daffodils, Dutch hyacinths, and tulips take longer to mature and must be planted in full sun in northern regions.

Summer-blooming bulbs such as cannas and dahlias require at least 6 hours of full sun to develop strong stems and large blooms. When planting these bulbs in the spring, take care that they won't be in the shade cast by a building or under the dense canopy of a tree later in the season. And in southern states

Depth and Spacing of Fall-Planted Bulbs

Soil depth

Plant spring-blooming bulbs and hardy summer-blooming bulbs in late summer to late fall, depending on the specific variety. This chart gives the recommended planting depth and spacing for a number of bulb varieties.

1"

Eranthis (winter aconite)
2-3 inches apart

2"

Crocus vernus (Dutch crocus)
2-3 inches apart

Anemone blanda (windflower)
2-3 inches apart

Muscari (grape hyacinth)
3 inches apart

3"

Chionodoxa (glory-of-the-snow)
2-3 inches apart

Iris reticulata (dwarf iris)
2-3 inches apart

4"

Allium aflatunense (ornamental onion)
4-6 inches apart

5"

6"

Iris hollandica (Dutch iris)
6 inches apart

7"

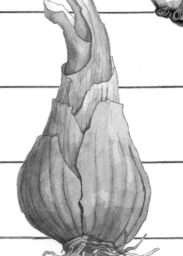

Tulipa (tulip)
6 inches apart

Narcissus (daffodil)
4-6 inches apart

8"

where the sun is very hot at noon, flowers that bloom from late spring through the summer months will last longer if they are planted in a part of the bed that receives filtered sun in the afternoon. Bulbs planted in a warm, protected southern exposure next to a building or wall will bloom earlier than those planted in an unprotected northern exposure.

Preparing the Soil

After you've decided on a spot for your bulbs, get to know your soil type. Most bulbs require soil that holds moisture—but not too much. Heavy clay is lethal to bulbs because it can become sodden and rot them. Be wary of sandy soils as well, since they can drain water away too fast. Loam, a crumbly combination of clay, sand, silt, and organic matter, is the ideal. (*Fritillaria meleagris* and several types of Siberian and Japanese iris are the exceptions to this rule—they prefer moist soil.)

If your soil has too much clay or sand to allow proper drainage, improve it by adding organic matter, which will open and aerate clayey areas and add substance and aid moisture retention in sandy soil. Compost, shredded leaves, or ground pine bark are good choices, as is commercial composted sewage sludge. Peat moss will do the job, although it doesn't last as long. For heavy clay, add sand

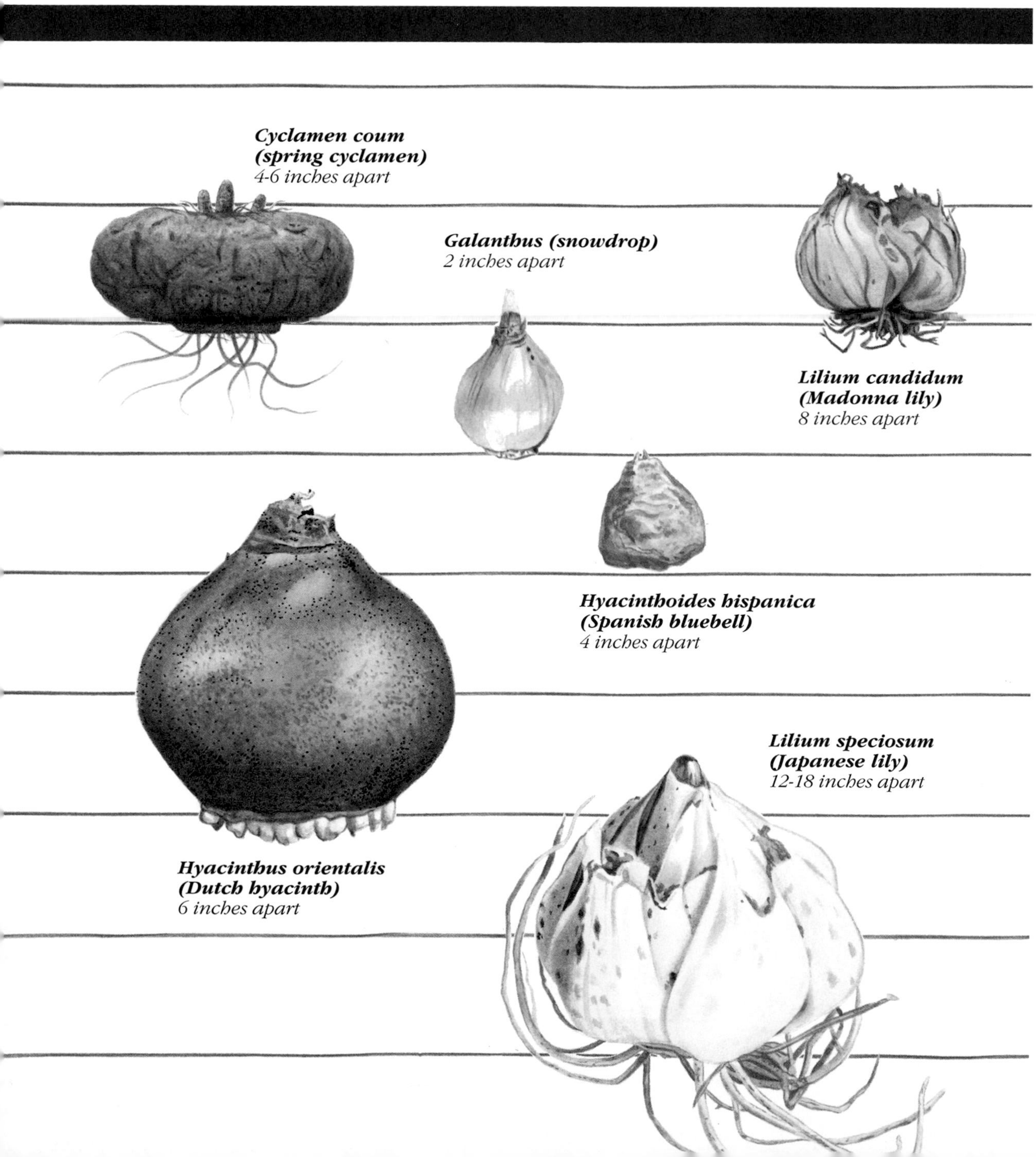

**Cyclamen coum
(spring cyclamen)**
4-6 inches apart

Galanthus (snowdrop)
2 inches apart

**Lilium candidum
(Madonna lily)**
8 inches apart

**Hyacinthoides hispanica
(Spanish bluebell)**
4 inches apart

**Hyacinthus orientalis
(Dutch hyacinth)**
6 inches apart

**Lilium speciosum
(Japanese lily)**
12-18 inches apart

to the amendments to further loosen the soil.

Besides improving drainage, organic matter will add nutrients and help maintain a pH of 6.0 to 7.0, the slightly acid to neutral level preferred by most bulbs. If your soil's pH is below 5.9, you will also need to add lime. The amount needed will depend on your soil type and its pH.

Work the soil to a depth of 10 to 12 inches for large bulbs and 6 to 8 inches for smaller bulbs; remove rocks, old roots, and weed clumps. For soil that is in good condition, cover the bed with a 1-inch layer of organic matter; if major improvement is in order, spread several inches of organic matter over the plot and dig it into the soil.

If you are preparing the bed at least several weeks before planting, you can also dig in a slow-release fertilizer such as a 9-9-6 or a low-nitrogen 5-10-20; these chemical granules need time to break down or they will burn the bulbs. If you are planting at the same time you are preparing the bed, avoid fertilizer burn by enriching the soil with compost and an organic fertilizer rather than a synthetic one. Several organic formulas that are specially suited for bulbs are available at your local garden center. Refer to the package to figure the application rate. If a test of your soil indicates adequate phosphorus, you can get by with a top dressing of compost and fertilizer rather than digging them in.

Depth and Spacing of Spring- and Summer-Planted Bulbs

Soil depth

Plant tender summer-blooming bulbs in late spring to early summer, and hardy fall-blooming bulbs as soon as they are available in late summer. This chart gives the recommended planting depth and spacing for a number of bulb varieties.

1"

2"

3"

4"

5"

6"

7"

8"

Ranunculus asiaticus (Persian buttercup)
4 inches apart

Gladiolus callianthus (Ethiopian gladiolus)
5 inches apart

Canna x generalis (canna lily)
16 inches apart
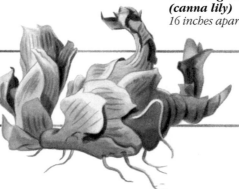

Galtonia candicans (summer hyacinth)
6-8 inches apart

Begonia x tuberhybrida (tuberous begonia)
10 inches apart

Crocosmia (montbretia)
6 inches apart

Zantedeschia aethiopica (calla lily)
10-12 inches apart
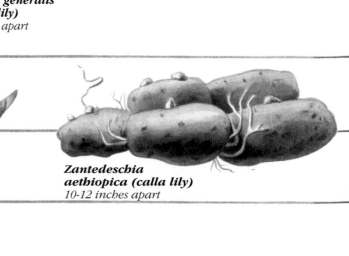

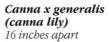
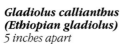

Planting Your Bulbs

A rule of thumb for planting most bulbs is to dig a hole 3 times as deep as the bulb is high. However, depth varies with soil type: In lighter soils, bulbs can be planted an inch or so deeper; in heavy soils, prepare a shallower hole and top with several inches of organic mulch. Exceptions include the Madonna lily, tuberous begonia, and *Hippeastrum* (amaryllis), which are always planted close to the surface. Refer to the charts below and on pages 32-33 for specific spacing and planting depths for the different bulb species.

When planting many bulbs in a new bed where the soil is loose and crumbly, a small trowel is the best tool for the job *(page 37)*. If you're planting bulbs in an established bed among perennials and shrubs, use a shovel to loosen the soil in small areas and a trowel to dig individual planting holes. If the soil is not compacted, a hand-held hollow bulb planter *(page 37)* can be used to remove plugs of earth. Dig several inches below where the bulb will sit, and work in organic matter or a slow-release synthetic fertilizer at the rate of 1 tablespoon per square foot. If you use a synthetic, prevent damage to the bulbs by covering the fertilized layer with untreated soil up to planting depth before placing the bulbs in the holes. Position the bulbs so that their pointed ends

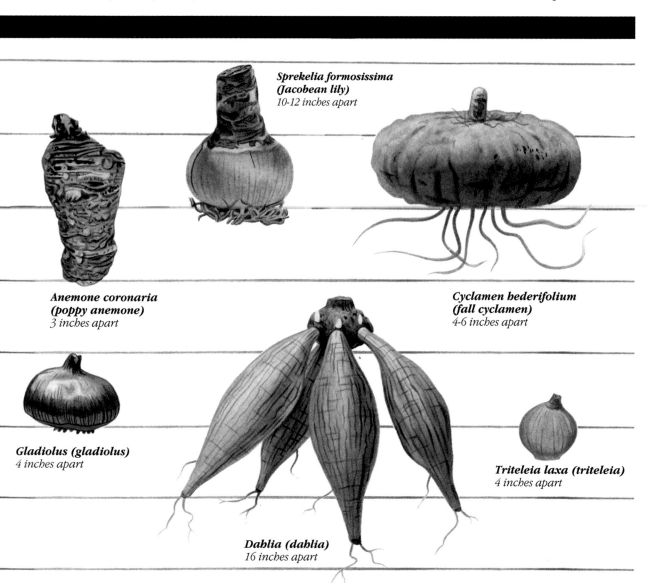

Sprekelia formosissima (Jacobean lily)
10-12 inches apart

Anemone coronaria (poppy anemone)
3 inches apart

Cyclamen hederifolium (fall cyclamen)
4-6 inches apart

Gladiolus (gladiolus)
4 inches apart

Dahlia (dahlia)
16 inches apart

Triteleia laxa (triteleia)
4 inches apart

COLOR IN THE FALL
Nestled among evergreens at the base of a fountain, purple Crocus speciosus 'Artabir' adds a pocket of color to a backyard Virginia garden. Plant the hardy autumn-flowering bulbs in late summer for blooms 6 to 8 weeks later.

also good because they can be cut, are flexible, and won't break in the cold. Or you can use labels made of sturdy plastic, which are pointed at one end for insertion into soft earth.

When to Plant

Hardy spring-blooming bulbs require a chilling period and should be planted in early fall. This gives them time to develop a good root system before the ground freezes. In northern areas the best planting time may be as early as September, in southern areas, as late as December. Hardy summer-blooming bulbs are usually planted in the fall. They can be planted in late spring with other flowering perennials, but in the North they may not get established sufficiently to bloom the same year.

Tender summer-blooming bulbs cannot be planted until the soil temperature reaches 65° to 70° F, because they will rot if planted in cold, wet earth. Some, such as caladium and tuberous begonia, should be started indoors in spring, 3 to 4 weeks before the last frost date, so they have several inches of growth before they're moved outdoors. Canna and dahlia benefit from being started indoors in northern areas where summers are short.

Use flats filled with an enriched potting mix containing peat moss. If you are starting caladium and begonia tubers, soak them in tepid water to remove the wax coating that is applied to prevent them from dehydrating during transit. If you are planting caladiums, encourage them to produce many leaves by breaking off the primary shoot with your thumb.

Arrange the tubers in the potting mix, cover them with another inch of it, and place the flats in a sunny window. Water regularly to keep the mix barely moist, and feed the growing plants every 2 weeks with a diluted fish or seaweed liquid fertilizer. Plant the tubers outdoors when they have sprouted several inches of foliage and the soil temperature is 70° F.

Growing Spring Bulbs in Mild Climates

If you live in the South, you can enjoy spring-blooming bulbs, but with few exceptions you'll have to accept them as annuals and replant each fall. No amount of soil preparation or careful tending can turn cold-loving bulbs into perennials when the weather is too hot.

face upward; flat tubers of anemones and cyclamens should be planted sideways.

Cover the bulbs with soil, tamp it down, and water thoroughly. Mulch the entire bed—new or established—with 2 to 4 inches of shredded pine bark, pine needles, or shredded leaves to control weed growth, retain moisture, and maintain soil temperature.

To keep track of the bulbs after they are planted and after the foliage has died back, you may want to mark their location. Metal labels, available at nurseries or garden centers, have tabs that can be marked with permanent ink, and their two pin legs keep them securely anchored in the ground. Vinyl markers are

Tools for Planting Bulbs

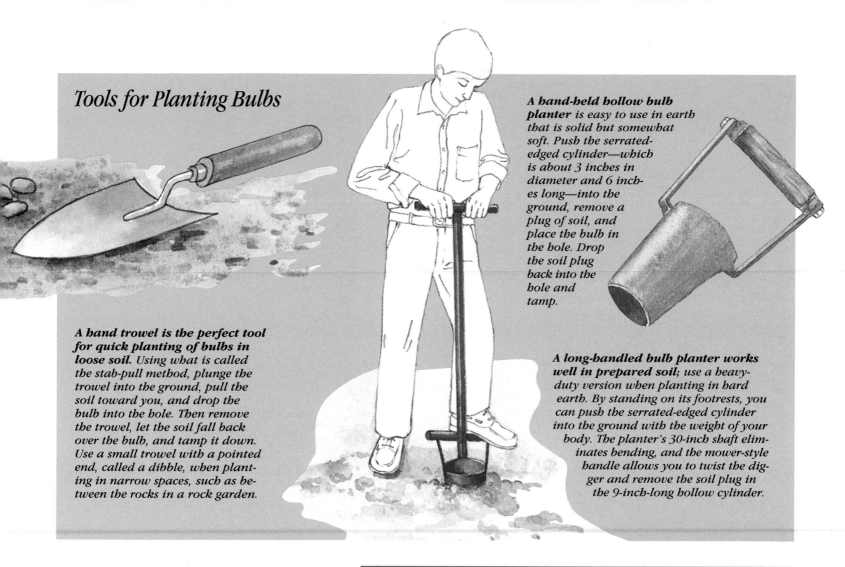

A **hand-held hollow bulb planter** is easy to use in earth that is solid but somewhat soft. Push the serrated-edged cylinder—which is about 3 inches in diameter and 6 inches long—into the ground, remove a plug of soil, and place the bulb in the hole. Drop the soil plug back into the hole and tamp.

A **hand trowel is the perfect tool for quick planting of bulbs in loose soil.** Using what is called the stab-pull method, plunge the trowel into the ground, pull the soil toward you, and drop the bulb into the hole. Then remove the trowel, let the soil fall back over the bulb, and tamp it down. Use a small trowel with a pointed end, called a dibble, when planting in narrow spaces, such as between the rocks in a rock garden.

A **long-handled bulb planter works well in prepared soil**; use a heavy-duty version when planting in hard earth. By standing on its footrests, you can push the serrated-edged cylinder into the ground with the weight of your body. The planter's 30-inch shaft eliminates bending, and the mower-style handle allows you to twist the digger and remove the soil plug in the 9-inch-long hollow cylinder.

However, some daffodil and tulip varieties will perennialize as far south as Zone 9.

Most hardy bulbs need an artificial pre-chilling period of 9 to 12 weeks in Zones 8, 9, and 10. As soon as they are purchased—usually in September—they should go right into the refrigerator. Don't store them with apples or pears, because these fruits release ethylene gas, which causes the bulbs to sprout prematurely and the flower to abort. Place the bulbs in a cloth or paper bag filled with moist vermiculite, perlite, or peat moss, fold the top loosely, and leave them in the refrigerator for 6 to 8 weeks. Then plant them in pots filled with a commercial potting soil. Return them, in their pots, to the refrigerator or put them in another cool location, such as an unfinished basement or crawlspace, for 3 to 4 weeks.

Water the potted bulbs occasionally, and at the first sign of growth, plant them in a sunny spot outdoors where they will be shielded from direct afternoon sun. The hotter and more direct the afternoon sun is, the faster the blooms will fade. In Zones 9 and 10, you can expect the bulbs to bloom about 6 weeks after

TIPS FROM THE PROS
Perennializing Hybrid Tulips

Though hybrid tulips are treated as annuals in many areas, it is possible for them to return year after year in Zones 3 to 7. For optimum life span, plant the bulbs of showy, large hybrids 8 to 10 inches deep in well-drained, loamy soil where they will receive full sun or, in the hot South, partial shade.

Well-fed bulbs produce healthier foliage, plus more and bigger flowers. At planting time, work a 9-9-6 fertilizer into the soil at the rate recommended on the package. In heavy soil, make holes only 4 to 6 inches deep, and loosen the soil before working in the bulb food. Put the bulbs in the holes and fill in with a soil-and-compost mix; tamp down and water thoroughly. Cover with a mulch of 4 to 6 inches of compost, aged shredded leaves, or shredded bark so the total depth of the bulbs is 8 to 10 inches.

When foliage emerges in the spring, fertilize the plants again. Remove the seedheads after the blooms fade, and allow the foliage to die back naturally.

Hybrid species tulips respond especially well to such care and can be counted on to bloom each spring. Those that readily perennialize include *Tulipa greigii*, *T. kaufmanniana*, *T. fosteriana*, Darwin hybrids, and tetraploid single late tulips.

Protecting Bulbs from Animals

Many small rodents are fond of tulip and crocus bulbs. To outwit them, place chipped stones at the bottom of the planting hole, position the bulb, and sprinkle more stones around it to reach but not cover the pointed tip. Fill in with soil.

Larger rodents—chipmunks and squirrels among them—also find tulip and crocus bulbs a tasty treat and will dig them up before the ground freezes. In the West, gophers can quickly destroy entire plantings. One way to prevent such foraging when putting in bulb beds is to plant in wire baskets. Dig a trench and line the bottom and sides with metal hardware cloth. Lay the bulbs on top, cover with several inches of soil, and tamp down. A top dressing of well-aged cow manure or commercial composted sewage sludge will further repel pests. Bulbs not bothered by rodents include daffodils, squills, glory-of-the-snow, and snowdrops.

planting. Papyraceus daffodils, a group that includes paper-whites, will bloom in these warm zones without a precooling period and can be planted directly outdoors. Most perform as annual bulbs, but some may perennialize.

Some hybrid species tulips also can forgo a cold period and will thrive for several years. Such varieties include *Tulipa clusiana* var. *Chrysantha, T. sylvestris,* and *T. bakeri.* In fact, in some areas these smaller species will spread freely when planted in well-drained, gravelly soil under ideal conditions. Wild tulips are smaller than hybrids and can be planted closer together—at the rate of 90 per square yard, 3 to 4 inches apart, compared with 45 hybrid bulbs per square yard.

Planting Mixed Bulbs

For a continuous show of color over several weeks, combine bulbs that bloom at different times. If your combinations include both large and small bulbs, plant them in layers. Start by digging a rectangular hole 12 inches

deep. Loosen the soil in the bottom of the trench, mix in a slow-release bulb food, and top with a layer of unfertilized soil to bring the depth of the prepared trench up to about 8 inches. Place large bulbs in the bottom and cover with 4 inches of soil. Set the smaller bulbs in the trench and fill to the top with soil. Tamp it down, and water thoroughly before covering the area with a layer of mulch.

Bulbs that can be layered include dwarf iris over early daffodils or early to midspring tulips, squill over late-spring ornamental onion, windflower over early to midspring daffodils, muscari over mid- to late-spring tulips, and crocus over early to midspring hyacinths.

If you're interplanting similar-size bulbs that bloom at different times in the spring, dig an area to the required depth and alternate the bulbs, placing them as close as possible *(see chart, pages 32-33).* Cover with soil, tamp down, and water. Bulbs that have sequential bloom times and can be planted at the same depth include late-blooming daffodils and ornamental onion, crocus and muscari, and dwarf iris and windflower.

Using Bulbs for Special Effects

Flowering bulbs are versatile as well as beautiful. They can be grown in a number of settings and in combination with many other plantings to add glorious—and sometimes unexpected—splashes of seasonal color.

Rock Gardens and Raised Beds

Almost any bulb that is small enough to grow in nooks and crannies can be used to brighten rock gardens and even the spaces between the flagstones of a patio or walkway—environments that drain water quickly. Crocus, scilla, winter aconite, glory-of-the-snow, snowdrop, species tulips, and botanical and dwarf daffodils do especially well in these settings.

If you'd like to see such cheerful rock garden flowers as *Tulipa kaufmanniana* and *T. greigii* in your regular garden beds, you will have more success if you duplicate rock garden conditions. Before planting, incorporate equal parts of builder's sand or gravel and leaf mold or peat moss into the soil. Amend an

CANDIDATES FOR THE ROCK GARDEN
Lavender-petaled species tulips and golden miniature daffodils are ideal plants for the dry soil of this Virginia rock garden. The hybridized wild species grow best in rocky ground where rainfall can drain off quickly.

FLOURISHING BULBS IN A RAISED BED
Red hybrid Darwin tulips thrive in the well-drained soil found in this Oregon raised bed, an informal mound of soil. Grape hyacinths—which tolerate most conditions as long as the soil drains well—soften the edge.

area large enough to accommodate a handful of bulbs and deep enough to allow water to drain completely away from the roots.

Raised beds are another way to create a well-drained home for virtually any bulb. Appealing to the eye, they are also practical in areas where the soil is heavy and clayey. The beds can be framed with wood, brick, or cobblestones, or they can be pleasingly informal mounds of earth. In any case, your bed should contain at least 12 inches of soil. Amend the soil and plant the bulbs—interplanting different varieties if you wish—as described on pages 32-38.

Naturalizing Bulbs

Many bulbs will take hold and spread rapidly in almost any location—under trees, on a slope, in a meadow, or on a lawn—as long as they are planted in well-drained soil. Left to grow undisturbed, they'll self-seed, multiply underground, and return in greater numbers year after year.

When choosing a site for naturalizing, consider your bulbs' decaying foliage. Small bulbs with low foliage—such as crocus, snowdrop, glory-of-the-snow, snowflake, and dwarf iris— are well suited for planting in a lawn at the front of the house. They bloom early in the season, and by the time the grass needs mowing their foliage is spent. Set your mower at 4 inches for the first few clippings; the blades will ride over short bulb foliage without cutting it, and the grass will conceal it as it dries.

Many of these same small bulbs—along with windflower, wood hyacinth, winter aconite, and spring and fall cyclamens—also naturalize well under deciduous trees. In a damp area of the garden where no other bulb will grow, *Fritillaria meleagris* will thrive, and in full sun, grape hyacinth, camassia, and ornamental onion are vigorous spreaders.

Naturalize larger bulbs such as narcissus at the back or side of the house rather than in front. These bulbs also do nicely in a meadow or an orchard, where the longer grasses and emerging wildflowers help disguise the decaying foliage. Some of the best narcissus cultivars for naturalizing include 'Peeping Tom', 'Jack Snipe', 'Minnow', 'Ice Follies', 'Tête-à-Tête', 'Fortune', 'February Gold', 'Carlton', 'Mount Hood', and 'Birma'.

To make your bulb plantings look natural, scatter them over the ground and plant them where they land. Holes should be 6 to 7 inches deep for narcissus and 3 to 4 inches deep for smaller bulbs. On a lawn or other grassy environment where the soil is not compacted, use a hand-held hollow bulb planter or a trowel to dig individual holes. Some garden centers and catalogs also offer a "naturalizing tool" for planting bulbs in a lawn; it can be used from a standing position. Or, to limit the number of holes you must bore through the sod, cut away 8-inch squares of turf with a spade or an edger, loosen the soil below, and arrange the bulbs in a random pattern on the soil. Dig holes accordingly, plant the bulbs, and replace the sod. Repeat this method until all of your bulbs have been planted.

Marrying Bulbs with Ground Covers

Flowering bulbs add seasonal beauty to evergreen ground covers and vines such as ajuga, pachysandra, creeping juniper, ivy, periwinkle, bunchberry, euonymus, and cotoneaster. Try planting crocus, squill, grape hyacinth, and daffodils among these ground covers un-

der deciduous trees for bright spring color before the tree leafs out. The ground covers not only set off the blooms but will help hide the bulb foliage as it wilts. When making these combinations, however, be sure to consider the mature heights of the bulb and the ground cover. A smaller bulb like crocus would be lost amid the tall, thick growth of pachysandra, for example, whereas daffodils would hold their own nicely.

You can also pair bulbs with blooming ground covers, synchronizing flowering times for an even more spectacular effect. In a sunny border, daffodils, tulips, grape hyacinths, and ornamental onions can be planted so they poke through moss pink, flowering thyme, creeping thyme, aubretia, snow-in-summer, candytuft, spurge, or sweet woodruff.

In new beds, you can plant bulbs and ground covers at the same time. If you are combining bulbs with shallow-rooted ground covers such as moss pink or thyme, bury the bulbs and tamp them down, then overplant the ground covers. For larger-rooted shrubby creepers such as juniper, cotoneaster, bunchberry, and euonymus, interplant the bulbs with the ground covers. When shallow-rooted

A FIELD OF MULTICOLORED BLOOMS
A bounty of diminutive, vaselike crocus blooms adds charm to an expanse of turf grass in early spring in the Pacific Northwest. Because their thin, short foliage quickly dies and shrivels, crocuses are perfect for naturalizing in a lawn.

AN ENCHANTMENT OF DAFFODILS
A magical sight in springtime, this sea of yellow daffodils in New Jersey is a powerful magnet that proved irresistible to a Canada goose. The bulbs have naturalized by multiplying underground and by setting seed. With space to spread, the clumps do not need division.

41

Growing and Staking Very Large Blooms

1. To stake tall, large-flowering plants such as dahlias, place one end of a 4-foot length of bamboo or plastic-coated metal next to the tuber or bulb in the bottom of the planting hole and fill in with amended garden soil. Tamp the soil down to remove air pockets and secure the stake, then water thoroughly. As the plant grows, rest its stem against the stake but do not yet secure it (Step 3).

2. As soon as flower buds form between the main stem and the side leaves, pinch them off so that only two or three buds are left at the top of the main stem. For exhibition-size plants, leave only one bud at the top of the stem. In this way, the top buds benefit from more of the plant's nutrients and develop into larger flower heads.

3. When the main stem is about 12 inches high, tie it to the stake with twine or raffia. Knot the ties firmly around the stake but leave a loose loop around the stem so as not to bruise or strangle it. Continue tying at intervals of 8 to 12 inches as the stem keeps growing toward its full height and the blossoms mature.

ground covers already occupy the planting area, use a shovel to ease back a clump at a time. Gently loosen the soil underneath with a trowel to the right depth for the bulbs you've chosen, and follow the soil preparation and planting procedures described on pages 32-38. Replace the ground cover, press it firmly into the soil, and water thoroughly.

Some ground covers with dense or deep root systems, such as sweet woodruff, periwinkle, dead nettle, and pachysandra, can't be peeled back. Instead, dig out a section with a pointed shovel or a trowel. After planting the bulbs, replace the ground cover, press down firmly, and water thoroughly.

Interplanting Bulbs with Annuals

Annual flowering and foliage plants are perfect for interplanting with established bulbs. Soil preparation for the shallow roots of annuals doesn't have to be as deep as for perennials, so disturbance of the area can be kept to a minimum. Choose annuals that are contained in cell packs or pots no larger than 4 inches, and plant them in small, shallow holes. Tamp soil around the plants, and water thoroughly.

Lobelia, moss rose, sweet alyssum, zinnia, forget-me-not, and pansy have such minor root systems they can be planted as close as the dying foliage of the bulbs allows. Larger-branching and deeper-rooted annuals such as impatiens, marigold, geranium, cornflower, and China pink should be interplanted only with bulbs buried at least 6 inches deep.

Growing Exhibition-Size Blooms

Several of the larger bulbs, such as dahlias, tuberous begonias, and some gladiolus and lilies, produce naturally large and beautiful blooms. To grow exhibition-size flowers for a spectacular show in the garden or for cut bouquets indoors, you must start with large, healthy bulbs. Plant them after the last spring frost in a protected, sunny spot with well-drained soil. Work an organic 9-9-6 fertilizer into the soil at planting time, and feed them with a low-nitrogen fertilizer when the buds emerge and again when the flowers show color. For the largest dahlia blooms, prune as shown at left; these plants will require staking.

Care and Maintenance

Once you've planted your bulbs in the proper soil, you can relax and enjoy the flowers of your labor. With just a minimum of upkeep, many bulbs will bloom year after year, delighting the eye and rewarding you for the care you took when putting them in the ground.

Fertilizing and Watering for Best Results

Although bulbs contain their own food supply for the next season's blooms, feeding them each year with commercial fertilizers ensures star performances. Fertilize established beds in mid- to late fall when the bulbs are sending out good root growth and before the ground starts to freeze. Use a 9-9-6 slow-release synthetic sprinkled over the ground at the rate of 1 pound per 100 square feet of surface area.

If your bulbs are in a mixed herbaceous bed that has been fertilized regularly, these additional feedings aren't necessary. Also, soils that have been amended with organic materials such as compost, shredded leaves, shredded bark, or aged manure don't need regular, additional fertilizing. Instead, layer compost around the plants in the spring and put down mulch in the fall. If the soil was not amended at planting time, periodic top-dressing with organic-rich materials will create nutrient-laden, moisture-retentive, loamy soils. Normal rainfall usually provides enough moisture. However, if your area experiences a long period of dry weather during the bulbs' active growth times, give them at least 1 inch of water each week. As with all plants, water is best delivered to bulbs in a long, slow soaking. To discourage fungus diseases, avoid overhead watering; water early in the morning to reduce evaporation caused by heat.

How to Avoid Staking

When tall or heavy bulb varieties are planted deep enough in loose loamy soil, they send out a good root system and grow sturdy

stems. If you plant the bulbs in a sheltered area where winds and rain can't topple them, the stems will rarely need staking.

Even gladiolus can be self-supporting when planted in a row, especially if the soil is mounded up slightly to bolster the growing stems. But if the flower heads are particularly large and top-heavy, they will need some help. The entire row can easily be supported with lengths of twine gently woven among the stems and secured to stakes at each end of the row.

Large-headed flowering bulbs such as tuberous begonias, true lilies, Dutch hyacinth, dahlias, giant ornamental onion, and ranunculus may need individual staking when they are planted in exposed locations, poor soil, or shade; when they have a profusion of naturally large blooms; or when they are cultivated for exhibition (opposite).

LONG LIVES WITH PROPER CARE
After globes of silver-lilac flowers have faded, the broad blue-green leaves of Allium karataviense (ornamental onion) will continue to add interest to this perennial border for several weeks. Properly fed, watered, and left undisturbed, clumps of ornamental onions will flower and multiply for 10 seasons or more.

Protecting Lilies and Tulips from Foragers

When deer and rabbits nibble on the tender new foliage and immature buds of single-stemmed tulips and lilies in spring, the bulbs will not recover to produce another flower in the same season—and may not recover at all. If the problem is limited to isolated plantings, surround the grouping with green or brown plastic-coated wire mesh cages as soon as the shoots begin to emerge. Remove the cages when the blooms are ready to burst open and the plant foliage is no longer tender.

Another effective deterrent is a top dressing of blood meal or commercial composted sewage sludge, which not only repels animals but also adds nutrients to the soil. Foul-smelling organic repellents—liquid sprays that contain putrescent egg, tar oil, or ammonium soaps—can help control damage as well. Start spraying foliage when it begins to emerge, and reapply every 2 weeks until the buds begin to open. Avoid the repellent sprays that are advertised as foul tasting, however; they contain a chemical that is toxic to wildlife, humans, and the environment.

After the Flowers Fade

Once the blossoms fade, cut off the heads to prevent seed formation. Keeping the plant from making seed will help to increase the size of the bulb so that it can produce a larger flower the next season. However, you don't want to deadhead bulbs that are naturalizing because, of course, setting seed is one of the ways they multiply and spread.

Don't pull, cut, bend, or knot the foliage or dig up the bulb before its leaves have turned yellow and withered. Some varieties—such as narcissus—can take as long as 10 or 12 weeks to die naturally. After the yellowed leaves have completely withered, tug them gently to remove them or cut them off neatly at soil level. Tender summer bulbs can be lifted from the ground and stored after the foliage has died.

Mulching for Frost Protection

When the weather turns cold in late fall or early winter, mulch your bulb beds with 2 to 4 inches of organic material such as shredded bark, pine needles, seedless salt hay, or shredded leaves. Avoid whole leaves because they mat down and make it difficult for bulbs to poke through. Applying a mulch in winter protects the bulbs from alternate freezing and thawing, which can cause the soil to heave and expose plant roots. Mulching will also help to maintain moisture in the soil.

Growing Bulbs in the Cutting Garden

Flowering bulbs are a natural source of beauty for cut bouquets. If you are reluctant to cut flowering bulbs from your beds and borders to enjoy indoors, consider planting several varieties in a special cutting garden. Plant such bulbs in rows spaced 1½ feet apart for easy access, and space larger bulbs 6 inches apart.

Some of the best bulbs for cutting are those with the largest flowers and the longest stems, such as hybrid tulips, daffodils, dahlias, gladiolus, and lilies. Other candidates that are shorter but provide a glorious display of color include poppy anemones, tuberous begonias, ranunculus, and the wonderfully perfumed hyacinths. Even the smallest blooms of such bulbs as grape hyacinth and dwarf narcissus make charming arrangements. To prolong the cutting season, plant different cultivars of daffodils, tulips, and lilies, and stagger gladiolus plantings so that you'll get a succession of blooms spanning many weeks.

The best time in the growth cycle to cut a flower is when it's just beginning to open. Daffodils—which should be picked by pinching the stem rather than cutting it—perform best when the bud starts to swell, stops pointing upward, and moves into a right angle. Cut tulips when the color starts to show through the green bud. At this stage, the flower will continue to open and last a long time. If a tulip is cut too soon, the bud will not develop into an open flower.

The best time of day to cut flowers is in the early morning or in the evening, when the stems contain the most water. Cut the stems on a slant with a sharp knife so as not to tear or crush them, and don't cut the foliage. Carry a pail of tepid water so that the fresh-cut stem can be submerged immediately.

Avoid placing daffodil stems in the same pail with tulips because they release a sap that is toxic to tulips; keep them separate for several hours before combining them in an arrangement. When cutting lilies, snip off the stamens so that the pollen won't stain your clothes, skin, and other flowers. Also, your lilies will bloom more readily in subsequent years if you remove no more than half the stem's length; the remaining stem continues to direct nutrients to the bulb for use the following year. For the same reason, cut individual stems only every second or third year; cutting more often will rob the bulb of fuel.

As soon as you get the flowers indoors, recut the stems with a sharp knife, making the cut under water to keep air bubbles out. (Daffodils are again the exception; do not recut their stems.) Submerge the stems immediately up to the base of the bud in fresh water in a container that keeps them standing straight. Place them in a dark, cool closet or basement for a few hours. During this time, the stems will continue to take in water and become firm.

To prolong the life of the flower, add a commercial floral preservative to the water in your vase, or make your own preservative by adding ¼ teaspoon of liquid laundry bleach and ½ teaspoon of sugar to a quart of water.

The bleach will inhibit the growth of bacteria that can clog the cut ends of the stems, and the sugar will provide food for the flowers. Change the water frequently and cut the stems ½ inch each time.

A favorite way to display flowers grown from bulbs is to arrange them in tall glass vases that support and show off their long, slender stems. If you use a shallow container, you'll need a "frog"—a wire, ceramic, or glass device with holes—to hold individual stems. A small piece of crumpled chicken wire or floral foam also can be used to hold the stems upright. Floral foam will be visible in a glass vase, but chicken wire, when placed at the top, can be disguised with foliage. Another, decorative solution is to place glass marbles in the bottom of a shallow glass vase. Or wrap florist's wire around the floppy stems of tulips, ranunculus, anemones, hyacinths, and other weak-stemmed bulbs. The stems of these bulbs have a tendency to stretch and may need cutting and repositioning daily.

Best Bulbs for Cutting

Allium
(ornamental onion)
Amaryllis belladonna
(belladonna lily)
Anemone coronaria
(poppy anemone)
Dahlia
(dahlia)
Eremurus
(foxtail lily)
Freesia
(freesia)
Hyacinthus orientalis
(Dutch hyacinth)
Iris hollandica
(Dutch iris)
Lilium
(lily)
Muscari
(grape hyacinth)
Narcissus
(daffodil)
Ornithogalum
(star-of-Bethlehem)
Ranunculus asiaticus
(Persian buttercup)
Scilla peruviana
(Peruvian lily)
Sprekelia formosissima
(Jacobean lily)
Tulipa
(tulip)

Calla lilies, Dutch iris, lilies, and poppy anemones

A Year of Bulbs

Versatile and adaptable, bulbs can flower during every season. From the first explosion of cheerful crocuses in the waning frosts of winter to the last splash of colorful dahlias amid the earth tones of late fall, bulbs provide an almost endless parade of color in the garden. They brighten both sunny and shady areas, and many produce appealing foliage and excellent cutting flowers. And when the harsh blasts of midwinter weather finally put an end to all outdoor flowering, you can defy the barrenness of the season with fragrant indoor blooms forced from hardy bulbs that seem oblivious of the calendar.

The gallery on the following pages shows bulbs in a variety of settings for all seasons; a planting guide for each garden appears on pages 58-61.

HEARTENING HINTS OF THINGS TO COME
Drifts of pale purple and silver-gray crocus brighten a late-winter scene in Oregon. Originally planted in 1938, the steadfast bulbs naturalized and spread through the garden over the years.

A TRAFFIC-STOPPING SPRING GARDEN

A riot of red Persian buttercups (Ranunculus asiaticus) grabs the eye in this mixed border fronting a street in a San Francisco suburb. A spring-blooming tuber, Persian buttercup is hardy in areas with dry summers and mild winters. Its hybrid strains yield a rainbow of hues, including the pink and white buttercups that, aided by the purple of French lavender and yellow of mountain alyssum, relieve and soften the garden's red theme.

49

EXOTIC INTERLUDE FOR A MIXED BED
Clusters of dazzling lilies—orange 'Milano' and creamy white 'Roma'—glow in the bright sun of a Virginia summer. Best planted in groups of three or more, these Asiatic hybrids, with an erect growth habit and flower heads that evoke faraway places, are effective high-lights in this terraced bed. Hardy and easy to grow, they are also perfect for cutting.

SUMMER BLOOMERS TO PUNCTUATE A HILLSIDE BORDER
Dense umbels of showy deep blue Agapanthus 'Bressingham Blue' (African lily) stand out in bold contrast to golden mounds of orange coneflower, slender trumpets of Cape fuchsia, and lemon yellow daylilies in this Washing-ton State garden. Vigorous summer-flowering tubers, the African lilies bloom throughout the season, preferring full sun but tolerating partial shade. Their large clumps of fleshy, straplike leaves provide handsome fill-in foliage even when the plant is not in flower.

COLORS TO BRIGHTEN
A SHADY HAVEN

The variegated green-and-white leaves of Caladium 'June Bride' seem to share the light-reflecting qualities of the water beyond, creating a focal point in this Pennsylvania meadow garden. Vivid red impatiens, accented by a white-flowering hosta, and impatiens in bright white are interplanted along paths and around a rustic walnut log bench, enhancing the summertime woodland setting. In sunnier spots, orange canna lilies, planted in tubs placed directly into the ground, produce bright vertical accents. The cannas can be lifted and stored for the winter in a frost-free area.

A LIVELY MIX OF FLOWERS AND FOLIAGE
*Overarching bronze leaves of canna lily
make a regal backdrop for the simple beauty
of low-growing, daisylike dahlias. Towering
sunflowers and a carpet of pink geraniums
complete the arresting combination in this
Washington State garden, where blooms
abound from mid-July to late October.*

**COLORS AND TEXTURES
FOR A FALL GARDEN**
*An array of cultivated dahlias—named cac-
tus, water lily, anemone, and decorative—
adds daubs of color to a Pennsylvania mixed
border. Blooming from summer to late fall,
these intrepid tubers extend the life of the garden when many other bedding plants are waning or have stopped flowering for the season.*

**BULBS TO LIFT
MIDWINTER SPIRITS**
*Red trumpets of 'Scarlet
Baby' amaryllis rise amid
a ring of bright red Tulipa
'Jingle Bells' to comple-
ment the warm copper
tones of the cookware in
this Virginia kitchen. Along
with flanking pots of deep
red cottage tulips, the
amaryllis belies the frigid
temperatures outside.
Bulbs are some of the easiest plants to grow indoors,
and many can be forced
into bloom at specific times
of winter; 'Jingle Bells'
tulips are some of the earliest, flowering in time for
the holiday season.*

**HEARTENING HINTS
OF THINGS TO COME**
pages 46-47

A. *Hamamelis x intermedia
'Jelena' (1)*
B. *Crocus tomasinianus
(drifts of 1,000s)*

C. *Galanthus sp. (many)*
D. *Hamamelis x intermedia
'Diane' (1)*
E. *Rhododendron sp. (1)*

**SUMMER BLOOMERS
TO PUNCTUATE A
HILLSIDE BORDER**
page 50

A. *Helianthus decapetalus (1)*
B. *Artemisia 'Huntington
Garden' (2)*
C. *Agapanthus 'Bressingham
Blue' (10)*
D. *Hemerocallis cv. (3)*

E. *Achillea ageratum
'W. B. Child' (3)*
F. *Phygelius capensis (1)*
G. *Rudbeckia fulgida
'Goldsturm' (6)*
H. *Hemerocallis 'Corky' (4)*

A TRAFFIC-STOPPING SPRING GARDEN
pages 48-49

A. *Rosa 'Abraham Darby' (1)*
B. *Ranunculus asiaticus cv. (3)*
C. *Ranunculus asiaticus cv. (10)*
D. *Papaver nudicaule 'Champagne Bubbles' (1)*
E. *Lavandula stoechas (1)*
F. *Chrysanthemum paludosum (3)*

G. *Pelargonium x hortorum (1)*
H. *Iris 'Beverly Sills' (4)*
I. *Ixia maculata (12)*
J. *Rosmarinus officinalis 'Tuscan Blue' (2)*
K. *Ranunculus asiaticus cv. (3)*
L. *Lychnis coronaria*

'Angel's Blush' (1)
M. *Alyssum montanum (1)*
N. *Chrysanthemum frutescens (2)*
O. *Lavandula angustifolia (1)*
P. *Mentha suaveolens 'Variegata' (1)*

EXOTIC INTERLUDE FOR A MIXED BED
page 51

A. *Lilium 'Roma' (3)*
B. *Lilium 'Milano' (9)*
C. *Veronica austriaca 'Crater Lake Blue' (2)*
D. *Tagetes erecta 'Inca Gold' (9)*

E. *Achillea 'Coronation Gold' (3)*
F. *Antirrhinum majus Wedding Bells Series (6)*
G. *Cosmos bipinnatus 'Seashells' (4)*

NOTE: The key lists each plant type and the total quantity needed to replicate the garden shown. The diagram's letters and numbers refer to the type of plant and the number sited in an area.

COLORS TO BRIGHTEN A SHADY HAVEN
pages 52-53

A. *Hosta plantaginea (1)*
B. *Impatiens 'Red Velvet' (4)*
C. *Impatiens 'Accent White' (6)*
D. *Caladium 'June Bride' (3)*
E. *Anemone x hybrida 'Alba' (2)*

F. *Hydrangea 'Blue Lacecap' (1)*
G. *Asclepias incarnata (1)*
H. *Ligularia dentata 'Desdemona' (2)*
I. *Canna x generalis 'Pretoria' (4)*

A LIVELY MIX OF FLOWERS AND FOLIAGE
page 54

A. *Helianthus annuus 'Autumn Beauty' (5)*
B. *Canna x generalis 'Red King Humbert' (4)*

C. *Dahlia hybrid (5)*
D. *Geranium x riversleaianum 'Mavis Simpson' (1)*
E. *Sedum x 'Autumn Joy' (4)*

60

COLORS AND TEXTURES FOR A FALL GARDEN
pages 54-55

A. *Pyrus cv. (1)*
B. *Cleome spinosa 'Helen Campbell' (12)*
C. *Dahlia cv. (5)*
D. *Salvia uliginosa (4)*
E. *Dahlia 'Snow Country' (3)*

F. *Dahlia 'David Howard' (4)*
G. *Daphne x burkwoodii 'Carol Mackie' (2)*
H. *Senecio vira-vira (6)*
I. *Bidens ferulifolia 'Golden Goddess' (10)*

J. *Dahlia 'Gerry Hoek' (9)*
K. *Verbena bonariensis (4)*
L. *Agastache mexicana 'Toronjil Mirado' (2)*
M. *Dolichos lablab (3)*
N. *Canna x generalis 'Striata' (3)*

BULBS TO LIFT MIDWINTER SPIRITS
pages 56-57

A. *Tulipa 'Burning Love' (11)*
B. *Hippeastrum 'Scarlet Baby' (3)*

C. *Tulipa 'Jingle Bells' (8)*
D. *Hyacinthus orientalis (1)*

NOTE: The key lists each plant type and the total quantity needed to replicate the garden shown. The diagram's letters and numbers refer to the type of plant and the number sited in an area.

CHAPTER THREE

Storage and Propagation

Being uniquely self-contained, bulbs are far easier to move than other plants. This trait allows gardeners in any climate to grow tender bulbs—plants whose vulnerability to frost would otherwise limit them to only the warmest regions—by digging them up and storing them over winter.

The large leaves of the two cultivars of Caladium shown at right, for example, can add their variegated beauty to this Richmond, Virginia, planting because the gardener has lifted the tubers each fall, dried them, packed them, and stored them, using a method presented in this chapter.

Bulbs out of the ground offer an opportunity for division, a remarkably easy way to propagate them. On the following pages you'll find instructions for dividing bulbs and other techniques for multiplying your stock of true bulbs, corms, tubers, and rhizomes—including, in some cases, growing them from seed. And if you're feeling particularly adventurous, on pages 75-77 you'll learn how to create your own lily hybrids—to deliciously unpredictable effect.

A. *Hosta undulata 'Variegata' (wavy-leaf plantain lily) (1)*
B. *Caladium cv. (caladium) (1)*
C. *Athyrium nipponicum 'Pictum' (painted lady fern) (3)*
D. *Impatiens 'Super Elfin Hybrids' (impatiens) (1)*
E. *Dicentra 'Luxuriant' (bleeding heart) (1)*
F. *Caladium cv. (caladium) (1)*

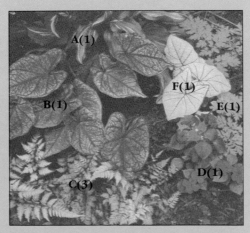

NOTE: The key lists each plant type and the total quantity needed to replicate the garden shown. The diagram's letters and numbers refer to the type of plant and the number sited in an area.

Storing Cold-Sensitive Tender Bulbs

Gardeners who grow only hardy bulbs such as tulips and daffodils, which typically bloom and are gone by late spring, can expand their horizons considerably with tender summer- and fall-blooming bulbs.

Tender bulbs look generally the same as their hardy cousins, and they grow the same way. Their difference can be attributed to place of origin. Tender bulbs are warm-climate plants and thus may not withstand the extremely cold ground temperatures that oc-cur in parts of the United States and Canada.

Tender and hardy are relative terms, however. A very few bulbs are extremely cold sensitive. Caladium, which tolerates no frost at all, must be lifted for winter even in Zone 9—an area that includes south Texas and much of southern California. Dahlia and gladiolus may find winter in Zone 8 too frigid. Yet so-called tender bulbs like crocosmia and tigridia can safely stay in the ground in Zone 7, where the average minimum temperature is 0° to 10° F.

Digging and Storing Dahlias

1. When the foliage has substantially yellowed, *as on the tall plant in the illustration at right, trim the stems back to about 6 to 8 inches. Using a garden spade, plunge the blade to nearly its full length into the soil about a foot away from the plant. Repeat all around the plant to thoroughly loosen the soil and sever the longest fibrous roots. Carefully lever the plant out of the soil by pressing down on the handle of the spade.*

2. Using a garden hose with a nozzle, *direct a gentle spray on the tubers to wash away all clinging soil without damaging them. Then, trim the stem or stems down to an inch or two. Allow the tubers to dry upside down in an airy place for a day or two.*

3. After the tubers have dried thoroughly, *dust them with a fungicide such as garden sulfur and place each one in a clear plastic bag filled with coarse vermiculite or a similar medium. Seal the bags and store them in a cool, dry place. Check the tubers after 1 month for rotting and for signs of excess moisture—indicated by a mist or beads of water on the inner surface of the bag—and then one or two more times during the winter. Let air in to reduce moisture, and discard any bad tubers.*

Rescuing Tender Bulbs from Frost

Being among the most tender of bulbs, caladiums and several other genera must be brought in well before the first frost. Trim away their dead foliage and dig them carefully by sinking a garden fork into the soil at least 6 inches out from the crown of the plant. If you inadvertently damage a bulb, discard it.

While a garden fork is fine for digging most bulbous plants, switch to a spade for dahlias *(opposite)* so you can lift out a fair-size rootball. Dahlia tubers send out long fibrous roots that hang on tenaciously to the soil, and lifting the tuber with the tines of a fork against the pull of the roots might tear it apart.

If you're digging and saving more than one variety or species, separate the bulbs according to type and mark them with plant tags.

Watsonia 'Pink Opal' (bugle lily)

Drying

Bulbs cannot go directly from the ground into storage. Moisture on their surfaces may cause rot, and clinging soil may harbor diseases. So they must first be cleaned and dried. Carefully brush or wash off loose soil. Then spread the bulbs out on a screen or in trays in a warm, dry place. After the surfaces are thoroughly dry, dip the bulbs in garden sulfur, which will act as a natural fungicide.

Some bulb types, such as dahlia and canna, are perishable and cannot be exposed for more than a day or two before desiccation sets in. But their surfaces should dry sufficiently in that time, especially if the process is accelerated with a bit of forced air from a fan.

Other tender bulbs, such as gladiolus, tuberous begonia, and acidanthera, are somewhat tougher, but all bulbs should be dried as quickly as possible to limit their exposure to fungal infection. If possible, try to dig and dry during a dry, clear spell of weather. Wet, raw conditions will make the job more difficult.

Packing and Storing

Once the bulbs are clean and dry, place them in bags filled with a sterile medium such as vermiculite, perlite, dry sand, or peat moss. Dahlia and canna require cool, moist storage conditions and do best when packed individually in sealed plastic bags to retain a modicum of moisture. Most other bulbs, such as watsonia, galtonia, gladiolus, tuberous begonia, and acidanthera, on the other hand, will do best packed in paper bags that are folded shut but not sealed. These bulbs can be packed several at a time, but make sure the bulbs don't touch each other inside the bag.

Environmental requirements for storing bulbs vary, making it difficult to find the ideal winter resting place for all your bulbs. For most, the temperature should fall somewhere between 40° and 55°F, with dahlia, gladiolus, tuberous begonia, and canna preferring the lower end of that range. Caladiums, hymenocallis, and gloriosa, by contrast, may suffer damage at temperatures below 60°F.

You should be able to keep most bulbs in a garage or a basement. If you are using an unheated garage, however, and the interior temperature falls below 35°F, you must bring the bulbs into your house. If your basement is heated, find the coolest area and place the containers on a portion of uncarpeted floor.

Tender bulbs growing in pots, such as tuberous begonia, chlidanthus, and zantedeschia, can be stored over winter in their containers. Trim the plants back to the soil line and store in open air in a cool, dry place with the pots resting on their sides.

Selected Bulbs That Must Be Lifted

ZONE 9 AND NORTHWARD
Achimenes
(orchid pansy)
Caladium
(caladium)
Gloriosa
(gloriosa lily)

ZONE 8 AND NORTHWARD
Dahlia
(dahlia)
Freesia
(freesia)
Gladiolus hybrids
(gladiolus)
Hymenocallis
(spider lily)
Ranunculus
(buttercup)
Sprekelia formosissima
(Jacobean lily)

ZONE 7 AND NORTHWARD
Canna
(canna)
Ornithogalum arabicum
(Arabian star-of-Bethlehem)
Ornithogalum dubium
(star-of-Bethlehem)
Ornithogalum thyrsoides
(wonder flower)
Watsonia hybrids
(bugle lily)
Zantedeschia
(calla lily)
Zephyranthes
(zephyr lily)

Propagating True Bulbs

Most gardeners are familiar with growing plants from seeds and increasing their number of plants by sowing seeds gathered from the original stock. The process of creating new plants from seed is termed sexual propagation, because the seeds originate from reproductive plant parts that are fertilized through pollination.

Since true bulbs produce viable seed, they can be propagated by this method. But the wait for bulbs to grow to maturity from seed may require more patience than many gardeners possess. Tulips and daffodils, for example, might take 4 or 5 years to flower from seed, hyacinths even longer. Furthermore, cultivars and hybrids that have been propagated from seed are susceptible to reverting to earlier forms in their genealogy. The resulting plants may not give you the look you were expecting from your flowers.

Starting from Seed

If you can commit yourself to a long-term proposition, the best approach to propagating true bulbs from seed is to sow a different variety of seed every year. Although the first crop will take years to come into flower, after that your waiting will be over. Each year a different planting will add its blooms to the existing bulb show.

Despite the long wait, propagating by seed is the best choice for a few true bulb genera, including *Scilla,* simply because they don't easily lend themselves to other propagation methods. Planting scilla seed will give you flowers in 3 to 4 years.

Nevertheless, for most true bulbs it's far easier and more reliable to propagate asexually—by dividing the bulbs and then planting

Separating True Bulbs

After the foliage has turned brown, dig the bulbs up in their naturally formed clumps. Taking care not do damage the roots, brush away clinging soil *(below, left)*. Discard any injured, diseased, or rotted bulbs. Ease the daughter bulbs away from the mother bulb *(below, right),* making sure each one includes a portion of the basal plate. The smallest, youngest bulbs may still be firmly attached to the mother. If they do not separate easily, leave them in place and allow them to mature for another year or two. Dust the separated mother and daughter bulbs with a fungicide such as garden sulfur and replant.

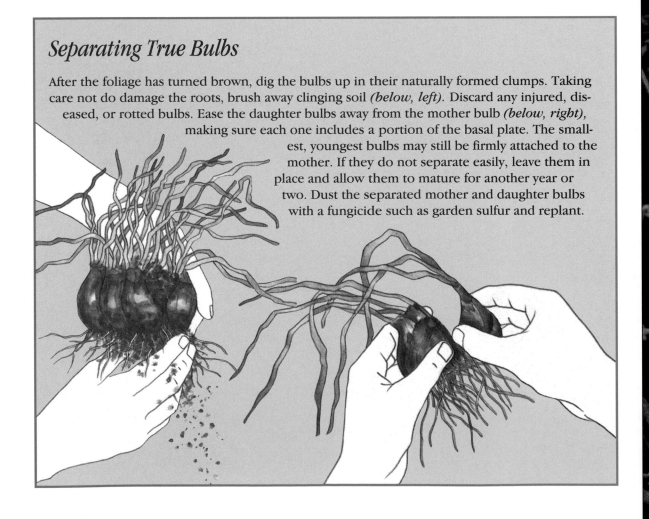

their offsets. Some bulbs, such as daffodils, have large offsets that will flower as early as the first season.

When and How to Propagate Asexually

The correct time for digging and dividing true bulbs depends on the growth habit of the plant. Most should be dug after their foliage has withered but while it still remains in place to show the location of the bulbs. If the foliage is not too far gone, it might even serve as a handle to help lift the bulbs. An exception is *Galanthus* (snowdrop), which should be dug immediately after flowering.

If you plan to propagate several varieties, it's a good idea to mark the foliage with an indelible pen while the plants are still in flower. That way, you'll be able to identify the bulbs later when all the withered, brown leaves look more or less the same.

Choose only healthy, disease-free plants for propagation. Dig the bulbs carefully with a spading fork, making sure not to damage them; cuts and bruises can give rise to rot. Imbricate bulbs such as lily and fritillary, which have scales but no papery outer covering, are especially fragile and vulnerable to injury. Gently brush away any clinging soil and carefully separate the bulbs as shown at far left.

Different Treatment for Different Bulbs

In general, hardy bulbs such as tulips and daffodils can be dug, divided, and replanted all in one operation. Tender summer bulbs, such as *Zephyranthes* and *Chlidanthus,* should be dug in fall, separated, stored over the winter, and planted in spring.

Once they are divided, sort the bulbs according to size—small, medium, or large. You can plant the largest ones in the garden to flower the following year. Medium-size bulbs

TRUE BULBS WITHIN A DIVERSE GENUS
Rising above tiny blue Myosotis sylvatica (forget-me-not) blossoms, these gloriously hued Dutch irises stand about 18 inches tall. One of the few irises that grow from bulbs, not rhizomes, the plants can be propagated by seed or by division.

Selected True Bulbs

Allium
(onion)
Amaryllis belladonna
(belladonna lily)
Calochortus
(mariposa lily)
Camassia
(camass)
Chionodoxa
(glory-of-the-snow)
Crinum
(spider lily)
Eucharis grandiflora
(Amazon lily)
Eucomis
(pineapple lily)
Fritillaria
(fritillary)
Galanthus
(snowdrop)
Galtonia
(summer hyacinth)
Habranthus
(habranthus)
Hippeastrum
(amaryllis)
Hyacinthoides
(hyacinthoides)
Hyacinthus
(hyacinth)
Hymenocallis
(spider lily)
Ipheion
(spring starflower)
Iris
(iris)
Lachenalia
(Cape cowslip)
Leucojum
(snowflake)
Lilium
(lily)
Lycoris
(spider lily)
Muscari
(grape hyacinth)
Narcissus
(daffodil)
Nerine
(nerine)
Ornithogalum
(star-of-Bethlehem)
Oxalis
(sorrel)
Puschkinia
(striped squill)
Scilla
(squill)
Sprekelia formosissima
(Jacobean lily)
Sternbergia
(winter daffodil)
Tulipa
(tulip)
Vallota
(Scarborough lily)
Zephyranthes
(zephyr lily)

can also go directly into the garden, but they may or may not bloom the following year.

The smallest bulbs will need further growing before they are mature enough to bloom. It's best to plant them in a nursery bed to allow them to develop.

Lily bulblets and bulbils, too, should be planted out in a nursery bed *(right)*. Separate the bulblets from the mother bulb and the bulbils from the stem in late summer, about 6 weeks after flowering, and then replant the mother bulb in the garden.

Nursery Beds

Immature bulbs, bulblets, and bulbils will do best in more carefully arranged growing conditions than you would use for full-size bulbs. The prime consideration is good drainage. Another is freedom from competition with larger plants for moisture and nutrients. Still another is the need to grow in a situation where the baby bulbs' tiny, grasslike sprouts will not be mistaken for unwanted grass or weeds and pulled out.

The arrangement that meets all these needs perfectly is a nursery bed. Set aside a small, sunny, out-of-the-way plot devoted exclusively to young plants. Here, without excessive effort, you can cultivate and amend the soil for ideal drainage and fertility.

Because the plants you start here will be transplanted as soon as they are mature enough, you can grow them relatively close together and in rows without worrying about aesthetics. And because you know that those wisps of vegetation that appear in the bed may well be something you planted, there's less danger you'll uproot them.

Water the bed amply to encourage good growth. Take pains to weed it carefully in the autumn, because when new shoots begin to emerge the following spring you may find it difficult to weed without jeopardizing them.

As soon as winter weather arrives, mulch the ground to moderate changes in the temperature of the soil. Otherwise, the expansion and contraction of earth that alternately freezes and thaws could heave the tiny bulbs out of the ground.

Allow the plants to grow for a year or two in the nursery bed; at the end of that time they should be ready to go into the garden. Dig them after the foliage dies back and plant where desired.

Planting Bulblets and Bulbils

Most lilies produce bulblets around the base of the flower stem, just underground; some also produce bulbils at the leaf axils. To use these for propagation, separate them from the plant after the foliage has withered.

Bulbils

Dig a trench 3 to 4 inches deep and lay down a 1-inch layer of sand. Place the bulblets several inches apart in the trench. For bulbils, which are considerably smaller, dig the trench about 2 inches deep and add 1 inch of sand. Fill in with loose, fertile soil topped with a sprinkling of a complete fertilizer.

Bulblets

Lilies That Produce Bulblets and Bulbils

BULBLETS		BULBILS
Lilium auratum (gold-banded lily)	*L. speciosum* (showy Japanese lily)	*L. lancifolium* (tiger lily)
L. henryi (Henry lily)	*L.* Asiatic hybrids (lily)	*L.* Asiatic hybrid 'Enchantment' (lily)
L. lancifolium (tiger lily)	*L.* Oriental hybrids (lily)	
L. longiflorum hybrids (Easter lily)	*L.* trumpet hybrids (lily)	
L. regale (regal lily)		

Scaling to Propagate Lilies

Most lily bulbs look something like artichokes, being made up of a series of overlapping fleshy scales that grow out in a spiral formation from a central, flowering axis. All of the scales are attached to the bulb's basal plate, but they grow in a loose configuration, and the outer ones can easily be removed without cutting and without harming the remaining bulb. This characteristic allows lilies and a few fritillaries—especially *Fritillaria imperialis*—to be propagated by a special technique called scaling. (Most fritillaries, which are composed of very few scales, may be destroyed in the process.)

Planted in a proper medium, at the right temperature, the scales will form bulblets at their base. These can be planted in turn, just like the bulblets from the underground portion of the stem of a growing lily bulb. Each scale will produce at least one bulblet, and each bulblet, potentially, will grow into a mature bulb. You can use scaling to supplement the bulblets and bulbils that grow naturally on lilies, particularly for varieties that produce few offsets. Scaling before you plant an expensive lily variety also helps ensure survival to the next generation should the original die during its first year, as sometimes happens.

How to Scale

Bulbs can be scaled at any time—even when you've just brought them home from the nursery. However, because lily and fritillary are hardy bulbs, meant to stay in the ground over winter, most bulblets produced by scaling will need to experience a period of chilling before they can begin to sprout. Therefore, the best time to scale is in late summer or early autumn, which will allow time for the bulblets to emerge and then be refrigerated for several months before planting out in spring. Also, completing the operation by au-

TWO POTENTIAL PAY-OFFS FROM SCALING
Brightening a garden in Washington, D.C., orange Fritillaria imperialis (crown imperial) and its purple-hued cousin, F. persica, both can be propagated by growing bulblets on scales removed from the original bulbs.

Propagation by Scaling

Scales will produce bulblets quite readily, but there are some minimum requirements for success. The scales will do best planted in a flat containing coarse vermiculite or a combination of coarse sand and peat moss. Keep the medium moist and the temperature between 60° and 70°F. The top of the refrigerator or a warm cupboard is a good place to keep the flat; light does not matter. After the bulblets emerge and the necessary chilling has taken place, plant them, with scales attached, in a nursery bed. Place the scales upright so that the tips of the scales are about 1 inch belowground and 6 inches apart.

1. Dig the bulb and gently remove the soil, taking care not to damage the roots. Cut off the top growth to about 6 to 8 inches.

2. Carefully pull off several outer scales, discarding any that are unhealthy, broken, or otherwise damaged. Rinse them, let them dry on newspaper, and dip them—and the wounded areas of the bulb—in a fungicide. Replant the bulb immediately; it will bloom normally again the next spring.

3. Plant the scales upright, about half to two-thirds submerged, in a flat filled with a suitable medium. Slip the flat into a plastic bag propped up with small sticks to protect the scales. Inspect occasionally for adequate moisture or rot.

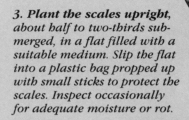

4. After 6 weeks, check one scale for bulblets with roots. Leaving the flat in plastic, chill over winter and plant the scales in spring.

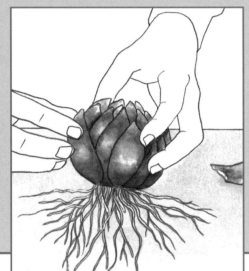

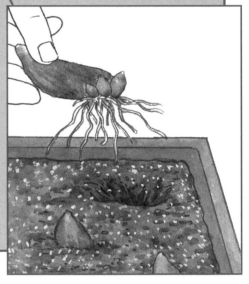

tumn will give the bulb time to reestablish itself after you replant it before winter sets in.

Choose the plants you'd like to scale, and mark them while they are still in flower. When the time is right, dig the bulbs carefully and remove and plant the scales as described above. Scales from most lilies will produce bulblets in 6 to 8 weeks; trumpet lilies will take about 12 weeks.

The newly emerged bulblets will be ready for chilling once they reach ¼ inch or more in height. You can accomplish the chilling in one of two ways. Either do your initial planting of the scales in a cold frame in the garden, where the emerging bulblets will remain to be chilled over winter. Or, once the bulblets have reached the proper size, place them in the refrigerator. They should be kept at 35° to 40°F—the temperature range in most refrigerators—for 2 months or longer.

If you keep them in the refrigerator, wait until the proper spring planting time to set them out. Don't remove the bulblets from the withered scales, as the tiny bulbs are fragile and easily damaged; also, the scales can still provide some nourishment to the bulblets after they are planted. Allow the bulblets to grow over the summer, then dig and replant them the following fall, setting them at a 6-inch depth, 4 to 6 inches apart.

Propagating Corms

Like other bulbs, cormous plants can be propagated from seed. Indeed, gladiolus produces abundant seed, is easy to grow from seed, and may bloom the first year. *Ixia, Sparaxis,* and *Tritonia* should bloom from seed within 2 years; *Babiana, Crocosmia, Tigridia,* and *Watsonia* within 3 years; *Crocus* and *Colchicum* in 3 or more years.

Still, unless you are growing only species, not cultivars or hybrids, the easiest and most reliable way to increase your stock of most cormous plants is to grow them from the corms and cormels they produce. For example, although hybrid gladiolus grows well from seed, the flowers that emerge may be throwbacks. Gladiolus also produces many cormels, however, which grow into clones of the original plant. So if you want your favorite gladiolus hybrids to reappear year after year, use this method to reproduce them.

Propagating from Cormels

Obtain cormels by lifting the desired plant when the foliage has withered but is still visible. Remove the cormels as illustrated at left and replant the mother corm in the garden.

In most climates, the cormels of gladiolus, freesia, and watsonia must be stored over the winter before being set out. And because their blooms will not appear until the second or third year, you will have to lift and store them once or twice more before they flower.

Prepare a shallow trench in a nursery bed and plant the cormels 1½ to 2 inches deep and 2 to 3 inches apart. In their first year, they will produce narrow, grasslike foliage. If need be at the end of the season, dig hardy corms such as crocus and replant them farther apart.

Separating Cormels

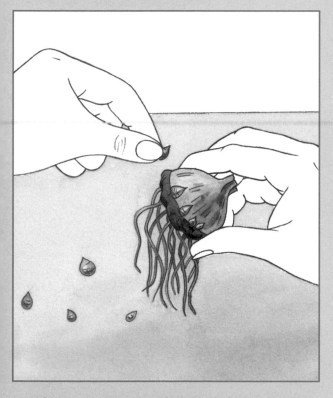

When propagating with cormels from a tender plant, such as the gladiolus hybrid above, wait until fall before digging. By then the mother corm has died, the daughter corm is fully mature, and cormels have emerged. Dry the new corm as quickly as possible, then gently pull off the cormels. Place the corm in a paper bag filled with dry peat moss and store over winter in a cool area such as a basement or garage. Sort the cormels by size and store them similarly. Plant them in a nursery bed in spring after all danger of frost has passed. If the plants you are propagating are hardy, you can simply lift them when the foliage has died, separate the cormels, and replant both corm and cormels immediately.

Crocus 'Snow Beauty'
(crocus)

Cormous Plants

Babiana
(baboon flower)
Bulbocodium vernum
(spring meadow saffron)
Colchicum
(autumn crocus)
Crocosmia
(montbretia)
Crocus
(crocus)
Dichelostemma congestum
(dichelostemma)
Erythronium
(dogtooth violet)
Freesia
(freesia)
Gladiolus
(gladiolus)
Ixia
(African corn lily)
Liatris spicata
(spike gay-feather)
Rhodohypoxis baurii
(rhodohypoxis)
Sparaxis
(harlequin flower)
Tigridia
(peacock flower)
Triteleia
(wild hyacinth)
Tritonia
(blazing star)
Watsonia
(bugle lily)

Note: The abbreviation "spp." stands for the plural of "species"; where used in lists it means that many, but not all, of the species in a genus meet the criterion of the list.

Propagating Tubers and Rhizomes

Some tuberous and rhizomatous plants can be started from seed. Seeds of dahlia and tuberous begonia, for example, are readily available through nursery catalogs. Or you can collect seeds from plants in your garden, though you run the risk of ending up with a different—and perhaps inferior—new generation. A tuber such as caladium, for example, grown solely for its strikingly colored foliage, may produce a good deal of undesirable variation when grown from seed.

Dahlia and tuberous begonia, if propagated from seed, require a long growing season to begin to flower. In all but the warmest regions, if the plants are to have time to flower the first year, the seeds must be started indoors in late winter, then planted out after the weather has warmed.

You will have a longer wait before you see flowers from other tubers and rhizomes started from seed. Achimenes, anemone, begonia, belamcanda, corydalis, ranunculus, and zantedeschia won't bloom until the second year. Gloriosa may take longer. If you don't want to wait that long, you must turn to asexual propagation techniques appropriate to tubers and rhizomes, such as division or stem cutting.

Asexual Propagation

The need to lift and store tender plants such as canna, dahlia, and tuberous begonia offers a convenient opportunity to propagate them asexually, by division. However, the process is a bit more invasive than that of separating true bulbs or plucking bulblets or cormels.

Instead of producing neatly sectioned or self-contained offsets that practically come off in your hand, tubers and rhizomes must be separated by force. Some tubers do grow offsets, but even these are firmly attached to the main body. To divide them, you must unflinchingly cut them into pieces.

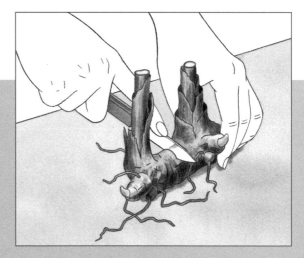

Dividing Tubers and Rhizomes

In dividing a dahlia tuber (below), cut it so that each section includes a root portion, a slice of the crown, and a growth bud. The buds, located around the crown, have been exaggerated for clarity in this illustration. Dip the cut surfaces in a fungicide and plant each section as shown in Chapter 2.

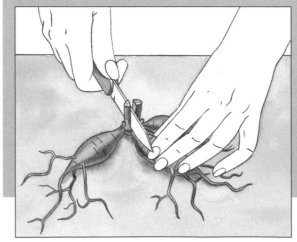

*Place tuberous bego-
nias (left) in a warm,
bright location to pro-
mote emergence of the
eyes, or growth points.
Cut a large tuber into 2
or 3 divisions, each of
which must contain an
eye. Dust the pieces with
a fungicide and let them
callus over for 2 days
before planting.*

*Canna rhizomes, like
the one at left, must be
stored over winter from
Zone 7 northward. In ear-
ly spring, remove the rhizomes from storage and
discard any withered or
diseased ones. Cut so that
each section contains a
growth node and roots.
Pot the sections or plant
in the garden, depending
on your climate.*

Nevertheless, division is a faster, easier, and more foolproof way to increase your stock of these plants than growing them from seed. The divided pieces usually will produce flowers their first year in the ground. And the offspring will be exact duplicates of the originals.

Dividing Tubers and Rhizomes

To propagate successfully by division, make sure you cut the tuber or rhizome so each piece contains one or more growth nodes. These nodes will appear on the tops of tubers and along the tops or sides of rhizomes.

Use a sharp knife sterilized in a solution of 1 part household bleach to 10 parts warm water. Dip the knife in the solution after each cut. If you are dividing tender plants that were lifted and stored for the winter, do your cutting just before spring planting. Hardy plants, by contrast, should be dug when the foliage has died back, divided, and replanted.

Before replanting, however, allow the cut pieces to "suberize," or heal, for 2 days in a warm place. During that time, a callus will form over the cut, protecting the tuber or rhi-

zome from rot once it is back in the ground.

Plant the divided pieces in the garden, following the planting instructions for different genera shown in Chapter 2. The pieces cut from tender bulbs will bloom later that season; those cut from hardy bulbs will bloom the following year.

Propagating from Stem Cuttings

Both dahlia and tuberous begonia produce branching plants and can therefore be propagated by stem cutting. Pick specimens that are the best and most representative examples of the hybrids or cultivars you wish to reproduce. Tag your choices early in the growing season and track their progress, switching to better ones should any originals falter.

Taking Cuttings from Your Garden

There are two ways to obtain stems for rooting. One is to cut them directly from desired varieties in your garden when the plants are

73

in full growth. Use a sterilized knife to cut approximately 4 to 6 inches off the growing end of a stem, making sure that the cut piece has a terminal bud or growth node, for further vertical growth, and intact nodes in the axils of its lowest set of leaves, for root growth. Make your cut just below the lowest leaves. You can also take a cutting from farther down on a stem; just be certain that you include at least two sets of leaves with growth nodes in their axils.

Whether you cut from the tip of a stem or farther down, proceed to steps 3 and 4 of the propagation process illustrated below. Once the stems of dahlias have rooted, it will be too late in the growing season to plant them in an outdoor bed. You will have to grow the cuttings indoors over the winter and plant them in spring. They will flower their first summer in the garden. However, tuberous begonias may form a tuber and come into flower in the same growing season you take the cutting.

Growing Shoots for Rooting

The other way to obtain cuttings is to grow shoots directly from tubers that have been in winter storage, as shown below. A dahlia tuber placed in a flat to grow shoots for stem cuttings will start sprouting in 2 to 4 weeks and may produce abundant shoots, which you can harvest periodically over a few weeks.

Begonia tubers and some dahlia cultivars, however, may grow no more than one or two shoots. If a tuber grows only one, you should leave it uncut so that the tuber will sprout when you replant it.

It takes another 6 weeks or so for a cutting from a tuber to grow roots and be ready to be planted out in the garden. And since dahlias and begonias grow best at temperatures above 55°F, you should begin the process at least 8 weeks before the time when minimum nighttime temperatures in your region are expected to rise to that level.

Propagating from Rooted Shoots

2. Shoots will appear in 1 to 2 weeks. *When they are 3 to 4 inches tall, cut them as close as possible to the surface of the tuber. If the tuber is a dahlia, take care not to nick it; if it is a begonia, cut away a bit of the tuber with the shoot.*

3. Trim stems below the lower leaves, *remove those leaves, and dip in rooting hormone. Fill a flat with fine vermiculite, poke holes in it, and plant the stems, pressing the medium around them. Put in a clear plastic bag and place under grow lights.*

4. After a few weeks, *gently tug at the cuttings. If you feel resistance, they have rooted. Once they reach this point, carefully dig out each cutting with its rootball and transplant it to its own peat pot filled with potting soil (below). Keep the shoots under grow lights for approximately 16 hours a day for another few weeks until it is time to plant them outdoors.*

1. In late winter or early spring, *divide the tubers of the plants you have selected for propagation. Set the tubers in a flat and fill with a moist potting soil, leaving the eyes or growth nodes exposed (left). Place the flat under grow lights in an area kept between 65° and 70°F.*

Creating Lily Varieties

Planting bulblets or bulbils, or dividing or scaling bulbs, lets you grow identical plants year after year. But what should you do if you want something different, something you've never seen in a garden before?

Part of the joy of gardening comes from the surprises it can offer, and sexual propagation —growing flowers from seeds, the product of pollination—is a sure way to create surprises. Not all the surprises are welcome ones, of course. Seeds sown from a cultivar that self-pollinated naturally in your garden may express earlier forms in the plant's ancestry. The offspring may be inferior in color, growth habit, bloom size, or scent. But you can improve the odds of getting a beautiful flower by seizing control of the propagation process from Mother Nature. You can create your own hybrids from existing varieties whose traits hold the potential to combine well.

Hybridizing may sound like a complex procedure best left to professionals, but the technique is actually rather simple. It helps to start with a plant such as a lily, which is relatively easy to hybridize because its sexual parts are easy to identify and handle. But as with any seed-grown lily, your hybrids won't produce flowers for at least 2 to 3 years.

How Lilies Procreate

Before you begin, you should understand that all lily flowers contain male and female parts *(page 76)* and can produce offspring through pollination. Tiny two-cell grains of pollen emerge on male parts called anthers. When a grain of viable pollen reaches the female part called the stigma, one of the cells begins to grow into a tube that extends down from the stigma to the ovary, searching for an opening into one of the ovules within.

The second cell divides to become two sperm that travel down the tube and enter the ovule, where one fertilizes it and the other combines with a cell in the ovule to become a food-storage unit called an endosperm. The fertilized ovule grows and matures into a seed. As the fertilized lily flower begins to fade and the petals dry and fall off, a seed pod forms. The pod eventually opens and the seeds are dispersed over the ground, where they may or may not germinate, depending on growing conditions.

Hybridizing

Plants form hybrids when pollen from the anthers of one variety, which becomes the male parent, reaches and fertilizes the ovules of another variety—the female parent. This is called cross-pollination, and it can happen naturally or be helped along by human hands.

FLOWERS THAT BEG TO BE CROSSED
Two lilies, a red 'Mid-Century' and a bicolored 'Sinai', display perfect readiness for hybridizing—some of their blooms open and making pollen, others still closed and shielded from being naturally pollinated by an unwanted donor.

75

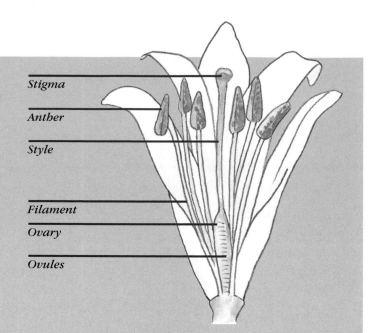

Anatomy of a Lily

The main reproductive parts of a lily flower are so highly visible that they are part of its charm. The female part, the pistil, is located at the center of the bloom. It consists of a tip, the stigma, which is connected to the ovary by a tube called the style. Inside the ovary are ovules, which become seeds after they are fertilized. The pistil is surrounded by six male parts called stamens, at the tip of which are anthers. Filaments hold the anthers away from the pistil.

Stigma

Anther

Style

Filament

Ovary

Ovules

Making your own hybrid simply means transporting pollen from an anther of a chosen male parent to the stigma of a chosen female. You must also make sure no other pollen reaches the female's stigma, either from its own anthers or from any other flower.

Successful hybridization begins with advance planning. First, to transfer pollen directly from one flower to another, you obviously must choose two varieties that bloom at approximately the same time in the garden.

If you are intrigued at the prospect of crossing lilies that bloom at different times, however, you can store pollen from a designated male parent to fertilize a later-flowering female parent. Remove several anthers from the male parent when the pollen is fresh, and dry them on blotting paper in a warm, dry room for a few days. Then place the anthers and paper in a small Mason jar with a tight-fitting lid. Label the jar and refrigerate it. When the female parent blooms, remove the anthers from the bottle and transfer their pollen to the female parent as shown on page 77.

Choosing Candidates for Hybridization

To minimize the wait for new flowers, select parent lilies that are known to bloom from seed within 2 or 3 years. Asiatic hybrids—one of nine divisions of lilies *(see encyclopedia, pages 106-151)*—meet that description and are among the easiest lilies to hybridize. Your best chance of success will come from cross-

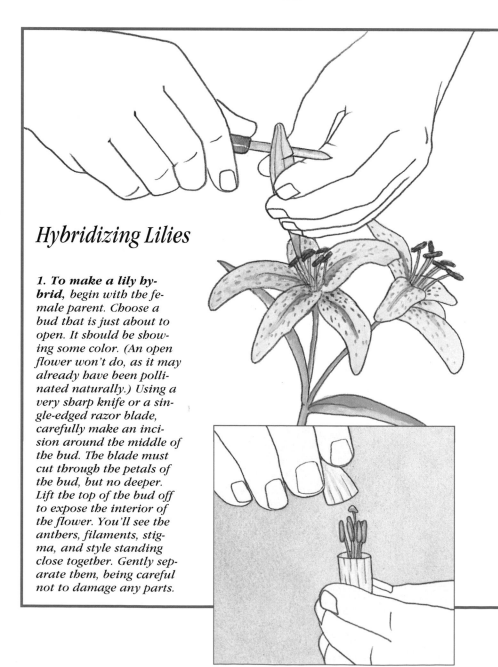

Hybridizing Lilies

1. To make a lily hybrid, begin with the female parent. Choose a bud that is just about to open. It should be showing some color. (An open flower won't do, as it may already have been pollinated naturally.) Using a very sharp knife or a single-edged razor blade, carefully make an incision around the middle of the bud. The blade must cut through the petals of the bud, but no deeper. Lift the top of the bud off to expose the interior of the flower. You'll see the anthers, filaments, stigma, and style standing close together. Gently separate them, being careful not to damage any parts.

ing parents within the same division. Also, look for plants whose pollen appears fluffy rather than waxy. And to further ensure success, pollinate several flowers on the female parent plant just in case some don't take.

There are several traits you can select for as you hybridize. Consider growth habit, vigor, strong stems, and, perhaps, abundant flowers. Then factor in form, size, scent, and color of the potential parent flowers. Try crossing several varieties at once, and cross a few more the next year, when your first hybrids are just sprouting. If you hybridize for several consecutive years, you'll have new flowers of your own creation every growing season. Keep track of them by marking each female parent with the names of both parent plants.

Sowing the Seed

If your cross succeeds, the female parent will display a seed pod after the flowers disappear. Collect the seeds and store them to sow in a nursery bed the following spring. Plant the seeds about ¼ inch deep and 2 inches apart in well-drained soil tilled and amended to a depth of 10 to 12 inches. The seeds should begin germinating in about 1 month.

After your new hybrids bloom, choose the best of them to plant out in the garden. There you can propagate them asexually to provide you with a supply of exact duplicates. Or you can continue crossing them with other flowers, recording the crosses you have made.

2. Pinch or cut off all the anthers. Since the flower hadn't opened, the anthers will be unripe and no pollen will be visible. By removing them, you prevent them from pollinating the stigma.

3. For the male parent, use a flower that is in full bloom. The anthers should be open and beginning to release their powdery pollen. Carefully pull off a single filament with its anther attached.

4. Steadying the filament between your fingers, brush the anther across the stigma of the female. The pollen will stick to the stigma.

5. Punch a few tiny holes in a clear plastic bag and label it with the parent names, female first—for example, Lilium 'Roma' x L. 'Montreux'. Cover the flower with the bag and secure it loosely with a twist tie.

6. Remove the plastic bag after 2 weeks. Later in the summer, if your cross-pollination was successful, you'll see a large seed pod. When it turns brown, but before it opens, snap it off.

7. Slice the pod open lengthwise and shake the seeds out onto a paper towel to dry for 2 to 3 days. Then store the seeds in a Mason jar in the refrigerator till planting time in spring.

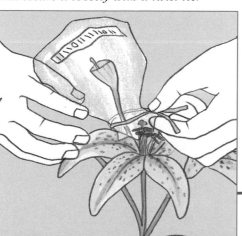

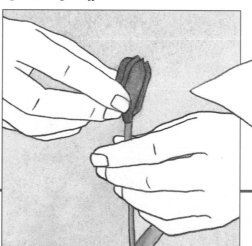

CHAPTER FOUR

The Indoor Bulb Garden

One sure way to banish winter's doldrums is to surround yourself with the fragrant scent of sweet garlic or the vivid, upswept blooms of cyclamen, such as those brightening the sun porch at right. With a little advance planning and a small amount of effort, you can experience these pleasures indoors long before your outdoor garden comes to life.

Bulbs are among the easiest plants to cultivate indoors, provided you understand the structure and needs of each type. As explained on the following pages, you can force hardy spring-flowering bulbs such as hyacinths into winter bloom by accelerating their natural growth cycles. Tender bulbs like Hippeastrum (amaryllis) and Narcissus papyraceus (paper-white narcissus) will naturally come into flower indoors during the cold months. Still other bulbs, including Sinningia speciosa (gloxinia) and Clivia miniata (Natal lily), thrive year round as houseplants.

A. *Oxalis bowiei (giant pink clover) (1)*
B. *Cyclamen persicum (florist's cyclamen) (3)*
C. *Pelargonium (rose-scented geranium) (1)*
D. *Tulbaghia fragrans (sweet garlic) (1)*
E. *Lotus berthelotii (coral-gem) (1)*

NOTE: The key lists each plant type and the total quantity needed to replicate the garden shown. The diagram's letters and numbers refer to the type of plant and the number sited in an area.

Forcing Hardy Bulbs to Bloom

No matter where they are planted, bulbs must go through three stages before they bloom —dormancy, deep root development, and sprouting. Dormancy, during which active growth stops, is usually brought on by winter's cold or summer's drought. For hardy bulbs, those that typically bloom from late winter through early spring, this period occurs during summer and early fall. Then the bulbs undergo about three cold months during which their roots develop; next, sprouts and blooms appear *(chart, pages 82-83)*.

To manipulate hardy bulbs into flowering early—during the winter holidays, for example—you must first put them through a cold storage period. Then you can force them, or stimulate the bulbs into bloom before their time, by exposing them to the artificial light and warm temperatures indoors.

Buying Your Bulbs

It's best to purchase hardy bulbs as soon as they are available in late summer or early fall, while you can still be sure of fine quality. Buy them at least 6 weeks or so before your region usually gets its first hard frost. Whether you buy bulbs from home garden centers or from mail-order nurseries, which generally have a large selection of high-quality bulbs, be sure to choose types specifically recommended for forcing *(left)*. Low-growing varieties work well and don't need staking.

Healthy bulbs are plump and solid, and their skins should be clean and free of cuts, bruises, mold, or other blemishes. If you purchase by mail and receive bulbs that you think may be damaged, talk to the supplier; some seeming flaws may be unimportant. But send damaged bulbs back promptly.

Some bulbs—hyacinths are the most common example—are sold already "prepared." They will bloom more quickly than unprepared bulbs and should be planted as soon as you get them. It's best to pot up any bulbs

BASKETS FULL OF SPRINGTIME
Forced for indoor winter display, cheerful yellow 'Tête-à-Tête' daffodils and the dainty white nodding bells of lily of the valley evoke a warmer season to come.

within a few days of purchase. But if potting is delayed for some reason, you can store most bulbs for up to 4 to 6 weeks in a well-ventilated, dark location at temperatures ranging from 45° to 55° F. One solution is to keep them in your refrigerator in a perforated plastic or paper bag. Don't be alarmed if your bulbs have already begun to sprout when you buy them. It's just an indication that they are ready to be potted and start growing; they won't sprout further until they have roots.

The Right Container

Plastic, terra-cotta, or ceramic pots are equally good for bulbs. It's very important that the containers be clean and have drainage holes—unless you are growing plants in water *(page 84)* or a water-and-pebbles medium *(page 88)*. In that case, of course, you'll need

Potting Tulips for Indoor Forcing

1. Select a pot just large enough to plant the bulbs you want, *close together but not touching. Cover the drainage holes in the bottom of the pot with rocks, pebbles, or pottery shards. Then add growing mixture (right) until the container is about ⅔ full. Moisten with water, but keep the soil loose, not compacted.*

2. Taking care not to pack the soil down, *place each bulb into the mix with the pointed end up and the bulb's flattened side against the wall of the pot (right). Thus the first leaves will emerge and grow over the edge of the pot, for an attractively uniform appearance. Also, as the first leaf will be wider than the rest, it would crowd later leaves if it grew inward. Do not allow the bulbs to touch.*

3. Use your fingers to sprinkle the potting mix over the bulbs (right), *adding soil until the main body of each bulb is buried about ½ inch below the surface. The bulbs' tips will be just peeking out of the soil. Again, be careful not to pack the soil tightly, which would hinder root development.*

4. Place the pot in a refrigerator *or other cool, dark place with temperatures of 32° to 45° F. Check the pot at about 12 weeks and weekly thereafter. When roots protrude through the drain holes and shoots emerge (right), place the pot in a moderately warm, bright spot to encourage growth.*

pots that don't drain; transparent plastic or glass containers are popular for this use. Bulb pans, which are shallower and wider than conventional pots, are exceptionally useful. One of them will hold more bulbs than a normal pot, and the broad base prevents top-heavy flowers from tipping over.

If you are reusing old pots, wash out soil residue that may carry disease. When using new clay pots, soak them overnight before planting so they won't draw moisture from the soil. Generally, your pot should be twice as deep as the length of a bulb. The inside of the receptacle should be only slightly bigger than the girth of the bulb or bulbs, so if you are planting three bulbs to a pot, you will need a container about 6 inches in diameter.

Potting Your Bulbs

Many bulbous plants can be grown in water alone, as is commonly done with hyacinths *(page 84)*. Bulbs grown without soil, however, use up all their nutrients and can't bloom again. If you plan to replant your indoor bulbs later, you must pot them in soil or a soil-based growing mix for this indoor cycle. Even so, it will take them a couple of years to absorb enough nutrients to bloom again.

You can prepare your own soil mix or buy a premixed growing medium. The soil must drain well but at the same time retain sufficient moisture for good root development. And the consistency has to be stiff enough to give the roots something to hold onto without being so dense it blocks root growth. A good growing mix is composed of ⅓ loam, ⅓ compost, humus, or peat moss, and ⅓ perlite, vermiculite, or sand.

It is not necessary to fertilize your bulbs unless you plan to replant them later in the garden. If that's the case, add a level teaspoonful of 10-10-10 slow-release dry fertilizer to each quart of soil mix before potting.

When you pot your bulbs *(page 81)*, plant them close together but not touching for a full, lush effect when they flower. Pack the potting mix fairly loosely around the bulbs, so root growth is not stunted by compacted soil and the bulbs won't push themselves up out of the soil as they grow. Water thoroughly and label each container with the date and the varieties it holds.

GROWING HARDY BULBS

BULB	NORMAL BLOOM SEASON	WHEN TO COOL	COOLING PERIOD	WHEN TO FORCE	
CHIONODOXA	Early Spring	Fall	Potted in moist soil, 10-14 weeks	Winter/Early Spring	
CONVALLARIA	Spring	Fall	Potted in moist soil, 10-12 weeks	Winter/Early Spring	
CROCUS	Winter/Spring	Fall	Potted in moist soil, 8-10 weeks	Winter/Spring	
ERANTHIS	Late Winter/Early Spring	Early Fall	Potted in fairly acid soil, 10 weeks (soak bulb 24 hours before potting)	Winter	
FRITILLARIA	Spring	Summer	Potted in dry soil, 10-12 weeks	Fall	
GALANTHUS	Late Winter/Early Spring	Fall	Potted in moist soil, 9-12 weeks	Winter	
HYACINTHUS (unprepared)	Spring	Fall	Potted in moist soil, 8-10 weeks	Early Winter/Early Spring	
IRIS (Dutch, reticulata)	Spring	Fall	Potted in moist soil, 10-14 weeks	Winter	
MUSCARI ARMENIACUM	Late Winter/Early Spring	Fall	Potted in moist soil, 10-12 weeks	Winter	
NARCISSUS	Late Winter/Spring	Fall	Potted in moist soil, 10-12 weeks	Winter	
SCILLA	Late Winter/Spring	Fall	Potted in moist soil, 12-16 weeks	Winter	
TULIPA	Spring	Fall	Potted in moist soil, 12-16 weeks	Winter	

The Chilling Phase

Your newly potted bulbs are now ready for the cold storage stage of their growth cycle. They must be kept moist and in a dark, cold place. For about 6 weeks, while the bulbs are rooting, the temperature should be between 40° and 55° F. After that, during bud formation, temperatures should range between 32° and 45° F. Check the soil in the pots weekly, and water if it feels dry. But don't let the soil get too wet, as dampness will rot the bulbs.

Most hardy bulbs need 10 to 16 weeks to develop strong roots. Bulbs taken prematurely from cold storage may sprout, but without healthy roots, blooms probably will fall off without opening. For the cooling periods of specific indoor bulbs, see the chart below.

If during the fall months your climate provides temperatures in the appropriate range, you can chill hardy bulbs outside. One easy way is to place your pots close together and cover them with a heavy blanket of mulch, piled into a mound so it will drain. The water that penetrates the mulch will keep the potting soil moist. Make a note of when the pots

should be removed, and when you shovel off the mulch, be careful not to break the new shoots. One way to avoid this is to place a piece of plywood or chicken wire in the pile, about 3 inches above the pots. When you dig down to the wood or wire, you'll know the pots—and tender shoots—are just below.

If you live where hard freezes are more common—say, from Zone 5 northward—you can bury the pots in a trench, preferably on a slope to assist drainage. Be sure to dig down below the frostline, usually 6 to 12 inches beneath the surface. Line the trench with newspapers or leaves for insulation and to keep the pots clean; cover the pots with leaves and then earth. Make a record of when to remove the pots.

In a mild climate, fall temperatures won't chill bulbs properly, and you'll need an indoor solution to the cold storage problem. Depending on the temperature, you might chill potted bulbs in an unheated garage, spare room, cellar, or basement. Cover the pots with news-

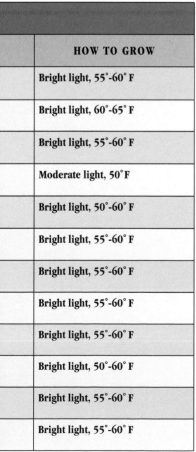

HOW TO GROW
Bright light, 55°-60° F
Bright light, 60°-65° F
Bright light, 55°-60° F
Moderate light, 50° F
Bright light, 50°-60° F
Bright light, 55°-60° F
Bright light, 55°-60° F
Bright light, 55°-60° F
Bright light, 55°-60° F
Bright light, 50°-60° F
Bright light, 55°-60° F
Bright light, 55°-60° F

Elegance in Water: Forcing a Hyacinth

You can force a hyacinth quickly, easily, and with eye-pleasing results by growing it in water. A helpful device is the hourglass-shaped container used at left, which holds the bulb so that its base is just touching the water. This prevents the bulb from rotting, while the roots have plenty of room to grow downward and create their own visual interest.

Hyacinths forced hydroponically, as this method is called, must be purchased already "prepared" and ready to grow. (If you can't plant right away, store your bulb in a ventilated paper bag in the refrigerator until you can.) Fill the glass up to its narrow waist with water. Add a small piece of horticultural charcoal to filter the water and stave off fungal diseases. Then set the bulb in the upper section of the container, so that the water is just touching its base, and put the glass in a dark corner to promote strong root growth. When your hyacinth is ready to bloom, in about 3 weeks' time, shift the glass to a bright, sunny location where temperatures range from 60° to 70° F. Rotate the glass so the flower will develop uniformly. Maintain the water level so it just touches the underside of the bulb. Discard the bulb after blooming.

paper so no light strikes them. You can also store potted bulbs in a refrigerator, where you can easily monitor the temperature. Old-fashioned refrigerators are ideal; modern, frost-free ones tend to dry out the bulbs. Wrap perforated paper or plastic bags around the pots to keep the soil moist, but watch out for mold. Also, be sure there is no ripening fruit in the refrigerator with your bulbs. Fruit gives off ethylene gas, which will abort the bloom. And *never* store bulbs in the freezer.

Forcing Bulbs to Bloom

Once your bulbs have completed their cooling phase, they are ready to be forced into bloom. This involves gradually introducing them to light and warmth, usually over a 2- to 4-week period. To make sure they're ready, check the drainage holes in your pots; they should be clogged with roots. And pale yellow shoots should be breaking the soil surface. If your bulbs have not yet reached this stage, check their progress every few days.

Exposing your plants to bright sun too quickly can cause "blasted buds," meaning the flower stalks dry up and wither immediately. Instead, place the pots in indirect light in temperatures between 50° and 55° F. When the

plants start to bloom, move them to bright sunlight. If you live in a very warm climate like that of Florida, beware of leaving your plants too long in sunny locations, where they can burn easily. By contrast, if the light is insufficient, the plants will stretch to reach it, producing tall, leggy stems that can topple over. In any case, rotate your pots regularly so that all leaves receive an equal amount of light.

The slower and cooler you bring the bulbs along, the better quality your plants will be. To keep them blooming longer, move the pots onto a porch at night—if the outside temperature is no colder than the mid-20°s F. A hot, dry house makes flowers age more quickly, so mist them daily. To stretch your indoor blooming season, bring in a few pots from cold storage each week, rather than all at once.

Once Blooming Is Over

After the blossoms on your soil-grown bulbs die, cut off the shriveled bloom and the seed pod. Don't remove the stem, as it has green cellular surfaces and will act as an extra leaf, converting light into nutrients for the bulb. After the danger of a hard spring freeze is over, you can transplant hardy bulbs into your garden. Discard those bulbs grown in water.

Growing Tender Bulbs Indoors

Recommended
Indoor
Tender Bulbs

Tender bulbs, those natives of tropical and subtropical climates, are far too delicate for the frequent freezes typical of winter and early spring in the temperate zone. Only in the warmest parts of North America can tender bulbs survive outdoors during winter.

Indoors, however, tender bulbs are valued as houseplants, especially during the winter holidays. Many adult gardeners recall as children growing their first *Hippeastrum* (amaryllis), with its great, trumpetlike blooms, or paper-white narcissus, which is easily forced in a dish of pebbles and water and fills the room with its unforgettably sweet fragrance.

In addition to these old favorites, you can grow other, less familiar, tender bulbs indoors to chase away winter blues, or even year round as houseplants. From the exotic gloxinia, with its velvet-textured flowers and ruffle-edged foliage, to cyclamen, with its upturned blossoms and heart-shaped leaves, the key to cultivating these bulbs indoors is to know where each comes from and to understand the growing conditions of its native climate. By reproducing their natural environments as best you can, you can make these plants flourish in your home all winter, where they will often bloom simultaneously with your indoor hardy bulbs. Two tender South African natives—*Freesia* in its many colors and *Lachenalia* (Cape cowslip) with its delightful bell-shaped blossoms—make arresting combinations when flowering alongside containers of bulbs such as daffodils or grape hyacinths.

And by starting bulbs in individual cell packs *(page 87),* you can make your plants movable units to combine in a single pot at blooming time, creating bedfellows of bulbs you could never have successfully forced together in the same container.

Duplicating Native Climates

Tender bulbs grow most profusely in the wild in areas of the world whose climates are characterized by warm, wet winters and hot, dry summers. South Africa is one such place, the natural habitat of such tender bulbs as freesia, *Zantedeschia* (calla lily), *Babiana* (baboon flower), lachenalia, *Agapanthus,* and *Veltheimia*. The greatest concentration of bulbs in the world is found in the Cape region of South Africa. But tender bulbs grow on South Africa's eastern coast as well, although it has a virtually reversed climate pattern, with summer rains followed by mild, dry winters. In the warm, frost-free climates of North America (Zones 9 to 11), these tender bulbs will grow outdoors during winter, but in temperate climates they adapt easily to life indoors, starting bud growth in the fall, before the first frost.

Other warm regions of the world contribute tender bulbs as well. *Hippeastrum,* commonly called amaryllis because its many species once were incorrectly classified as such, is native to the tropics of South America. So are tuberous begonia and *Sinningia,* the genus that includes gloxinia. *Cyclamen persicum* (florist's cyclamen) and *Ranunculus* (buttercup) are found in Asia Minor,

Babiana
(baboon flower)
Begonia x tuberhybrida
(tuberous begonia)
Clivia miniata
(Natal lily)
Cyclamen persicum
(florist's cyclamen)
Eucharis grandiflora
(Amazon lily)
*Hippeastrum 'Apple Blossom',
'Red Lion', 'White Christmas',
'Lady Jane'*
(amaryllis)
Ixia maculata
(corn lily)
Ixia viridiflora
(green ixia)
Lachenalia aloides
(tricolor Cape cowslip)
Lachenalia bulbiferum
(nodding Cape cowslip)
Narcissus papyraceus
(paper-white narcissus)
Ornithogalum
(ornithogalum)
Oxalis regnellii
(wood sorrel)

Oxalis triangularis 'Adenophila'
(wood sorrel)
Ranunculus asiaticus
(Persian buttercup)
Sprekelia formosissima
(Jacobean lily)
Veltheimia bracteata
(red-hot poker)
Veltheimia capensis
(winter-red-hot poker)
Zantedeschia aethiopica
(common calla)

*Hippeastrum
'Apple
Blossom'
(amaryllis)*

GROWING TENDER BULBS

BULB	NORMAL BLOOM SEASON	WHEN TO STORE	HOW TO STORE AND HOW TO GROW	WHEN TO GROW
BABIANA	Spring	Fall/Early Winter	Store potted in dry soil, 50°F, 8-16 weeks. Repot and grow in well-drained soil, bright light, 55°F.	Late Winter/Early Spring
BEGONIA (tuberous)	Spring/Summer/Fall	Fall/Winter	Store in dry peat moss, 50°-60°F, 8-12 weeks. Repot and grow in rich, organic soil, limited light, 65°-75°F.	Spring/Summer
CALADIUM	Spring/Summer	Summer/Fall	Store potted in dry soil, 50°-60°F, 8-12 weeks. Repot and grow in well-drained soil, limited light, 50°-60°F.	Fall/Winter/Early Spring
CLIVIA	Spring/Summer	N/A (does not go dormant)	Do not store. Grow in organic soil, bright light, 50°-60°F. Raise temperature 5° -10°F to flower.	Winter/Late Spring
CYCLAMEN PERSICUM	Winter	Late Spring/Summer	Store potted in dry peat moss, 50°-60°F, 8-12 weeks. Repot and grow in organic soil, limited light, 50°-60°F, high humidity.	Fall/Winter
EUCHARIS GRANDIFLORA	Spring/Summer/Fall	Winter	Store potted in dry soil, 50°-60°F, 8-12 weeks. Repot and grow in organic soil, bright light, 65°-75°F, high humidity.	Spring
FREESIA	Winter/Spring	Summer/Fall	Store potted in dry peat moss, 50°-60°F, 8-12 weeks. Repot and grow in organic soil, bright light, 50°-60°F.	Fall/Winter/Spring
HIPPEASTRUM	Winter/Spring	Late Summer/Fall	Store potted in dry soil, 50°-60°F, 8-12 weeks. Repot and grow in well-drained soil, bright light, 65°-75°F.	Late Fall/Winter
NARCISSUS (paper-white)	Early Spring	Do not store	Grow in bright light, 65°-75°F, in almost any soil that retains moisture.	Late Fall/Winter/Early Spring
OXALIS (certain species)	Late Spring/Early Summer	Late Summer	Store in dry peat moss, 50°-60°F, 8-12 weeks. Repot and grow in rich, organic soil, bright light, 65°-75°F.	Winter
RANUNCULUS	Spring/Summer	Late Summer/Fall	Store in dry peat moss, 8-10 weeks. Repot and grow in rich, sandy, well-drained soil, bright light, 50°-55°F.	Winter/Spring
SINNINGIA SPECIOSA	Fall/Winter/Spring	Summer	Store potted in dry soil. Repot and grow in rich, organic soil, bright light, 60°-75°F.	Fall/Winter/Spring

while *Bletilla* (Chinese ground orchid) is from China and *Smithiantha* (harlequin flower) is from Mexico.

To cope with the natural dry periods in their native climates, most tender bulbs, including hippeastrum and babiana, undergo a period of dormancy after flowering, during which all growth ceases and foliage dies back. Indoors, you would duplicate this natural dry period by withholding water. Other tender bulbs, including *Clivia, Oxalis, Caladium,* and *Eucharis* (Amazon lily), are native to locations where rainfall occurs throughout the year. These plants, which can be maintained

indoors as houseplants, also undergo a period of rest after flowering but need occasional watering to stay green year round.

Planting Tender Bulbs

Generally, the time to plant your tender bulbs for indoor winter blooming is in the fall, following the natural summer dormancy period and before the first frost. Containers can be clay, plastic, or ceramic and, just as with hardy bulbs, the most important considerations are that the pot be clean and have

To grow an amaryllis bulb in a cell pack, as shown in the cutaway illustration above, first half-fill the container with potting mix. Set the bulb on top of the soil and add soil around it until one-quarter to one-half of the bulb is buried. Water well, but then only sparingly until the bud emerges from the top of the bulb.

Mixing and Matching Cell Pack Blooms

If you grow your indoor bulbs in the small, deep plastic pots called cell packs, you can create imaginative displays by mixing and matching plants with diverse growing needs. The arrangement below combines a tender bulb, a bright pink cyclamen, along with the hardy bulbs narcissus, *Iris reticulata*, and *Convallaria majalis* (lily of the valley). Boston and button ferns add textural contrast.

Once a bulb has developed deep roots that are visible at the bottom of the cell pack and the flower is ready to bloom, lift the bulb—with its soil plug intact—and place it in a container half-filled with soil. Add other plants, moving them about to test combinations of shape and color until you achieve the effect you want. Then fill in with soil and, if you like, tuck sphagnum moss around the base of the plants.

drainage holes. To prevent soil from escaping through the drainage holes, cover the holes with broken pottery shards, pebbles, or even the plastic "popcorn" used in packaging goods for shipping. A 6-inch-diameter pot or bulb pan will hold four to eight bulbs, set close but not touching, depending on the size and type of bulb. As with hardy bulbs, the pot should be about twice as deep as the length of the bulb.

Tender bulbs need a rich soil that is free-draining but won't dry out too quickly. A growing mixture identical to that used with hardy bulbs is recommended—⅓ loam, ⅓ compost, humus, or peat moss, and ⅓ perlite, vermiculite, or sand.

Potting varies slightly with the type of bulb. Most true bulbs, such as eucharis or the exotic *Bowiea* (climbing onion), need plenty of soil underneath them to develop strong roots; they are planted close to the soil surface. Likewise, sinningia, tuberous begonia, cyclamen, and other tubers should be planted at or just below the soil surface. Pot up corms like *Ixia* (corn lily) and *Sparaxis* (wand flower) so that they are covered with an inch of soil; freesia, however, needs to be buried about 5 inches deep. Pot a hippeastrum so that the upper half to three-quarters of the bulb protrudes above the soil. It should fit fairly snugly in its container, with the pot no more than 2 to 4 inches wider than the bulb.

The Cool Storage Stage

Once you have potted your tender bulbs, store them in a relatively cool, dark location *(chart, page 86)*. Most prefer temperatures of 50° to 60° F while they are developing roots, although ixia and freesia root better in warmer conditions. Water the bulbs thor-

oughly at the outset of cool storage, but then just enough to keep them damp until they have sprouted top growth.

There are exceptions to this chilling regimen, however. If you purchase a prepotted hippeastrum, it can skip the cool storage stage. The plant will mature in about 6 weeks if given a daytime temperature of 70° F. If you wish to delay its blooming, keep the bulb in cooler temperatures. Cool storage is not a necessity for paper-white narcissus either. Once you have planted the bulbs, in soil or in water with gravel or pebbles, keep them fairly warm—about 50° to 70° F—and they should bloom in 2 to 3 weeks. For best results, first put them in a shaded, warm spot. Then, when growth is under way, bring them gradually into sunlight. If you start different containers of paper-whites at 2-week intervals, you can have blooms throughout the winter.

Light and Water

When sprouts appear on your cool storage plants, move the pots to a warm, sunny location and begin watering regularly. Watering needs vary greatly. Zantedeschia likes lots of

An Easy Way to Grow Paper-Whites

1. In a wide container—preferably clear glass—arrange a 2-inch layer of pebbles. Sprinkle horticultural charcoal over the pebbles to absorb odors.

2. Place bulbs on the pebbles, *growing tips up. Bulbs may be set as close as ½ inch apart. Add more pebbles to the container until bulbs are firmly positioned.*

3. Add water until it just reaches the bulbs' bottoms. *Put the container in a cool, dark place; when sprouts appear, in about 2 weeks, move it to a cool, bright spot. Flowers will follow in 4 weeks. Keep water level constant and rotate container daily to expose all sides to the sun.*

water, while clivia stores moisture in its fleshy stems and doesn't need as much (clivia is a very vigorous plant, though, and can survive occasional overwatering). Since frequent watering leaches nutrients from the soil, the bulbs may require additional fuel. Each week give them a dose of houseplant fertilizer at half-strength, mixing it into their water.

Many tender bulbs grow best if given a little bottom heat during the warming stage. For a small pot, this can be as simple as setting the pot on top of the refrigerator. If you have a large pan or container filled with bulbs such as hippeastrum or *Sprekelia formosissima* (Aztec lily), it may be more practical to place the container on a heating mat specifically designed for this purpose. (A personal heating pad is not safe for this use.) Or you can install a heating coil, available at hardware stores and garden centers, that sits at the bottom of the pot. If you choose this method, it is very important to follow explicitly the instructions that come with the device: The coil should be raised slightly above the floor of the container and should never sit in water.

Light and Temperature

Because many tender bulbs come from environments that offer abundant sunshine, these bulbs require a great deal of light in order to grow successfully indoors. To lachenalia, sparaxis, ixia, freesia, and other South African varieties, light is critical. If they don't get enough, their stems are apt to become soft, causing the plants to collapse. Tender bulbs also control growth and set bud according to the length of the day. This can be a problem if you are growing bulbs indoors in winter, when daylight hours are shorter. To add a few extra hours of light a day, you can use grow lamps or fluorescent lights. They will help keep your bulbs from becoming too leggy and toppling over.

Other tender bulbs, native to tropical forests, grow better in indirect light—behind a gauzy curtain, for example—rather than in direct sunlight. Tuberous begonia, native to the Andes Mountains, zantedeschia, from the swampy areas of South Africa, and clivia, which grows in the forests of the Natal region of its native South Africa, prefer light shade. Cyclamen also thrives in filtered sunlight, as does caladium, a popular houseplant grown primarily for its showy foliage.

Narcissus papyraceus 'Jerusalem'

Many tender plants respond to daytime temperatures of 65° to 75° F while growing, but others vary. Cyclamen needs to be chillier (no higher than 65° F during the day and even cooler at night), and you should keep it out of direct sunlight. The *Eucharis grandiflora*, or Amazon lily, on the other hand, should never be exposed to temperatures below 65° F. It will flourish in very warm and humid conditions; a bathroom might be an ideal location. It, too, wants only indirect light.

After Flowers Fade

Once the plants have flowered, cut off the stems and continue to water as long as foliage remains green. When leaves begin to wither, slowly discontinue watering until the leaves have dried, meaning the plant is dormant. For

Paper-White Narcissus Cultivars

'Bethlehem'
(3 weeks to bloom)

'Galilee'
(3 weeks to bloom)

'Grand Soleil d'Or'
(4-5 weeks to bloom)

'Israel'
(3 weeks to bloom)

'Jerusalem'
(3 weeks to bloom)

'Nazareth'
(3 weeks to bloom)

'Ziva'
(2 weeks to bloom)

the majority of tender bulbs, leaving them dry during their dormant periods is essential. This is their time to store up nutrients for a burst of growth the following year. Watering bulbs that don't need water can cause them to rot. Others may survive in a feeble state but probably will not flower. To remind yourself not to water dormant plants, turn the pots over on their sides. Bear in mind, though, that if your plant is a nonseasonal, or evergreen, tender bulb, such as clivia or eucharis, it should never go completely dry. These plants require occasional dampening during dormancy, as does *Cyclamen persicum*. It flowers indoors during fall and winter and experiences its natural resting period in spring and summer, when it will drop most, but not all, of its foliage.

Humidity is also a factor with tender bulbs. Some need a higher humidity level than is typically available indoors during the winter. There are a number of simple ways to elevate the humidity level for your plants. You can run a humidifier, as long as you keep the plants at a sufficient distance from it and make sure that it doesn't make the room too humid for them. You can mist the plants daily with a hand sprayer, or group plants together, so that their evaporating moisture creates its own microclimate with a higher humidity level. Another well-known technique is to spread pebbles or stones in a tray or pan and pour in just enough water to come almost—but not quite—to the top of the stones. Then place the plants atop the stones, making sure the pots themselves aren't sitting in water.

Washing the foliage of your plants works both to raise the humidity level and to keep the plants clean, which helps reduce pest and disease infestation. Wash the leaves about every 2 weeks using lukewarm water and a soft sponge.

Repeat Blooming

Tender bulbs will keep blooming year after year if you treat them properly, particularly during dormancy periods. Some tender bulbs will become dormant in the spring, others not until summer, and some, of course, will stay green all year. You can set the pots of dormant plants outside in a cool, dry, and shady location and just leave them alone until fall. Then some bulbs will need a top dressing of new soil, and others will need repotting, so be sure you are familiar with the particular requirements of your plants.

If the climate where you live is warm enough, you can plant the bulbs in the garden before they go into their dormant period (once the possibility of frost has passed), and let them continue blooming there. Fertilize them until the foliage dies off and then leave the bulbs alone through the dormant stage. Bring the bulbs indoors before the first fall frost and begin watering them again for another season of bloom.

Contrary to some beliefs, forced hippeastrum does not have to be discarded after one blooming season. With some care, the amaryllis will happily bloom indoors year after year. After flowers die, continue watering

Tropical Beauties That Feel at Home

Because they thrive in indoor warmth, many tropical and semi-tropical plants—gloxiana, *Tulbaghia*, clivia, and certain *Oxalis* species among them—make good houseplants. Some are evergreen; others have dormant periods. They are not forced to bloom early but flower indoors at their normal times. Gloxinia blooms off and on throughout the year, with dormant interludes of 2 to 4 months. Tulbaghia has evergreen leaves and flowers year round; it performs best if kept at about 45° F at night and around 60° F during the day. *Clivia miniata,* shown here, flowers in late winter or early spring. Tolerant of a wide range of temperature and light conditions, it remains green all year and can stay in the same pot for years. *Cyclamen persicum* also blooms profusely and makes an eye-catching display with its heart-shaped marbled foliage and delicate, upturned flowers.

the plant to keep the foliage alive during spring and summer. In the fall, withhold water completely until the leaves wither. Then add new soil to the top of the pot and store in a cool, dark place, between 50° and 60° F, for about 8 weeks, until new growth appears. Gardeners in the southern part of North America can transplant a house-grown amaryllis to the garden after it has bloomed indoors. There, with a little coaxing, it will bloom again.

Cyclamen needs to be replanted afresh each year in order to bloom again. After its summer dormancy, remove the dormant tuber from its pot and replant it in a container of the same size; cyclamen like being pot-bound. Water it well and place it outdoors in the shade. Bring it in before the first frost and fertilize it, and it will bloom again for you early in the new year.

Musings of a Bulb Master

Brent Heath, a third-generation bulb grower and owner of a daffodil nursery in Virginia, offers a potpourri of aesthetic and practical suggestions to help make indoor bulb-growing easier:

• By selecting the shorter cultivars and varieties recommended for forcing, you can usually eliminate the need for staking. When you must do it, however, green plastic rings, green twine, or even green twist ties blend in with the foliage and are relatively unobtrusive. Green bamboo sticks or natural-colored stakes also blend well.

• Tuck sprigs of ivy into your bulb pots, as shown in the photograph above. The ivy takes root easily and unifies the various elements of your flower arrangements.

• Select bulbs with upfacing blooms, such as some varieties of trumpet daffodils. The arrangement will be showier because you get more focal value when flowers look up.

• Choose bulbs with flowers that bloom well above the foliage, not those with blossoms concealed by the leaves.

• Purchase bulbs that produce flowers with thick petals. They last longer.

• Do not add gin to paperwhite narcissus to keep them from growing too tall and leggy. It is true that gin stunts the growth of the stalks, but it also burns tender root hairs and shortens the plant's life span.

Answers to Common Questions

What is the last date I can plant hardy spring-blooming bulbs?

Plant no later than 6 weeks before the ground freezes in your area. The bulbs need that much time to establish roots to protect them from freezing. Water them well to initiate root growth and mulch to help stabilize the soil temperature. In frost-free climates, plant before Christmas for best results.

What is the best soil pH for bulbs?

Tulips, hyacinths, and most other members of the lily family, as well as most iris family members, do best in a slightly alkaline soil, one having a pH between 7 and 7.5. Most members of the amaryllis family—such as daffodils, snowdrops, and lycoris—prefer a soil that is on the acid side, its pH slightly below 7. However, most bulbs, including these, will do fine in neutral soil.

What kinds of mulches are preferred for bulbs?

Bulb mulches should be of material that stays light and fluffy, as the shoots will have an easier time emerging through a covering that has not become compacted. Pine or evergreen needles are the best. Nut and seed hulls and pine bark are very good. Hardwood bark is good as long as it is well pulverized and has only a small percentage of woodchips or cellulose in it.

I would like to grow bulbs in partial shade, but I understand they don't do well under some trees. Which kinds of trees should I avoid?

Maples, beeches, and other trees with shallow, fibrous roots are the ones to avoid. Bulbs and most other kinds of plants have a hard time competing with them for nutrients, water, and growing space. Also avoid evergreens and other trees with low canopies that prevent at least a half-day of filtered light from getting through.

I have more bulbs than I need for this fall. Can I hold some to plant next fall?

Unlike some seeds, bulbs cannot be held from one year to the next, because the moisture in their tissues will dry out and they will die.

I received a potted Easter lily for Easter. Must I discard it after the bloom goes, or can I plant it in the garden or leave it in the pot and try to make it bloom again next year?

The Easter lily *(Lilium longiflorum)* is native to East Asia and has nothing to do with the holiday except that it will flower in spring in greenhouses. After the soil warms up in late spring, you can plant the bulb in the garden, where it will bloom in mid- to late summer the following year. You can also put the potted plant outside, watering and feeding it until the foliage dies back, at which time you can plant the bulb in the garden. It is not a good idea to keep the lily in its pot; it usually won't produce a good plant the second year.

We have had a mild winter so far, and my daffodils and tulips are coming up too early. Now we are expecting some hard freezes. How do I protect my bulbs?

The surprisingly tough foliage of these plants can take temperatures down to around 15°F. Below that point, the leaves may be "burned"—dried out by the cold—unless you cover or surround the plants with a light mulch. Even if the foliage is damaged, however, it doesn't seem to greatly affect later bloom and overall plant performance.

I think my newly planted bulbs must have frozen, because we had a very cold winter and they didn't come up this spring. When I dug them, they were soft and mushy. How can I keep this from happening again?

You can do several things: Plant your bulbs early, and at a depth at least 3 times their height; water well after planting to initiate root growth, because well-rooted bulbs resist frost damage better; mulch after planting to keep the soil temperature stable while the bulbs are rooting; and make sure the area is well drained, because soil that holds too much moisture is more likely to freeze and to encourage rot.

My double daffodils send up nice big fat buds that never open. What is the problem?

Your plants are experiencing "blasting." Double daffodils are especially susceptible to blasting, which happens when the plump buds are subjected to sudden freezing, high temperatures, or insufficient moisture. Protect buds from temperature extremes and water well. Some new cultivars have been developed that are blast resistant.

Can I plant my paper-whites outside after I force them?

In USDA Zones 8 to 11 you can plant paper-whites outside, once all danger of frost has passed, with a good chance of their surviving and blooming again in a few years. From Zone 7 northward, however, their chances of survival would be poor.

My bulb foliage gets too long and flops over, leaving an unsightly mess in my garden. How can I keep my plants from getting so tall?

Plants grow too tall and leggy when they do not have enough light. Most bulbs that do not get at least a half-day of sun are likely not only to flop over but also to have sparse blooms. Transplant the bulbs to a sunnier location; fertilize and water well; and thin out overhanging vegetation to let in more light. For future plantings on this site, choose cultivars that are more shade tolerant.

How do I keep my paper-whites from getting too leggy?

Put them in a sunny window prior to blooming. If you are forcing for bloom during the December holidays, when the days are at their shortest, keep the plants under fluorescent or grow lights in the evening.

Why do new bulbs that I buy and plant bloom 2 weeks later than those of the same cultivar already in the ground?

The new bulbs were probably imported from Holland or England, where they matured in a cooler climate than ours. This causes the flower buds to develop later. Next year, they will all bloom together.

Will picking or cutting their flowers hurt my bulbs?

Not at all, as long as you do not harm the leaves. Bulbs that have their foliage on the same stem as their flowers, such as tulips and lilies, can suffer foliage damage if the flowers are not removed carefully. If you're using a knife, make sure it's sharp and cut the stem on a slant. If picking, place forefinger and thumb as low as possible on the stem and pick with a pulling, snapping motion; this will yield a better stem that will help the flower last longer.

Should I be taking the dead blooms off my bulb plants?

There is no single answer for all bulbs. Hybrid daffodils, for example, will look better if you remove the dead blossoms, but deadheading is not necessary for plant health. And since very few are pollinated, their energy will not be wasted on making unwanted seed. By contrast, species narcissus are best spread by reseeding, so if you want to increase your planting, leave the blooms alone to produce seed. Tulips do benefit from the removal of spent blooms, because most of them will be pollinated, and if the flowers are left intact, 30 percent of the plants' energy will go to make unwelcome seed. Stems from which you remove dead flowers will act as extra leaves, helping with the plant's photosynthesis.

I love fragrant spring-blooming bulbs. Are there any besides Dutch hyacinths that are fragrant?

Many tulip cultivars are fragrant. Single early tulips such as the orange-and-purple 'Princess Irene', the orange 'General de Wet', the yellow 'Bellona', and the pastel pink 'Apricot Beauty' are extremely fragrant and make excellent cut flowers. There are also many fragrant narcissus: Jonquilla, Tazetta, and Poeticus are perhaps the narcissus divisions with the greatest number of fragrant cultivars; 'Actaea' and 'Sugarbush' are outstanding examples. But double daffodils such as 'Cheerfulness', 'Lingerie', and 'Bridal Crown' are also wonderfully fragrant.

F E R T I L I Z I N G

When is the best time to fertilize my bulbs? Old garden books tell me to do it after they bloom.

Bulbs send out new roots in the fall, when the soil temperature drops toward 60°F. Those roots begin to take up nutrients and continue to do so until the foliage turns yellow in late spring. Therefore, the best time to fertilize is in the fall, using a top dressing of slow-release bulb fertilizer or compost. Fertilizing after bloom will do no good.

How can I figure out where to put down fertilizer for my bulbs in fall when there is no remaining foliage to guide me?

Plant *Muscari* (grape hyacinth) bulbs around the edges of your other bulbs. The muscari foliage emerges in the fall and will show you where to fertilize. Or place markers such as vinyl plant labels or even golf tees around the edge of your planting in the spring; they will stay around to show you the way. Finally, you could take photographs of your plot in the spring and use them as a guide.

I use bone meal as the fertilizer for my bulbs, like the old gardening books advise. But the bulbs just aren't blooming well. What's going wrong?

Bone meal is not a complete fertilizer. It supplies only phosphorus and calcium. Bulbs also need nitrogen, potash, and trace elements. If you wish to fully fertilize your bulbs using only organic nutrient sources, you must add blood meal or cottonseed meal for nitrogen and "New Jersey Greensand" or wood ashes for potash and trace elements. An alternative is to use a ready-formulated fertilizer made just for bulbs. A 9-9-6 slow-release formula is best for tulips and members of the lily family but can be used for all bulbs. A 5-10-20 slow-release formula with trace elements is best for daffodils and members of the amaryllis family.

Many of my bulbs have stopped blooming, and others aren't blooming as well as they used to. Do I need to dig and divide them?

That is one solution, but perhaps an easier and more efficient way would be to fertilize the clumps to resupply the nutrients the bulbs have used up as they multiplied over the years. Once they again have enough nutrients, along with moisture and sunshine, most of those old clumps will bloom gloriously.

LIFTING BULBS

Can I lift my bulbs in the spring? I am moving and want to take them with me.

From the time they put down new roots in the fall until the foliage begins to die in the summer, bulbs are best left in the ground. If you must move them, try to disturb the tender roots as little as possible. Take up a large ball of soil with each bulb, get them back into the ground as soon as you can, and water them well.

When I dig my hardy bulbs to divide them, is it necessary to hold them out over the summer?

No, you can put them right back in the ground. If for any reason you need to delay replanting, however, dry their surfaces and make sure they have good air circulation in storage. Hang them in mesh fruit bags or place them on wire racks in trays in the shade until you replant them in fall.

PESTS AND DISEASES

Something is eating my tulip and crocus bulbs underground. Could it be moles, and how do I deal with this problem?

Moles are carnivorous, eating only insects. The underground bulb monster is more than likely a vole, also known as a field mouse. One way to protect your bulbs is to plant them a bit deeper than normal. Voles work in the top 3 to 4 inches of soil. Another is to put a handful of sharp-edged crushed gravel—pieces about the size of a fingernail—around the bulb. Voles do not like to dig through or move around in gravelly soil.

How can I keep my tulips from rotting in summer?

Tulip bulbs prefer to be dry during their dormancy. Plant them in raised beds if your soil drains slowly, and water them sparingly. You can also put in perennial, annual, or ground cover companion plantings over the tulips. These will keep them not only cool, by shading the soil from the sun, but also dry, by taking up considerable moisture.

Troubleshooting Guide

Although most bulbs have few serious pest and disease problems, even the best-tended gardens can come under attack. By using preventive measures combined with correct cultural practices, you can protect your bulbs from stress and, thus, from increased susceptibility. Purchase high-quality USDA-inspected bulbs from reliable sources, examining them closely for signs of mold or insect infestation. Bulbs should be firm and odor free. When possible, choose cultivars with improved resistance to pests and diseases. Store bulbs properly according to their type *(pages 64-65).*

Good drainage and air circulation, proper light, and soil with the proper pH and the correct amounts of moisture and fertilizer help bulbs resist pests and diseases. Encourage beneficial insects, such as ladybird beetles and lacewings, that prey on pests; keep the garden clean and free of weeds. Natural solutions to problems are best, but if you must use chemicals, treat only the affected plant. Try to use insecticidal soaps, horticultural oils, or the botanical insecticide neem; these products are the least disruptive to beneficial insects and will not destroy the soil balance that underlies a healthy garden.

PESTS

PROBLEM: Leaves curl or become distorted, may be sticky and have a black, sooty appearance, and may yellow. Buds and flowers may be streaked and malformed; new growth is stunted.

CAUSE: Aphids, wingless ⅛-inch-long insects of varying color, suck plant sap and may spread viruses. Most prevalent in spring and summer, aphids cluster on new shoots, on the undersides of leaves, and on petals and buds. They secrete a sticky substance that fosters sooty mold. *SUSCEPTIBLE PLANTS: MOST BULBS, ESPECIALLY ANEMONE, DAFFODIL, DAHLIA, GLADIOLUS, IRIS, LILY, AND TULIP.*

SOLUTION: Spray plants with a steady stream of water from a garden hose to knock aphids off. Introduce ladybird beetles and lacewings into the garden. Treat a severe infestation with insecticidal soap, horticultural oil, neem, or a pyrethrin-based insecticide. Inspect purchased or stored bulbs for aphids around growth points or under the tunic. Swab aphids off stored bulbs with alcohol or immerse them in a dip of insecticidal soap.

PROBLEM: Ragged holes appear on leaves, especially near the ground. Flowers may also be eaten; slugs will eat daffodil blooms but avoid the foliage, which is toxic to them. Emerging shoots may be partly eaten or may disappear entirely. Telltale shiny silver streaks appear on leaves and garden paths.

CAUSE: Slugs and snails feed on low-hanging leaves and emerging shoots at night or on overcast or rainy days. They prefer damp soil in a shady location and are most damaging in summer, especially in wet regions or during rainy years.

SOLUTION: Remove debris and control weeds to minimize hiding places. Trap by placing saucers of beer near plants. Salt kills pests but may hurt plants. Poison bait, available at garden centers, can be applied at dusk. Strips of coarse sand or cinders around beds will deter them. Spading in spring destroys dormant slugs and snails. *SUSCEPTIBLE PLANTS: MOST BULBS, BUT ESPECIALLY AGAPANTHUS, AMARYLLIS, ANEMONE, GLADIOLUS, LILY, AND TULIP.*

PROBLEM: Leaves develop silvery white or brownish streaks and flecks, and leaf tips turn brown. Eventually, leaves wither and die. Flower buds turn brown and may not open; if they do open, they are streaked and distorted.

CAUSE: Thrips, insects that are barely visible to the naked eye, look like slivers of yellow, black, or brown wood. They emerge in early spring and are especially active in hot, dry weather. The larvae are wingless and feed on stems, leaves, and flower buds. Adults are easily dispersed by wind and can travel great distances. *SUSCEPTIBLE PLANTS: GLADIOLUS AND THE WHITE AND PASTEL FLOWERS OF OTHER BULBS ARE HIGHLY SUSCEPTIBLE.*

SOLUTION: Control of thrips is difficult, especially during their migratory periods in early summer. Lacewings, minute pirate bugs, and several predaceous mites feed on them; late in the growing season such predators often check thrips populations. Remove and destroy damaged or infested buds, flowers, and foliage. Keep garden well weeded. In severe cases, spray plants with an insecticidal soap, horticultural oil, or neem.

PROBLEM: Small yellow to orange-brown or gray-brown spots appear or flowers, foliage, and stems, which may also look pinpricked or bruised. The spots then develop into blotches of fuzzy gray or brown mold. Flowers are distorted; buds may not open. Stem bases blacken and rot. Affected parts eventually turn brown and dry. Bulbs have dark, sunken areas and are covered with brown growth.

CAUSE: Botrytis blight, also known as gray mold, is a fungus disease that is most prevalent in damp spring-to-summer weather and often occurs if a bulb has been stressed by a late freeze or frost or has suffered physical damage. The blight is spread easily by water and wind. It survives the winter as hard, black lumps in the soil or on dead plant parts.
SUSCEPTIBLE PLANTS: MOST BULBS, ESPECIALLY TULIP.

SOLUTION: Inspect bulbs for blight before purchase; use a preplant dip; plant in well-drained soil; water early in the day and avoid overhead watering; thin out plants to provide more light and air or transplant them to a drier location. Cut off and destroy all infected plant parts. Spray plants with fungicide in spring when shoots emerge to keep any disease from spreading.

PROBLEM: Leaves turn blue, red, or yellow, then wilt and die. Growth is stunted. Flowers do not develop. Bulbs are either soft and mushy with a bad smell, or hard and dried out. They may be covered with sunken lesions. White, pink, gray, or black mold may form on bulbs or on the stem near the soil line. Roots become dark and slimy.

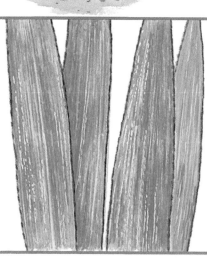

CAUSE: Root rot and bulb rot—specifically, bacterial soft rot, fusarium basal rot, and pythium root rot—are fungal and bacterial diseases that may occur either while the bulb is in the ground or during storage. Cultivar susceptibility and stressful conditions such as water-logged soil are the major causes. Rot occurs most often in warm, wet soil when bulbs are not actively growing, a time when spores multiply rapidly.
SUSCEPTIBLE PLANTS: MOST BULBS.

SOLUTION: Discard infected bulbs and all the soil for 6 inches around them. Be careful not to cut or bruise bulbs when digging or handling them; bulbs naturally carry the spores on their surface, and damage makes them highly susceptible to invasion. Good drainage is essential. Store bulbs properly; immediately after digging and cleaning, dry thoroughly, then pack and store according to the requirements of each type. Examine bulbs for white mold or brown splotches near the basal plate and for overall softness. Choose resistant cultivars. Never put fertilizer in a hole immediately before planting a bulb; it will burn the roots and cause root rot.

PROBLEM: Leaves become streaked with yellow to green, eventually turning completely yellow. Leaves may curl or become distorted. Flowers are smaller than normal and may be streaked or spotted with yellow, blue, or green. The plant may be stunted or cease to grow.

CAUSE: Infection by mosaic, yellows, ring spot, and tulip-breaking viruses.

SOLUTION: There are no chemical controls for viruses. Remove and destroy infected bulbs. Disinfect gardening tools with rubbing alcohol after working on infected plants. To help prevent virus, control aphids, which spread viral diseases. Plant virus-resistant species of lilies.
SUSCEPTIBLE PLANTS: MOST BULBS, ESPECIALLY DAFFODIL, LILY, AND TULIP.

Plant Selection Guide to Bulbs

Organized by flower color, this chart provides information needed to select species and varieties that will thrive in the particular conditions of your garden. For additional information on each plant, refer to the encyclopedia that begins on page 106.

WHITE

	Zone 3	Zone 4	Zone 5	Zone 6	Zone 7	Zone 8	Zone 9	Zone 10	Zone 11	Sandy	Well-drained	Moist	Full Sun	Partial Shade	Shade	Spring	Summer	Fall	Winter	Under 1 foot	1-3 feet	Over 3 feet	Naturalizing	Forcing	Container Plant	Fragrance	Cut Flowers
ACHIMENES TUBIFLORA								✓	✓	✓	✓		✓	✓	✓	✓					✓					✓	
AGAPANTHUS AFRICANUS 'ALBA'						✓	✓	✓		✓	✓	✓	✓				✓				✓					✓	✓
ANEMONE CORONARIA 'THE BRIDE'			✓	✓	✓	✓				✓	✓		✓			✓				✓					✓	✓	✓
ARISAEMA SIKOKIANUM		✓	✓	✓	✓	✓						✓	✓	✓	✓	✓				✓							
ARUM ITALICUM 'MARMORATUM'		✓	✓	✓	✓	✓						✓		✓	✓	✓				✓					✓		
BLETILLA STRIATA 'ALBA'			✓	✓	✓	✓					✓	✓	✓	✓			✓			✓					✓	✓	
BRIMEURA AMETHYSTINA 'ALBA'		✓	✓	✓	✓	✓	✓				✓		✓			✓				✓			✓	✓	✓		
CAMASSIA LEICHTLINII 'SEMIPLENA'		✓	✓	✓	✓	✓					✓	✓	✓	✓		✓							✓				
CARDIOCRINUM GIGANTEUM			✓	✓							✓	✓		✓			✓					✓				✓	
CHIONODOXA LUCILIAE 'ALBA'	✓	✓	✓	✓	✓	✓					✓	✓	✓			✓		✓	✓				✓				
CONVALLARIA MAJALIS 'FLORE PLENA'	✓	✓	✓	✓								✓		✓	✓	✓				✓			✓	✓		✓	✓
CRINUM ASIATICUM					✓	✓	✓	✓		✓	✓	✓	✓	✓			✓					✓			✓	✓	
DAHLIA X 'BAMBINO WHITE'					✓	✓	✓				✓	✓	✓				✓	✓		✓							✓
EREMURUS HIMALAICUS		✓	✓	✓	✓	✓				✓	✓		✓				✓	✓				✓					✓
ERYTHRONIUM DENS-CANIS 'CHARMER'	✓	✓	✓	✓	✓						✓	✓	✓	✓	✓	✓				✓			✓				
EUCHARIS AMAZONICA							✓	✓	✓		✓	✓		✓	✓				✓		✓			✓	✓	✓	
EUCOMIS COMOSA					✓	✓	✓	✓		✓	✓		✓	✓			✓				✓				✓		✓
GALANTHUS ELWESII		✓	✓	✓	✓	✓					✓	✓	✓	✓					✓	✓			✓	✓			
GALTONIA CANDICANS				✓	✓	✓	✓			✓	✓	✓	✓				✓				✓					✓	✓
GLADIOLUS CALLIANTHUS 'MURIALAE'				✓	✓	✓	✓				✓		✓				✓				✓					✓	✓
HAEMANTHUS ALBIFLOS							✓	✓	✓		✓		✓	✓				✓		✓					✓		
HIPPEASTRUM X 'DOUBLE RECORD'							✓	✓	✓		✓	✓	✓						✓		✓				✓		
HYACINTHOIDES HISPANICA 'WHITE TRIUMPHATOR'		✓	✓	✓	✓	✓					✓	✓	✓	✓		✓				✓			✓				
HYACINTHUS ORIENTALIS 'SNOW WHITE'			✓	✓	✓	✓					✓	✓	✓			✓				✓					✓	✓	✓
HYMENOCALLIS X FESTALIS						✓	✓	✓			✓	✓	✓	✓			✓				✓					✓	✓
LEUCOCORYNE IXIOIDES							✓	✓	✓		✓		✓			✓					✓					✓	✓
LEUCOJUM AESTIVUM		✓	✓	✓	✓	✓	✓			✓	✓	✓	✓	✓		✓				✓			✓			✓	✓
LILIUM REGALE	✓	✓	✓	✓	✓	✓					✓		✓	✓			✓					✓				✓	✓

	COLOR	PLANT	ZONES									SOIL			LIGHT			BLOOMING SEASON				PLANT HEIGHT			NOTED FOR				
			Zone 3	Zone 4	Zone 5	Zone 6	Zone 7	Zone 8	Zone 9	Zone 10	Zone 11	Sandy	Well-Drained	Moist	Full Sun	Partial Shade	Shade	Spring	Summer	Fall	Winter	Under 1 Foot	1-3 Feet	Over 3 Feet	Naturalizing	Forcing	Container Plant	Fragrance	Cut Flowers
	WHITE	LYCORIS ALBIFLORA				✔	✔	✔	✔				✔	✔	✔	✔				✔		✔						✔	✔
		MUSCARI BOTRYOIDES 'ALBUM'			✔	✔	✔	✔	✔			✔	✔		✔	✔		✔				✔			✔	✔		✔	✔
		NARCISSUS X 'MOUNT HOOD'	✔	✔	✔	✔	✔	✔	✔				✔		✔	✔	✔	✔					✔			✔	✔	✔	✔
		ORNITHOGALUM ARABICUM				✔	✔	✔					✔	✔	✔	✔		✔					✔				✔	✔	
		OXALIS TRIANGULARIS SSP. PAPILIONACEA			✔	✔	✔	✔	✔				✔		✔	✔			✔			✔					✔	✔	
		PANCRATIUM MARITIMUM					✔	✔	✔	✔	✔	✔	✔		✔				✔	✔		✔					✔	✔	
		POLIANTHES TUBEROSA 'THE PEARL'					✔	✔					✔	✔	✔				✔	✔			✔						✔
		SCILLA SIBERICA 'ALBA'	✔	✔	✔	✔	✔	✔					✔	✔	✔	✔	✔	✔				✔			✔	✔			
		TIGRIDIA PAVONIA 'ALBA'				✔	✔	✔	✔				✔	✔	✔				✔			✔							
		TRITELEIA HYACINTHINA			✔	✔	✔					✔	✔		✔	✔						✔		✔					✔
		TULIPA X 'WHITE TRIUMPHATOR'		✔	✔	✔	✔					✔	✔		✔			✔					✔			✔		✔
		URGINEA MARITIMA					✔	✔	✔			✔	✔		✔					✔		✔							
		WATSONIA X 'MRS. BULLARD'S WHITE'					✔	✔	✔				✔		✔			✔				✔		✔					
		ZANTEDESCHIA AETHIOPICA 'PERLE VON STUTTGART'					✔	✔	✔			✔	✔	✔	✔	✔			✔	✔		✔		✔			✔	✔	✔
		ZEPHYRANTHES CANDIDA					✔	✔	✔			✔	✔	✔	✔				✔	✔		✔					✔	✔	
	YELLOW	ALLIUM MOLY 'JEANNINE'	✔	✔	✔	✔	✔	✔	✔				✔	✔	✔	✔			✔			✔			✔				✔
		BEGONIA X TUBERHYBRIDA						✔	✔				✔	✔		✔	✔		✔	✔		✔					✔		
		CANNA X GENERALIS 'PRETORIA'					✔	✔	✔	✔			✔	✔	✔				✔					✔					
		CHLIDANTHUS FRAGRANS					✔	✔	✔			✔	✔	✔	✔	✔			✔			✔					✔	✔	✔
		CLIVIA MINIATA 'AUREA'					✔	✔	✔	✔			✔		✔	✔	✔	✔	✔			✔					✔	✔	
		CROCOSMIA X CROCOSMIIFLORA 'CITRONELLA'				✔	✔	✔	✔				✔	✔	✔				✔	✔			✔	✔			✔		✔
		CROCUS ANGUSTIFOLIUS 'MINOR'	✔	✔	✔	✔	✔						✔		✔			✔				✔			✔	✔			
		ERANTHIS HYEMALIS		✔	✔	✔	✔						✔	✔	✔	✔		✔			✔	✔			✔				
		EREMURUS STENOPHYLLUS		✔	✔	✔	✔	✔				✔	✔		✔			✔	✔					✔					✔
		ERYTHRONIUM X 'CITRONELLA'	✔	✔	✔	✔	✔	✔					✔	✔		✔	✔	✔				✔							
		GLADIOLUS X 'NOVA LUX'					✔	✔	✔	✔			✔		✔				✔	✔				✔			✔	✔	✔
		HYACINTHUS ORIENTALIS 'CITY OF HAARLEM'			✔	✔	✔	✔	✔				✔	✔	✔			✔				✔					✔	✔	✔
		IRIS DANFORDIAE			✔	✔	✔	✔	✔			✔	✔		✔			✔				✔						✔	
		LILIUM X 'CONNECTICUT KING'	✔	✔	✔	✔	✔	✔	✔				✔		✔				✔					✔					✔
		LYCORIS AUREA					✔	✔	✔	✔			✔	✔	✔	✔				✔	✔	✔							✔
		NARCISSUS 'DUTCH MASTER'	✔	✔	✔	✔	✔	✔	✔				✔		✔	✔	✔	✔					✔			✔	✔		✔
		NARCISSUS JONQUILLA	✔	✔	✔	✔	✔	✔	✔				✔		✔	✔	✔	✔				✔			✔	✔			✔

	ZONES									SOIL			LIGHT			BLOOMING SEASON				PLANT HEIGHT			NOTED FOR				
	Zone 3	Zone 4	Zone 5	Zone 6	Zone 7	Zone 8	Zone 9	Zone 10	Zone 11	Sandy	Well-Drained	Moist	Full Sun	Partial Shade	Shade	Spring	Summer	Fall	Winter	Under 1 Foot	1-3 Feet	Over 3 Feet	Naturalizing	Forcing	Container Plant	Fragrance	Cut Flowers
YELLOW																											
RANUNCULUS 'TECOLOTE GIANTS'						✓	✓	✓		✓	✓	✓	✓			✓					✓				✓		✓
STERNBERGIA LUTEA			✓	✓	✓	✓	✓			✓	✓		✓					✓		✓					✓		
TIGRIDIA PAVONIA 'AUREA'				✓	✓	✓	✓				✓	✓	✓				✓			✓	✓		✓		✓		
TULIPA BATALINII	✓	✓	✓	✓	✓						✓		✓			✓				✓				✓			✓
URGINEA MARITIMA					✓	✓	✓			✓	✓		✓					✓			✓			✓			
ZANTEDESCHIA X 'SOLFATARE'					✓	✓	✓				✓	✓	✓				✓	✓		✓			✓		✓	✓	✓
ZEPHYRANTHES SULPHUREA					✓	✓	✓			✓	✓	✓					✓	✓		✓					✓	✓	
ORANGE																											
ACHIMENES HETEROPHYLLA						✓	✓			✓	✓		✓	✓	✓					✓					✓		
BEGONIA X TUBERHYBRIDA						✓	✓			✓	✓		✓	✓		✓	✓			✓					✓		
BELAMCANDA CHINENSIS		✓	✓	✓	✓	✓	✓	✓			✓		✓				✓				✓						✓
CANNA X GENERALIS 'PFITZER'S CHINESE CORAL'					✓	✓	✓	✓			✓	✓	✓				✓				✓				✓		
CANNA X GENERALIS 'STADT FELLBACH'					✓	✓	✓	✓			✓	✓	✓				✓				✓						
CROCOSMIA X CROCOSMIIFLORA 'EMILY McKENZIE'					✓	✓	✓	✓			✓	✓	✓				✓	✓			✓		✓	✓	✓		✓
DAHLIA X 'ORANGE JULIUS'						✓	✓	✓			✓		✓				✓	✓			✓						✓
SANDERSONIA AURANTIACA						✓	✓	✓	✓	✓	✓		✓				✓				✓						✓
TRITONIA CROCATA				✓	✓	✓	✓				✓		✓			✓	✓			✓							✓
TULIPA 'PRINCESS IRENE'		✓	✓	✓	✓	✓					✓		✓			✓				✓				✓			✓
WATSONIA X 'DAZZLE'					✓	✓	✓				✓		✓			✓	✓			✓			✓				✓
RED																											
AMARYLLIS BELLADONNA 'CAPE TOWN'						✓	✓	✓		✓	✓	✓	✓					✓			✓				✓	✓	✓
ANEMONE CORONARIA X 'HOLLANDIA'	✓	✓	✓	✓	✓	✓	✓				✓	✓	✓	✓		✓				✓					✓	✓	✓
BEGONIA X TUBERHYBRIDA						✓	✓			✓	✓		✓	✓		✓	✓			✓					✓		
CANNA X GENERALIS 'BRANDYWINE'					✓	✓	✓	✓			✓	✓	✓				✓					✓					
CLIVA MINIATA 'FLAME'					✓	✓	✓	✓			✓	✓	✓		✓	✓	✓			✓					✓	✓	
COLCHICUM GIGANTEUM		✓	✓	✓	✓	✓	✓				✓		✓					✓		✓			✓	✓			
CRINUM MOOREI					✓	✓	✓	✓		✓	✓	✓	✓				✓				✓	✓			✓	✓	
CROCOSMIA MASONIORUM					✓	✓	✓	✓			✓	✓	✓				✓	✓			✓	✓			✓		✓
CYCLAMEN GRAECUM				✓	✓	✓					✓	✓		✓		✓				✓					✓	✓	
DAHLIA X 'JUANITA'						✓	✓	✓			✓		✓				✓	✓			✓						✓
FRITILLARIA IMPERIALIS 'RUBRA MAXIMA'	✓	✓	✓	✓	✓	✓				✓	✓		✓	✓		✓					✓		✓			✓	
GLADIOLUS COMMUNIS SSP. BYZANTINUS			✓	✓	✓	✓	✓	✓			✓		✓			✓					✓			✓			✓
HAEMANTHUS COCCINEUS						✓	✓	✓		✓	✓	✓	✓	✓				✓	✓	✓					✓		
HIPPEASTRUM X 'RED LION'						✓	✓	✓		✓	✓		✓			✓			✓		✓				✓	✓	

		Zone 3	Zone 4	Zone 5	Zone 6	Zone 7	Zone 8	Zone 9	Zone 10	Zone 11	Sandy	Well-Drained	Moist	Full Sun	Partial Shade	Shade	Spring	Summer	Fall	Winter	Under 1 Foot	1-3 Feet	Over 3 Feet	Naturalizing	Forcing	Container Plant	Fragrance	Cut Flowers
RED	HYACINTHUS ORIENTALIS 'HOLLYHOCK'			✔	✔	✔	✔	✔			✔	✔	✔		✔		✔				✔					✔		✔	✔
	LILIUM PUMILUM	✔	✔	✔	✔	✔	✔					✔		✔				✔			✔							✔
	LYCORIS RADIATA				✔	✔	✔	✔			✔	✔	✔	✔				✔			✔							✔
	NERINE SARNIENSIS 'CHERRY RIPE'					✔	✔	✔	✔		✔	✔	✔						✔		✔					✔		
	RANUNCULUS 'TECOLOTE GIANTS'						✔	✔	✔	✔	✔	✔	✔				✔				✔					✔		✔
	SCHIZOSTYLIS COCCINEA 'MAJOR'			✔	✔	✔	✔	✔				✔	✔						✔		✔					✔		✔
	SPREKELIA FORMOSISSIMA						✔	✔	✔	✔		✔						✔			✔					✔		
	TULIPA X 'PARADE'		✔	✔	✔	✔	✔					✔		✔			✔				✔				✔			✔
	VALLOTA SPECIOSA						✔	✔	✔	✔		✔						✔	✔		✔			✔				
PINK	ACHIMENES 'FASHIONABLE PINK'							✔	✔		✔	✔			✔	✔		✔			✔					✔		
	ALLIUM CERNUUM	✔	✔	✔	✔	✔	✔	✔			✔	✔	✔	✔			✔				✔							✔
	AMARYLLIS BELLADONNA						✔	✔	✔		✔	✔							✔		✔			✔			✔	✔
	ANEMONE BLANDA 'PINK STAR'	✔	✔	✔	✔	✔	✔				✔	✔	✔	✔		✔	✔				✔			✔		✔		
	BEGONIA X TUBERHYBRIDA							✔	✔		✔	✔			✔	✔		✔	✔		✔					✔		
	COLCHICUM AUTUMNALE		✔	✔	✔	✔	✔	✔				✔			✔				✔	✔	✔			✔	✔			
	CONVALLARIA MAJALIS 'ROSEA'	✔	✔	✔	✔	✔							✔		✔	✔	✔				✔			✔	✔		✔	✔
	X CRINODONNA						✔	✔	✔		✔	✔	✔	✔				✔			✔						✔	✔
	CYCLAMEN CILICIUM				✔	✔	✔	✔				✔	✔		✔			✔	✔		✔					✔		
	DAHLIA X 'CURLY QUE'						✔	✔	✔		✔	✔	✔					✔	✔			✔						✔
	FREESIA X 'ROSE MARIE'						✔	✔	✔	✔	✔	✔			✔		✔			✔	✔						✔	✔
	HYACINTHOIDES HISPANICA 'ROSE QUEEN'			✔	✔	✔	✔					✔	✔	✔			✔					✔		✔	✔			
	HYACINTHUS ORIENTALIS 'PINK PEARL'			✔	✔	✔	✔					✔	✔	✔			✔				✔					✔	✔	✔
	LILIUM X 'CASA ROSA'				✔	✔	✔	✔				✔		✔				✔					✔				✔	
	NERINE UNDULATA 'CRISPA'						✔	✔	✔	✔	✔	✔							✔		✔					✔		
	OXALIS ADENOPHYLLA			✔	✔	✔	✔	✔				✔		✔				✔			✔			✔		✔		
	RHODOHYPOXIS BAURII				✔	✔	✔	✔	✔		✔	✔						✔			✔			✔		✔		
	SCHIZOSTYLIS COCCINEA 'MRS. HEGARTY'				✔	✔	✔	✔	✔			✔	✔						✔		✔					✔		✔
	SCILLA SCILLOIDES			✔	✔	✔	✔	✔				✔	✔	✔	✔			✔			✔			✔		✔		
	TRITONIA CROCATA 'PINK SENSATION'					✔	✔	✔	✔			✔	✔				✔	✔			✔							✔
	TULIPA X 'ANGELIQUE'		✔	✔	✔	✔	✔					✔		✔			✔				✔				✔			✔
	WATSONIA X 'PINK OPAL'					✔	✔	✔	✔			✔		✔				✔					✔			✔		✔
	ZANTEDESCHIA X 'PINK PERSUASION'						✔	✔	✔		✔	✔	✔		✔			✔	✔			✔			✔		✔	✔

		ZONES									SOIL			LIGHT			BLOOMING SEASON				PLANT HEIGHT			NOTED FOR				
		Zone 3	Zone 4	Zone 5	Zone 6	Zone 7	Zone 8	Zone 9	Zone 10	Zone 11	Sandy	Well-Drained	Moist	Full Sun	Partial Shade	Shade	Spring	Summer	Fall	Winter	Under 1 Foot	1-3 Feet	Over 3 Feet	Naturalizing	Forcing	Container Plant	Fragrance	Cut Flowers
PURPLE	ALLIUM AFLATUNENSE	✓	✓	✓	✓	✓	✓	✓				✓	✓	✓	✓		✓					✓					✓	
	ALLIUM X 'PURPLE SENSATION'	✓	✓	✓	✓	✓	✓	✓				✓	✓	✓			✓					✓						✓
	BABIANA STRICTA 'PURPLE SENSATION'						✓	✓	✓			✓	✓	✓			✓					✓				✓	✓	
	BULBOCODIUM VERNUM	✓	✓	✓	✓	✓	✓				✓	✓		✓	✓		✓		✓	✓		✓						
	CALOCHORTUS SPLENDENS			✓	✓	✓	✓	✓				✓	✓	✓				✓				✓				✓		✓
	COLCHICUM AGRIPPINUM		✓	✓	✓	✓	✓					✓		✓					✓		✓			✓	✓			
	CORYDALIS SOLIDA			✓	✓	✓	✓	✓				✓	✓	✓	✓		✓				✓							
	CROCUS SEROTINUS SSP. CLUSII	✓	✓	✓	✓	✓						✓		✓					✓		✓			✓	✓		✓	
	CROCUS SIEBERI 'HUBERT EDELSTEIN'	✓	✓	✓	✓	✓	✓					✓		✓			✓				✓			✓	✓		✓	
	FRITILLARIA PERSICA	✓	✓	✓	✓	✓	✓				✓	✓		✓	✓		✓					✓						
	IRIS X HOLLANDICA 'PURPLE SENSATION'			✓	✓	✓	✓				✓	✓		✓			✓				✓	✓						✓
	LIATRIS SPICATA	✓	✓	✓	✓	✓	✓	✓	✓			✓	✓	✓				✓					✓					✓
	TULIPA BAKERI 'LILAC WONDER'		✓	✓	✓	✓	✓					✓		✓			✓				✓					✓		
BLUE	ACHIMENES X 'INDIA'						✓	✓			✓	✓		✓	✓		✓				✓					✓		
	AGAPANTHUS X 'PETER PAN'						✓	✓	✓		✓	✓	✓	✓			✓				✓					✓		
	ALLIUM CAERULEUM	✓	✓	✓	✓	✓	✓	✓				✓	✓	✓			✓				✓							✓
	ANEMONE BLANDA 'BLUE STAR'	✓	✓	✓	✓	✓	✓					✓	✓	✓	✓		✓				✓			✓	✓			✓
	CAMASSIA SCILLOIDES	✓	✓	✓	✓	✓						✓	✓	✓			✓					✓		✓				
	CHIONODOXA SARDENSIS	✓	✓	✓	✓	✓						✓	✓	✓			✓		✓	✓	✓							
	CROCUS SPECIOSUS 'ARTABIR'	✓	✓	✓	✓	✓	✓					✓		✓					✓		✓					✓		
	DICHELOSTEMMA CONGESTUM			✓	✓	✓					✓	✓		✓				✓				✓				✓		✓
	FREESIA 'ROMANY'						✓	✓	✓	✓	✓	✓		✓	✓					✓	✓						✓	✓
	HYACINTHOIDES HISPANICA 'DANUBE'			✓	✓	✓	✓					✓	✓		✓		✓				✓			✓	✓			
	HYACINTHUS ORIENTALIS 'BLUE MAGIC'			✓	✓	✓	✓					✓	✓	✓			✓				✓					✓	✓	✓
	IPHEION UNIFLORUM 'WISLEY BLUE'			✓	✓	✓	✓	✓				✓	✓	✓	✓		✓				✓			✓		✓	✓	✓
	IRIS X HOLLANDICA 'BLUE MAGIC'			✓	✓	✓	✓				✓	✓		✓				✓			✓	✓						✓
	IXIOLIRION TATARICUM				✓	✓	✓	✓			✓	✓		✓			✓	✓			✓						✓	✓
	MERTENSIA PULMONARIODES	✓	✓	✓	✓	✓	✓					✓	✓		✓	✓	✓					✓						
	MUSCARI ARMENIACUM 'BLUE SPIKE'	✓	✓	✓	✓	✓	✓	✓			✓	✓		✓	✓		✓				✓			✓	✓		✓	
	PUSCHKINIA SCILLOIDES VAR. LIBANOTICA	✓	✓	✓	✓	✓	✓	✓				✓	✓	✓	✓		✓				✓			✓				
	SCILLA LITARDIEREI			✓	✓	✓	✓					✓	✓	✓	✓	✓	✓				✓			✓	✓			
	TRITELEIA TUBERGENII 'QUEEN FABIOLA'				✓	✓	✓	✓			✓	✓		✓			✓	✓				✓						✓

MULTICOLORED

	Zone 3	Zone 4	Zone 5	Zone 6	Zone 7	Zone 8	Zone 9	Zone 10	Zone 11	Sandy	Well-Drained	Moist	Full Sun	Partial Shade	Shade	Spring	Summer	Fall	Winter	Under 1 Foot	1-3 Feet	Over 3 Feet	Naturalizing	Forcing	Container Plant	Fragrance	Cut Flowers
ACHIMENES LONGIFLORA							✓	✓			✓	✓	✓	✓	✓				✓						✓		
ALSTROEMERIA AUREA			✓	✓	✓	✓	✓	✓			✓	✓	✓				✓				✓				✓		✓
ALSTROEMERIA LIGTU HYBRIDS			✓	✓	✓	✓	✓	✓			✓	✓	✓				✓				✓				✓		✓
BEGONIA X TUBERHYBRIDA							✓	✓			✓	✓		✓	✓		✓	✓		✓					✓		
BELLEVALIA PYCNANTHA			✓	✓	✓	✓	✓	✓			✓		✓			✓				✓			✓				
CALADIUM 'FANNIE MUNSON'							✓	✓			✓	✓		✓	✓		✓				✓				✓		
CALADIUM 'WHITE CHRISTMAS'							✓	✓			✓	✓		✓	✓		✓				✓				✓		
CALOCHORTUS VENUSTUS			✓	✓	✓	✓	✓			✓	✓		✓	✓		✓					✓				✓		✓
CANNA X GENERALIS 'ROSAMUND COLE'					✓	✓	✓	✓			✓	✓					✓					✓					
CROCUS SIEBERI SSP. SUBLIMIS 'TRICOLOR'	✓	✓	✓	✓	✓	✓					✓		✓			✓				✓			✓	✓	✓		
CROCUS VERNUS 'PICKWICK'	✓	✓	✓	✓	✓	✓					✓		✓			✓				✓			✓	✓			
DAHLIA X 'MICKEY'					✓	✓	✓				✓	✓	✓				✓	✓			✓						✓
FREESIA X 'BALLERINA'					✓	✓	✓	✓	✓		✓		✓			✓			✓	✓						✓	✓
FRITILLARIA MELEAGRIS	✓	✓	✓	✓	✓	✓				✓	✓		✓	✓		✓				✓	✓						
GLADIOLUS 'PRISCILLA'					✓	✓	✓	✓			✓		✓				✓	✓			✓		✓				✓
GLORIOSA SUPERBA							✓	✓			✓	✓	✓	✓			✓				✓						✓
HABRANTHUS ROBUSTUS						✓	✓	✓			✓	✓	✓				✓	✓	✓								
HERMODACTYLUS TUBEROSUS			✓	✓	✓	✓					✓	✓	✓			✓				✓						✓	✓
HIPPEASTRUM X 'PICOTE'					✓	✓	✓	✓			✓	✓	✓			✓			✓	✓					✓	✓	
INCARVILLEA DELAVAYI			✓	✓	✓	✓	✓				✓	✓	✓				✓			✓							
IRIS RETICULATA 'CANTAB'		✓	✓	✓	✓	✓				✓	✓		✓			✓				✓	✓					✓	✓
IRIS RETICULATA 'SPRING TIME'		✓	✓	✓	✓	✓				✓	✓		✓			✓				✓	✓					✓	✓
IXIA X 'BLUEBIRD'					✓	✓	✓				✓	✓	✓			✓				✓					✓	✓	✓
LACHENALIA BULBIFERUM							✓	✓		✓	✓	✓	✓	✓					✓	✓							✓
LILIUM SPECIOSUM 'UCHIDA'		✓	✓	✓	✓	✓					✓		✓				✓				✓					✓	✓
NARCISSUS POETICUS	✓	✓	✓	✓	✓	✓	✓				✓		✓	✓	✓	✓				✓			✓	✓			✓
NECTAROSCORDUM SICULUM			✓	✓	✓	✓	✓				✓	✓	✓			✓					✓						
RANUNCULUS 'TECOLOTE GIANTS'					✓	✓	✓	✓		✓	✓	✓	✓			✓				✓					✓		✓
SAUROMATUM VENOSUM							✓	✓			✓	✓	✓	✓				✓		✓					✓		
SPARAXIS TRICOLOR						✓	✓	✓			✓		✓			✓	✓		✓	✓					✓	✓	✓
TULIPA X 'FLAMING PARROT'		✓	✓	✓	✓	✓					✓		✓			✓				✓				✓			✓
VELTHEIMIA BRACTEATA							✓	✓	✓		✓		✓						✓	✓					✓		

A Zone Map of the U.S. and Canada

A plant's winter hardiness is critical in deciding whether it is suitable for your garden. The map below divides the United States and Canada into 11 climatic zones based on average minimum temperatures, as compiled by the United States Department of Agriculture. Find your zone and check the zone information in the Plant Selection Guide *(pages 98-103)* or the encyclopedia *(pages 106-151)* to help you choose the plants most likely to flourish in your climate.

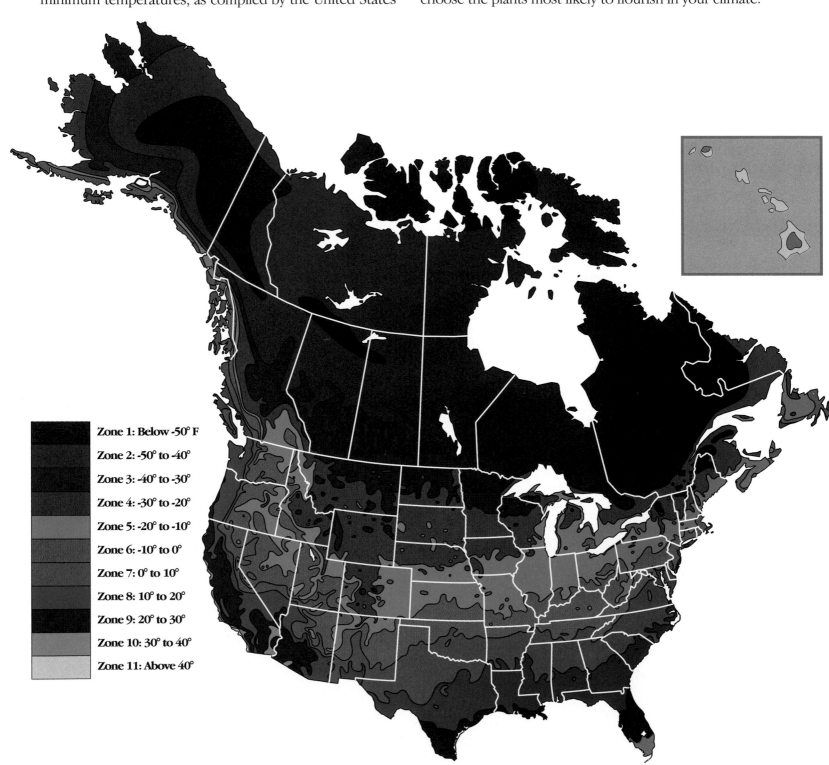

Zone 1: Below -50° F

Zone 2: -50° to -40°

Zone 3: -40° to -30°

Zone 4: -30° to -20°

Zone 5: -20° to -10°

Zone 6: -10° to 0°

Zone 7: 0° to 10°

Zone 8: 10° to 20°

Zone 9: 20° to 30°

Zone 10: 30° to 40°

Zone 11: Above 40°

Cross-Reference Guide to Plant Names

African lily—*Agapanthus*
Alpine hyacinth—*Brimeura*
Amaryllis—*Hippeastrum*
Amazon lily—*Eucharis*
Angel-wings—*Caladium*
Arabian starflower—
Ornithogalum arabicum
Arum lily—
Zantedeschia aethiopica
Atamasco lily—
Zephyranthes atamasco
Autumn crocus—*Colchicum*
Autumn daffodil—
Sternbergia
Aztec lily—*Sprekelia*
Baboon flower—*Babiana*
Basket flower—*Hymeno-
callis narcissiflora*
Belladonna lily—*Amaryllis*
Blackberry lily—
Belamcanda
Blazing star—*Tritonia*
Blood lily—*Haemanthus*
Bluebells—*Hyacinthoides,
Mertensia*
Bugle lily—*Watsonia*
Buttercup—*Ranunculus*
Button snakewort—
Liatris spicata
Calla lily—*Zantedeschia*
Cape Coast lily—
Crinum moorei
Cape tulip—
Haemanthus coccineus
Catherine-wheel—
Haemanthus katherinae
Checkered lily—
Fritillaria meleagris
Chincherinchee—
Ornithogalum
Chinese ground orchid—
Bletilla
Chinese lantern lily—
Sandersonia aurantiaca
Christmas-bells—
Sandersonia aurantiaca
Clover—*Oxalis*
Corn lily—*Ixia*
Cowslip—*Lachenalia,
Mertensia*
Crimson flag—*Schizostylis*

Crowfoot—*Ranunculus*
Crown imperial—
Fritillaria imperialis
Daffodil—*Narcissus*
Delicate lily—*Chlidanthus*
Desert-candle—*Eremurus*
Dogtooth violet—
Erythronium
Dragonroot—*Arisaema*
Eucharist lily—*Eucharis*
Fairy lily—*Chlidanthus,
Zephyranthes*
Fawn lily—*Erythronium*
Feather hyacinth—
Muscari comosum
Flag—*Iris*
Flame freesia—*Tritonia*
Foxtail lily—*Eremurus*
Fritillary—*Fritillaria*
Fumewort—
Corydalis solida
Garlic—*Allium*
Gay-feather—*Liatris*
George lily—*Vallota*
Giant lily—*Cardiocrinum*
Glory lily—*Gloriosa*
Glory-of-the-snow—
Chionodoxa
Glory-of-the-sun—
Leucocoryne
Grape hyacinth—*Muscari*
Green-dragon—
Arisaema dracontium
Guernsey lily—
Nerine sarniensis
Guinea hen tulip—
Fritillaria meleagris
Hardy gloxinia—*Incarvillea*
Hardy orchid—*Bletilla*
Harebell—*Hyacinthoides
non-scripta*
Harlequin flower—
Sparaxis tricolor
Heart lily—*Cardiocrinum*
Hyacinth—*Hyacinthus*
Indian turnip—
Arisaema triphyllum
Jacinth—*Scilla peruviana*
Jack-in-the-pulpit—
Arisaema triphyllum
Jacobean lily—*Sprekelia*

Jonquil—*Narcissus jonquilla*
Kamchatka lily—
Fritillaria camschatcensis
Leek—*Allium*
Leopard lily—*Belamcanda*
Leper lily—
Fritillaria meleagris
Lily—*Lilium*
Lily-of-the-Nile—
Agapanthus
Lily of the valley—
Convallaria
Loddon lily—
Leucojum aestivum
Lungwort—*Mertensia*
Magic flower—*Achimenes*
Magic lily—
Lycoris squamigera
Mariposa lily—*Calochortus*
Monarch-of-the-East—
Sauromatum
Montbretia—*Crocosmia*
Mysteria—
Colchicum autumnale
Natal lily—*Clivia*
Onion—*Allium*
Orchid amaryllis—*Sprekelia*
Orchid pansy—*Achimenes*
Painted lady—
Gladiolus carneus
Peacock flower—*Tigridia*
Persian violet—*Cyclamen*
Peruvian lily—*Alstroemeria,
Scilla peruviana*
Pineapple lily—*Eucomis*
Poison bulb—
Crinum asiaticum
Quamash—*Camassia*
Ramsons—*Allium ursinum*
Red calla—*Sauromatum*
Red-hot poker—*Veltheimia*
Red star—*Rhodohypoxis*
Resurrection lily—
Lycoris squamigera
River lily—*Schizostylis*
Saffron—*Crocus sativus*
St. James's lily—*Sprekelia*
Scarborough lily—*Vallota*
Sea daffodil—*Hymenocallis,
Pancratium*
Sea lily—*Pancratium*

Sea onion—*Urginea*
Sea squill—*Urginea*
Shamrock—*Oxalis*
Siberian lily—*Ixiolirion*
Snake's-head iris—
Hermodactylus
Snowdrop—*Galanthus*
Snowflake—*Leucojum, Or-
nithogalum umbellatum*
Sorrel—*Oxalis*
Spider lily—*Crinum,
Hymenocallis, Lycoris*
Spring meadow saffron—
Bulbocodium
Spring starflower—*Ipheion*
Squill—*Scilla*
Star-of-Bethlehem—
*Eucharis, Ornithogalum
umbellatum*
Stars-of-Persia—
Allium christophii
Striped squill—*Puschkinia*
Summer hyacinth—
Galtonia
Swamp lily—*Crinum*
Tassel hyacinth—*Muscari
comosum*
Tiger flower—*Tigridia*
Triplet lily—*Triteleia laxa*
Trout lily—
Erythronium americanum
Trumpet lily—
Zantedeschia aethiopica
Tuberose—*Polianthes*
Tulip—*Tulipa*
Voodoo lily—*Sauromatum*
Wake-robin—*Trillium*
Wand flower—*Sparaxis*
Widow iris—*Hermodactylus*
Wild hyacinth—
*Camassia scilloides,
Triteleia hyacinthina*
Windflower—*Anemone*
Winter aconite—*Eranthis*
Winter daffodil—*Sternbergia*
Wood hyacinth—
Hyacinthoides non-scripta
Wood lily—*Trillium*
Yellow bell—
Fritillaria pudica
Zephyr lily—*Zephyranthes*

Encyclopedia of Bulbs

Presented here in compact form is pertinent gardening information on most of the bulbs mentioned in this volume. The plants are listed alphabetically by their Latin botanical names; genus common names appear in bold type below the Latin. If you know a plant only by its common name, see the cross-reference chart on page 105 or see the index.

A botanical name consists of the genus and a species, both usually printed in italics. Species may also have common names, and many species contain one or more cultivars, whose names appear between single quotation marks. An "x" preceding the name indicates a hybrid.

"Hardiness" refers to the zones described on the USDA Plant Hardiness Zone Map for the United States and Canada (page 104). Those bulbs designated as "tender" are able to survive winter in the ground only in warm zones. Elsewhere, they must be dug up in fall for winter storage or grown in pots.

Achimenes
(a-kim-EE-neez)
ORCHID PANSY

Achimenes longiflora

Hardiness: *tender or Zones 10-11*

Type of bulb: *tuber or rhizome*

Flowering season: *summer to fall*

Height: *12 to 24 inches*

Soil: *moist, well-drained*

Light: *partial to full shade*

Clusters of flat-faced flowers up to 2½ inches across with long, tubular necks bloom in masses amid fleshy, downy leaves on slender arching or trailing stems. Blossom throats are often splashed or veined in a contrasting color. New flowers appear over a long season of bloom. Excellent as houseplants, orchid pansies can also be used outdoors in containers and hanging baskets on shady patios in locations with mild temperatures. Their graceful mounded, sometimes cascading habit shows to good advantage in this setting.

Selected species and varieties: *A. erecta*—deep red late-summer-to-fall-blooming flowers on stems to 18 inches tall. *A. heterophylla* (yellow mist)—red-orange blossoms with yellow throats on 12-inch stems in late summer. *A. longiflora* (trumpet achimenes)—white, pink, red, lavender, or violet flowers, sometimes with contrasting throats, in midsummer amid whorls of extremely hairy leaves on stems to 12 inches; 'Paul Arnold' has blue-violet blossoms; 'Ambroise Verschaffelt' is white with a deep purple throat. *A. tubiflora* [also classified as *Sin-*

ningia tubiflora]—fragrant white waxy summer flowers on 24-inch stems. *A.* hybrids—'Cascade Cockade' has deep pink petals surrounding a white eye; 'Cascade Evening Glow', deep salmon flowers; 'Cascade Fairy Pink', pink petals and white centers; 'Cascade Fashionable Pink', pink blossoms; 'Cascade Great Rosy Red', rose blooms; 'Cascade Violet Night', blue-violet petals and a white throat; 'Elke Michelssen', red-orange flowers; 'English Waltz', salmon petals; 'India', deep blue flowers; 'Quick Step', blue flowers; 'Viola Michelssen', rose red blooms.

Growing conditions and maintenance: Plant achimenes in spring, setting tubers 1 inch deep and 3 to 4 inches apart. Flowers appear 12 to 14 weeks after planting; staggering plantings over several weeks provides a continuous show of blossoms for several months. For earliest bloom, start tubers indoors 6 to 8 weeks shortly before nighttime temperatures warm to 50°F. Plants grow best in a 24-hour temperature range of 60° to 80°F. Keep soil moist but not soggy, and fertilize while the plants are blooming. Gradually with-

Achimenes 'Ambroise Verschaffelt'

hold water after flowering ceases. Store potted tubers over the winter in dry soil, or lift and dry tubers in fall for replanting in spring. Tubers do best stored at 50° to 60°F. Propagate by dividing dormant tubers into ½-inch pieces before repotting in spring or by removing and potting tiny rhizomes, which sometimes appear in leaf joints. Achimenes can also be grown from seed, but hybrids may revert to parent species.

Agapanthus
(ag-a-PAN-thus)
LILY-OF-THE-NILE

Agapanthus africanus

Hardiness: *tender or Zones 8-10*

Type of bulb: *rhizome*

Flowering season: *summer*

Height: *18 inches to 5 feet*

Soil: *moist, well-drained*

Light: *full sun*

Domed clusters of five-petaled, star-shaped flowers with prominent stamens rise on leafless, hollow stalks from graceful clumps of straplike evergreen leaves that persist after the flowers fade. Agapanthus makes dramatic border specimens or pot plants and can be used as long-lasting cut flowers. Its seed pods add interest to dried arrangements.

Selected species and varieties: *A. africanus* 'Albus' (African lily)—clusters of 30 or more 1½-inch white flower stars on stems to 3 feet tall. *A. praecox* ssp. *orientalis* (Oriental agapanthus)—up to 100 white or blue flowers clustered on stems to 5 feet tall above 3-foot-long leaves that are up to 3 inches wide and sometimes striped yellow; 'Peter Pan' is an 18-inch dwarf cultivar with blue blossoms.

Growing conditions and maintenance: Plant rhizomes 24 inches apart in spring for summer bloom, setting the tops of the bulbs just below the soil line. In colder areas, grow plants in pots, moving them indoors before frost. They bloom best when slightly potbound. Cut stems back after flowers fade. Propagate by dividing rhizomes every 4 or 5 years in spring.

Allium
(AL-lee-um)
ONION

Allium 'Globemaster'

Hardiness: *Zones 3-9*

Type of bulb: *true bulb*

Flowering season: *spring to summer*

Height: *6 inches to 5 feet*

Soil: *moist, well-drained, sandy*

Light: *full sun to light shade*

Related to edible culinary species, flowering onions produce showy 2- to 12-inch flower clusters, usually in dense spheres or ovals composed of hundreds of tiny blooms packed tightly together, but sometimes in loose, dangling or upright airy domes of larger flowers. Each stout, leafless hollow stem holds a single flower well above a low rosette of grassy or straplike leaves that die back after the bulbs produce their blooms. Many species smell faintly like onion or garlic when cut or bruised, but a few are sweetly fragrant. Mass alliums for effect in spring or summer beds or borders; strategically site larger flowering onions as dramatic garden accents; and interplant smaller species with ground covers or in a rock garden. Alliums are striking as cut flowers or in dried bouquets. Some flowering onion species will naturalize, and a few are suitable for forcing. Rodent pests find flowering onion bulbs unappealing.

Selected species and varieties: *A. aflatunense* (ornamental onion, Persian onion)—4-inch purple flower globes in late spring on 2- to 4-foot-tall stems above 4-inch-wide foliage; Zones 4-8. *A. atrop-urpureum*—2-inch wine red spheres on 2- to 3-foot stems in late spring above narrow 18-inch leaves; Zones 3-9. *A. caeruleum* (blue garlic, blue globe onion)—deep blue blossoms in dense 2-inch globes on 2-foot stems in late spring above narrow 10- to 18-inch leaves; Zones 3-9. *A. carinatum* ssp. *pulchellum* (keeled garlic)—carmine flower clusters on stems to 2 feet in summer; 'Album' has white flowers; Zones 3-9. *A. cernuum* (nodding wild onion)—loose clusters of 30 to 40 delicate pink flowers dangle atop 8- to 18-inch stems in late spring above rosettes of grassy 10-inch leaves; Zones 3-9. *A. christophii* (stars-of-Persia)—spidery late spring flowers with a metallic luster growing in lacy clusters up to 10 inches across on stout stems to 2 feet growing from rosettes of inch-wide leaves up to 20 inches long; Zones 4-8. *A.*

Allium christophii

flavum (small yellow onion)—dangling 2-inch clusters of yellow bell-shaped flowers on 1-foot stems in summer; Zones 4-9. *A. giganteum* (giant ornamental onion, giant garlic)—lilac-colored summer flower globes 6 inches across on stems to 5 feet rising from clumps of leaves 2 inches wide and up to 30 inches long; Zones 5-8. *A. jesdianum*—dense clusters of deep violet flowers; Zones 4-9. *A. karataviense* (Turkestan onion)—pale rose 3-inch or larger flower clusters on 10-inch stems above broad straps of attractive, spreading blue-green foliage in late spring; Zones 4-9. *A. macleanii*—red-violet blossoms clustered at the tips of 3-foot stems in late spring above broad, shiny foliage; Zones 4-9. *A. moly* (lily leek, golden onion)—flat clusters of ¾- to 1-inch flowers; 'Jeannine' has long-lasting 2- to 3-inch vivid yellow flowers on 12-inch stems in summer above blue-green leaves with a metallic sheen; Zones 3-9. *A. neapolitanum* 'Grandiflorum' (daffodil garlic, Naples garlic)—loose, open 3-inch clusters of up to 30 fragrant 1-inch white flower stars on 12- to 18-inch stems in late spring; Zones 6-9. *A. nigrum*—white spring flowers touched with gray on 2-foot stems; Zones 4-9. *A. oreophilum*—open clusters of fragrant 2-inch rosy pink blossoms on 4-inch stems

Allium moly

in late spring; Zones 4-9. *A. rosenbachianum* 'Album'—silvery white 4-inch flower clusters on stems to 3 feet in late spring above 2-inch-wide leaves up to 20 inches long; Zones 5-9. *A. roseum* 'Grandiflorum' (bigflower rosy onion, rosy garlic)—3-inch pinkish white flower globes in late spring on stems to 15 inches, frequently with tiny bulbils appearing after the flowers fade; Zones 5-9. *A. schubertii*—spidery pink-violet flowers in clusters up to a foot or more across on 1- to 2-foot stems in summer above distinctively wavy, inch-wide foliage; Zones 4-9. *A. sphaerocephalum* (drumstick chive, roundheaded leek, roundheaded garlic)—densely packed 2-inch oval heads of deep purple, bell-shaped summer flowers on 3-foot stems rising from clumps of hollow cylindrical leaves up to 24 inches long; Zones 4-8. *A. stipitatum* 'Album'—6-inch spheres of white flowers on stems to 4 feet in late spring above 2-inch-wide leaves; Zones 4-9. *A. triquetrum* (three-cornered leek, triangle onion)—dangling white flowers striped with green on unusual triangular 18-inch stems rising from clumps of deep green leaves 10 to 15 inches long throughout spring; Zones 4-

9. *A. unifolium*—rose flowers on 12- to 18-inch stems in late spring; Zones 4-9. *A. ursinum* (bear's garlic, ramsons, wood garlic)—2½-inch flat-topped clusters of white flowers with a strong garlicky odor on 12- to 15-inch stems in late spring; Zones 4-9. *A. zebdanense*—white blossoms clustered on 12-inch stems in late spring; Zones 4-9. *A.* hybrids—'Globemaster' has durable large purple blooms on 2- to 3-foot stems; 'Lucy Ball', deep lilac clusters on stems to 4 feet in summer; 'Purple Sensation', purple flowers on 30-inch stems in spring; Zones 4-9.

Growing conditions and maintenance: Plant flowering onions in fall in northern zones, in spring or fall in warmer areas. Set bulbs at a depth two to three times their diameter, spacing smaller bulbs 4 to 6 inches apart, larger ones 12 to 18 inches. Alliums suitable for naturalizing include *A. aflatunense, A. karataviense, A. moly, A. neapolitanum, A. oreophilum, A. sphaerocephalum,* and *A. triquetrum,* although *A. triquetrum*

Allium sphaerocephalum

can be invasive. Alliums may be left undisturbed in the garden for years until diminished bloom signals that bulbs are overcrowded. Both pleasantly scented *A. neapolitanum* and low-growing *A. schubertii* are suitable for forcing; plant several bulbs per 6-inch pot or bulb pan. Cut stems back after flowers fade, but allow foliage to die back before removing it. Protect bulbs with winter mulch north of Zone 5. Propagate by separating and replanting tiny bulblets that develop at the base of parent bulbs, by potting tiny bulbils that appear amid flower clusters, or by sowing seed, which will grow blooming-size bulbs in 2 years.

Alstroemeria
(ahl-strum-EE-ree-a)
PERUVIAN LILY

Alstroemeria Ligtu Hybrids

Hardiness: *Zones 6-11*

Type of bulb: *tuber*

Flowering season: *summer*

Height: *3 to 4 feet*

Soil: *moist, well-drained*

Light: *full sun to light shade*

Peruvian lily's 2-inch flowers bloom in clusters atop stiff stems lined with narrow leaves. The intricately patterned, funnel-shaped flowers with curving stamens resemble exotic azaleas with inner petals often speckled, splotched, striped or tipped in contrasting colors. Use Peruvian lilies as border plants, container specimens, and cut flowers.

Selected species and varieties: *A. aurea*—clusters of up to 50 flowers on 3-foot stems; 'Dover Orange' is orange; 'Lutea' yellow. *A.* Ligtu Hybrids—inner and outer petals in contrasting shades of white to pink, salmon or orange on stems to 4 feet.

Growing conditions and maintenance: Plant Peruvian lily tubers in spring or fall setting them 6 to 9 inches deep and 12 inches apart. *A. aurea* can be invasive. Protect with winter mulch in Zones 6-8. North of Zone 6, grow Peruvian lilies in containers and bring indoors in winter. Propagate by carefully dividing in spring or fall or from seed.

Amaryllis
(am-a-RIL-lis)
BELLADONNA LILY

Amaryllis belladonna

Hardiness: *tender or Zones 9-11*

Type of bulb: *true bulb*

Flowering season: *summer to fall*

Height: *1½ to 3 feet*

Soil: *moist, well-drained*

Light: *full sun*

Amaryllis belladonna, the sole species within this genus, produces clusters of 6 to 12 flower trumpets up to 3½ inches across. The straplike foliage, which appears in early to late spring, dies by summer. Fragrant flowers appear separately on a leafless stalk several months later. Force belladonna lilies indoors as houseplants or use as border plantings in Zones 9-11. Blossoms last a week as cut flowers.

Selected species and varieties: *A. belladonna* (belladonna lily)—white to pale pink or rose blossoms; 'Cape Town' has deep rose red flowers.

Growing conditions and maintenance: Pot with the neck of the bulb at the soil surface or set bulbs outdoors 4 to 6 inches deep and 12 inches apart. Begin watering when foliage appears, then withhold all water between foliage dieback and the appearance of the flower stalk; resume watering then and fertilize until flowers fade. Propagate from seed, planting the fleshy seeds as soon as they appear after flowers fade, or by removing bulblets from parent bulbs. Caution: Belladonna lily bulbs are poisonous and must be kept out of the reach of children.

Anemone
(a-NEM-o-nee)
WINDFLOWER

Anemone coronaria

Hardiness: *Zones 3-9*

Type of bulb: *tuber or rhizome*

Flowering season: *spring*

Height: *3 to 18 inches*

Soil: *moist, well-drained*

Light: *full sun to light shade*

Windflowers carpet a border with drifts of daisylike flowers held above whorls of attractively divided leaves resembling flat parsley. Single or double rows of petals surround a prominent cushion of anthers in a contrasting color, often with a halo of cream or white separating it from the main petal color. Mass windflowers for a tapestry of color beneath spring-flowering shrubs and trees or allow them to naturalize in woodland gardens. Anemones can be forced as houseplants, and the taller ones make good cut flowers.

Selected species and varieties: *A. apennina* 'Alba' (Apennine windflower)—inch-wide white flowers tinged blue on 6- to 12-inch stems; Zones 6-9. *A. blanda* (Grecian windflower)—2-inch single- or double-petaled flowers with prominent yellow centers on 3- to 8-inch stems; 'Blue Star' has light blue flowers; 'Blue Shades', light to dark blue blooms; 'Charmer', deep pink flowers; 'Pink Star', very large pink blossoms; 'Radar', reddish purple flowers with a white center; 'Rosea', rosy pink blooms; 'Violet Star', violet flowers with a white center; 'White Splendor', long-lasting, large white flowers; Zones 5-8. *A. coronaria* (poppy anemone)—'de Caen' hybrids grow 18 inches tall with single rows of petals; 'Mr. Fokker' has blue flowers; 'Sylphide', deep violet blooms; 'The Bride', pure white flowers. St. Brigid hybrids produce semidouble rows of petals; 'Lord Lieutenant' has bright blue flowers; 'Mt. Everest', white flowers; 'The Admiral', red-violet blooms; 'The Governor', deep scarlet flowers. 'Hollandia' has bright red flowers; Zones 6-9. *A. nemorosa* (wood anemone)—inch-wide white flowers tinged pink with yellow centers

Anemone blanda

on 6- to 10-inch stems; 'Alba Plena' has double petals; Zones 4-8. *A. ranunculoides* (buttercup anemone)—yellow blossoms on 6-inch stems; 'Flore Pleno' has semidouble yellow petals giving a ruffled appearance; 'Superba', large flowers above bronzy foliage; Zones 3-9.

Growing conditions and maintenance: Plant windflowers in the fall, massing them for best effect. Soak tubers overnight before setting them out 2 inches deep and 3 to 6 inches apart. *A. apennina* and Grecian windflower can be grown north of Zone 6 by setting tubers out in spring, then lifting them for storage in fall. *A. apennina,* Grecian windflower, and poppy anemone can be forced for houseplants. *A. apennina,* Grecian windflower, wood anemone, and buttercup anemone all naturalize well, although the latter two can be invasive. Anemones need constant moisture, though not soggy conditions, to bloom at their best. Propagate windflowers from seed or by division in late summer after foliage fades.

Arisaema
(a-ris-EE-ma)
DRAGONROOT

Arisaema triphyllum

Hardiness: *Zones 4-9*

Type of bulb: *tuber*

Flowering season: *spring*

Height: *1 to 3 feet*

Soil: *moist, acid*

Light: *partial to full shade*

Arisaemas produce a fleshy spike called a spadix nestled within an outer leaflike spathe, which folds over the spadix like a hood. Glossy, three-lobed leaves taller than the spathe and spadix persist throughout the summer. The spadix ripens to a cluster of attractive red fruit in fall. Use arisaemas in wildflower or woodland gardens or along stream banks, where they will slowly spread and naturalize.

Selected species and varieties: *A. dracontium* (green-dragon)—green spathe enfolding a 4- to 10-inch green or yellowish green spadix on 1-foot stems. *A. sikokianum*—ivory spadix within a spathe that is deep maroon banded in green on the outside and ivory at its base on the inside, on 1-foot stems. *A. triphyllum* (jack-in-the-pulpit, Indian turnip)—green to purple spadix within a green to purple spathe striped purple, green, white, or maroon inside on 1- to 2-foot stems.

Growing conditions and maintenance: Plant arisaemas in fall, setting tubers 4 inches deep and 1 foot apart in soil that is constantly moist but not soggy. Propagate by division in early fall.

Arum
(A-rum)
ARUM

Arum italicum

Hardiness: *Zones 6-9*

Type of bulb: *tuber*

Flowering season: *spring*

Height: *12 to 18 inches*

Soil: *moist, acid*

Light: *partial shade*

Italian arum *(Arum italicum)* is noteworthy for its attractively marbled, arrow-shaped leaves, which appear in fall and persist through the winter. Inconspicuous flowers appear in spring, lining a fleshy, fingerlike spadix enfolded by a leaflike hood called a spathe, which rises to a sharp point. Most gardeners grow arum for the plump cluster of glossy, brightly colored berries that follows the flowers in summer. Arum will naturalize in moist woodland or wildflower gardens.

Selected species and varieties: *A. italicum* 'Marmoratum' [also called 'Pictum'] (Italian arum)—narrow, waxy leaves veined in cream or silver followed by a creamy yellow or yellow-green spadix and thick clusters of brilliant orange berries.

Growing conditions and maintenance: Plant Italian arum in late summer, setting tubers 3 inches deep and 1 foot apart in soil that is moist but not soggy. Propagate from seed or by division in late summer. Caution: Both the foliage and berries of Italian arum are poisonous and must be kept out of the reach of children.

Babiana
(bab-ee-AH-na)
BABOON FLOWER

Babiana stricta

Hardiness: *tender or Zones 9-11*

Type of bulb: *corm*

Flowering season: *spring*

Height: *8 to 12 inches*

Soil: *moist, well-drained*

Light: *full sun*

Baboon flowers produce 1½-inch fragrant flowers with pointed petals surrounding a contrasting eye; the blooms last as long as 5 weeks in the garden. Flowers grow in clusters on stems rising from stiff, sword-shaped leaves. Use baboon flowers in borders or grow them in containers as patio specimens.

Selected species and varieties: *B. stricta*—flowers in shades of cream, blue, lilac, and crimson; 'Purple Sensation' produces white-throated purple flowers; 'White King', white petals streaked blue on their undersides surrounding a deep blue eye; 'Zwanenburg Glory', lavender to violet petals splashed with white.

Growing conditions and maintenance: Plant baboon flowers in fall, setting corms 6 inches deep and 6 inches apart. North of Zone 9, plant corms in spring and lift after foliage fades in fall for replanting the following spring. Propagate from seed or by removing and planting the cormels that develop around parent bulbs every 3 to 4 years.

Begonia
(be-GO-nee-a)
TUBEROUS BEGONIA

Begonia Picotee Group

Hardiness: *tender or Zones 10-11*

Type of bulb: *tuber*

Flowering season: *summer to fall*

Height: *8 to 18 inches*

Soil: *moist, well-drained*

Light: *partial to full shade*

Tuberous begonias produce an abundance of large flowers over a long season of bloom with soft, waxy petals in vivid tones of red, orange, apricot, rose, pink, yellow, cream, or white, sometimes bicolored, on fleshy upright or trailing stems. Blossoms open in succession amid pointed, crenelated green to bronze foliage that is deeply veined, sometimes in contrasting colors. Their diverse flower forms have plain, frilled, or fringed petals arranged to mimic the blossoms of roses, camellias, carnations, and other garden favorites. Thousands of hybrids offer almost limitless combinations of forms and colors for varying purposes. Upright tuberous begonias are striking when massed as bedding plants or grown as specimens in patio containers, whereas cascading forms are appealing when allowed to trail gracefully from hanging baskets.

Selected species and varieties: *B.* x *tuberhybrida*—flowers to 4 inches or more across, with hundreds of hybrids classified in 12 groups according to flower form and color. SINGLE GROUP—broad, flat-faced flowers composed of four enormous petals surrounding a central cluster of prominent stamens. CRISPA OR FRILLED GROUP—flat-faced flowers with large petals whose edges are ruffled or fringed, surrounding a colorful cluster of stamens. CRISTATA OR CRESTED GROUP—raised, frilled crests punctuating the center of each of several large tepals. NARCISSIFLORA OR DAFFODIL-FLOWERED GROUP—double rows of petals in an arrangement that resembles a flat-faced narcissus. CAMELLIA OR CAMELLIIFLORA GROUP—smooth petals of a single color arranged in overlapping layers like camellia flowers on upright plants. RUFFLED CAMELLIA GROUP—overlapping layers of ruffled petals that conceal the stamens. ROSI-

Begonia Camelliiflora Group

FLORA OR ROSEBUD GROUP—center petals tightly furled like a pointed, unopened rosebud. FIMBRIATA PLENA OR CARNATION GROUP—finely fringed petals overlapping in double rows. PICOTEE GROUP—double rows of overlapping petals edged in a narrow or broad band of a deeper shade of the main petal color. MARGINATA GROUP—double rows of petals edged in a narrow or broad band of a contrasting color. MARMORATA GROUP—double rows of pink or rose petals dappled with white. PENDULA OR HANGING-BASKET GROUP —a profusion of single- or double-petaled blossoms on trailing stems. MULTIFLORA GROUP—small single- or double-petaled blossoms on bushy plants with compact stems.

Most hybrid tuberous begonias are identified in the garden trade simply by form and color rather than by cultivar names, with the camellia-flowered, carnation-flowered, crispa marginata, picotee, and hanging basket—some-times called cascade or pendula—types most common. Nonstop hybrids have smaller flowers than the double hybrid begonias they resemble, but their blossoms appear throughout the summer and fall until frost.

Begonia Pendula Group

Growing conditions and maintenance: Plant tuberous begonias outdoors in spring for summer bloom, setting tubers 1 to 2 inches deep with their concave side up and 12 to 15 inches apart. For potted plants, space three or four tubers evenly in each pot or hanging basket, with the top of the tuber at the soil line. For earliest flowering, start tuberous begonias indoors 6 to 12 weeks before planting outside. Keep soil constantly moist but not soggy. Prune small tubers to a single stem, larger ones to 3 or 4 stems, and pinch early buds to encourage more prolific flowering. Provide support for upright forms. Fertilize while blooming with a dilute balanced houseplant fertilizer. North of Zone 10, lift tubers in fall after the first light frost, allow them to dry, and store them for replanting in spring. Propagate tuberous begonias from stem cuttings taken in spring; by dividing tubers, making sure to maintain at least one growth bud in each section; or from seed sown indoors in January to bloom in June.

Belamcanda
(bel-am-CAN-da)
BLACKBERRY LILY

Belamcanda chinensis

Hardiness: *Zones 5-10*	
Type of bulb: *rhizome*	
Flowering season: *late summer to fall*	
Height: *2 to 3 feet*	
Soil: *well-drained*	
Light: *full sun to light shade*	

Blackberry lilies carry sprays of lilylike flowers with narrow, curving, pointed petals on zigzag-branching flower stalks above fans of swordlike foliage. Each flower lasts only a day, but new blossoms open over several weeks. Flowers are followed by attractive seed pods, which burst open to reveal berrylike seeds. Use blackberry lilies in a sunny border or as cut flowers. Dried seed pods decorate the winter garden and can be used in dried arrangements.

Selected species and varieties: *B. chinensis* (leopard lily)—2-inch orange flowers with pointed, curving petals liberally spotted with red.

Growing conditions and maintenance: Plant blackberry lilies in spring or fall, setting rhizomes 1 inch deep and 6 to 8 inches apart. Blackberry lilies do best in full sun; in light shade, they may require staking. Propagate from seed to produce flowering plants in 2 years or by dividing rhizomes in spring or fall.

Bellevalia
(bel-VAH-lee-a)
BELLEVALIA

Bellevalia pycnantha

Hardiness: *Zones 6-10*	
Type of bulb: *true bulb*	
Flowering season: *spring*	
Height: *6 to 18 inches*	
Soil: *well-drained*	
Light: *full sun*	

Bellevalia's cylindrical flower clusters composed of 20 to 30 small flower bells open from bottom to top on a single stalk rising from a clump of straplike leaves. The blooms resemble *Muscari* as they begin to open, small *Hyacinthus* when fully open. Clusters of blue-black seeds follow in fall. Use bellevalia in borders or rock gardens, where they may naturalize.

Selected species and varieties: *B. pycnantha*—dull blue-black flowers with yellow edges that unfold on 12-inch-tall stalks above 12-inch-long leaves. *B. romana* [also called *Hyacinthus romanus*]—gray flower buds opening into dull white, ¼-inch flowers sometimes tinged with violet, brown, or green on 6- to 18-inch flower stalks.

Growing conditions and maintenance: Plant bellevalias in fall, setting bulbs 3 inches deep and 3 inches apart. Bulbs tolerate both wet spring conditions and summer drought. Propagate by removing and replanting the small bulblets that develop at the base of parent bulbs in fall.

Bletilla
(ble-TIL-la)
HARDY ORCHID

Bletilla striata

Hardiness: *Zones 5-9*	
Type of bulb: *rhizome*	
Flowering season: *late spring*	
Height: *1 to 2 feet*	
Soil: *moist, well-drained*	
Light: *partial shade*	

Hardy orchids bear up to six or more delicate flowers resembling small cattleya orchids on arching, branched stalks rising above clumps of narrow, oval, pointed leaves. Appearing over a long season of bloom, each nodding, multicolored flower has waxy petals and petal-like sepals rimming an elaborate lip with several crested ridges resembling ruffled pleats. Plant hardy orchids in woodland gardens where they can expand into handsome clumps, or pot them as houseplants.

Selected species and varieties: *B. striata*—inch-wide pink to purple flowers with decoratively spotted and mottled lips appearing for up to 6 weeks; 'Alba' is pure white.

Growing conditions and maintenance: Plant hardy orchids in spring or fall, placing rhizomes and the small pseudobulbs growing from them 4 inches deep and 6 inches apart in soil enriched with organic matter. In winter, mulch hardy orchids in Zones 5-7, or move potted hardy orchids to locations where they will not freeze. Propagate in spring or fall by dividing rhizomes.

Brimeura
(bri-MURE-ra)
ALPINE HYACINTH

Brimeura amethystina

Hardiness: *Zones 4-10*

Type of bulb: *true bulb*

Flowering season: *spring*

Height: *6 to 12 inches*

Soil: *well-drained*

Light: *full sun to light shade*

Alpine hyacinths produce up to a dozen nodding flower bells loosely spaced along one side of an arching flower stalk growing from a clump of grassy leaves. They resemble *Hyacinthus* but bloom later in the spring. Allow these dainty plants to naturalize in borders, rock gardens, or wildflower gardens. They can also be forced as houseplants.

Selected species and varieties: *B. amethystina* [formerly *Hyacinthus amethystinus* and *Scilla amethystina*] —up to 15 tiny ½-inch blue bells lining one side of the stalks; 'Alba' yields pure white flower bells.

Growing conditions and maintenance: Plant alpine hyacinths in fall, setting bulbs 1 to 2 inches deep and 4 to 5 inches apart. The small bulbs make the best show when planted closely and left to multiply. Save bulbs forced as potted plants to set out in the garden in fall. Propagate by removing and replanting the small bulblets that form alongside parent bulbs.

Bulbocodium
(bul-bo-KO-dee-um)
BULBOCODIUM

Bulbocodium vernum

Hardiness: *Zones 3-10*

Type of bulb: *corm*

Flowering season: *late winter to spring*

Height: *4 inches*

Soil: *well-drained, sandy*

Light: *full sun to light shade*

One of the earliest flowers to brighten the garden, bulbocodium sends up blossoms that open into upright trumpets of narrow, ribbonlike petals. The narrow, grassy leaves appear after the flowers bloom. The plant will naturalize in a border, rock garden, or wildflower garden.

Selected species and varieties: *B. vernum* (spring meadow saffron)—one to three 2- to 3-inch-wide rose-violet flower trumpets on each short stalk.

Growing conditions and maintenance: Plant spring meadow saffron in late summer or fall, spacing corms 3 to 4 inches apart and setting them 3 inches deep. Locations that provide moisture in spring, when bulbs are blooming and foliage is ripening, but are slightly dry in summer are ideal. Propagate by removing and replanting the small cormels that grow at the base of each corm every 3 or 4 years after the grassy leaves die back in early summer.

Caladium
(ka-LAY-dee-um)
ANGEL-WINGS

Caladium bicolor 'Aaron'

Hardiness: *tender or Zones 10-11*

Type of bulb: *tuber*

Flowering season: *summer*

Height: *1 to 2 feet*

Soil: *moist, well-drained*

Light: *partial shade to shade*

Exotic caladiums form clumps of intricately patterned translucent leaves that eclipse their insignificant flowers. The arrow-shaped leaves, rising continuously throughout summer, are vividly marbled, shaded, slashed, veined, and flecked in contrasting colors to brighten shady borders or decorate indoor gardens.

Selected species and varieties: *C. bicolor* [formerly *C. x hortulanum*]—foot-long arrow- or heart-shaped leaves; 'Aaron' has green edges feathering into creamy centers; 'Candidum' is white with green veining; 'Fannie Munson', pink veined red edged in green; 'Festiva', rose veined green; 'Irene Dank', light green edged in deeper green; 'June Bride', greenish white edged in deep green; 'Pink Beauty', a pink dwarf spattered with green; 'White Christmas', white with green veining.

Growing conditions and maintenance: Plant in spring when night temperatures remain above 60°F, setting the tubers 2 inches deep and 8 to 12 inches apart. North of Zone 10, lift and dry tubers in fall to replant the next spring. Provide high humidity and temperatures of 60°F or more. Propagate by division in spring.

Calochortus
(ka-lo-KOR-tus)
MARIPOSA LILY

Calochortus venustus

Hardiness: *Zones 6-10*

Type of bulb: *true bulb*

Flowering season: *spring*

Height: *8 inches to 2 feet*

Soil: *very well drained, sandy, acid*

Light: *full sun*

The furled, overlapping petals of mariposa lilies form tuliplike, upright cups. Each erect stem rises from a small clump of shiny, fleshy, narrow leaves. Grow mariposa lilies in a rock garden or as potted plants, or use them in arrangements.

Selected species and varieties: *C. splendens* (lilac mariposa)—2-inch lilac flowers on 1- to 2-foot stems. *C. venustus* (white mariposa)—white, yellow, purple, or red 2-inch flowers with throats splotched in darker shades or contrasting colors on 8-inch to 2-foot stems.

Growing conditions and maintenance: Plant mariposa lilies in fall, setting the bulbs 2 inches deep and 4 to 6 inches apart. The bulbs must dry out after foliage dies back; if necessary, lift them in late summer to replant in fall. Alternating freeze/thaw cycles reduce blooming; where this occurs, mulch after first frost or grow bulbs in pots to overwinter in cold frames. Avoid fertilizing. Propagate from seed or by removing and replanting bulblets growing alongside bulbs in fall.

Camassia
(ka-MA-see-a)
CAMASS, QUAMASH

Camassia quamash

Hardiness: *Zones 5-9*

Type of bulb: *true bulb*

Flowering season: *spring*

Height: *1 to 4 feet*

Soil: *moist, well-drained, sandy*

Light: *full sun to light shade*

Camass's spires of inch-wide flowers like tiny stars with a fringe of narrow, pointed, sometimes double petals open from bottom to top over several weeks. Naturalize camass in damp wildflower gardens, alongside streams or ponds, or among other spring-blooming bulbs.

Selected species and varieties: *C. cusickii* (Cusick quamash)—up to 300 flowers on stalks 3 to 4 feet tall; 'Zwanenburg' has horizontal stalks upturned at their ends. *C. leichtlinii* (Leichtlin quamash)—up to 40 flowers on stems to 4 feet; 'Alba' produces white blossoms; 'Blue Danube', very dark blue; 'Sempiplena', double-petaled creamy white to yellow. *C. quamash* (common camass)—foot-long spires on 2-foot stems; 'Orion' is very deep blue. *C. scilloides* (Atlantic camass, eastern camass, wild hyacinth)—blue or white ½-inch flowers on 2½-foot stems.

Growing conditions and maintenance: Plant camass bulbs in fall, setting them 4 inches deep and 6 to 9 inches apart. Provide shade where summers are dry. Bulbs can be lifted to remove offsets but are best left undisturbed unless flowering declines. Otherwise, propagate from seed.

Canna
(KAN-ah)
CANNA

Canna 'Pretoria'

Hardiness: *tender or Zones 8-11*

Type of bulb: *rhizome*

Flowering season: *summer to fall*

Height: *18 inches to 6 feet*

Soil: *moist, well-drained*

Light: *full sun*

Cannas produce a continuous show of bold 4- to 5-inch flowers with a tousled arrangement of petal-like stamens in strong colors from summer through frost. The flowers, which are sometimes bicolored, are carried on clumps of stiff, erect stems. The broad, bold leaves, up to 24 inches long, are usually a deep, glossy green but are sometimes bronzy red or striped or veined in white or pink. They line the stems to provide a dramatic backdrop to the flowers. Mass these coarse-textured plants at the back of borders in casual groupings or formal patterns, or grow dwarf cultivars as edgings or in patio containers.

Selected species and varieties: *C.* x *generalis* (canna lily)—standard varieties grow 4 to 6 feet tall; 'Black Knight' has deep velvet red flowers and bronze foliage; 'City of Portland', rosy salmon flowers above green leaves; 'Gaiety', yellow flowers edged in orange; 'Los Angeles', coral pink blooms above green foliage; 'The President', bright red flowers and deep green leaves; 'Red King Humbert', red flowers above bronzy foliage on very tall stems; 'Richard Wallace', canary yellow blossoms and green foliage; 'Rosamund Cole', red-and-gold bicolored blossoms; 'Stadt Fellbach', peach flowers with yellow throats fading to pink; 'Wyoming', rugged red-orange flowers and reddish bronze leaves. Dwarf varieties of this species grow to less than 3 feet tall; 'Ambrosia' has pinky orange blossoms on 18-inch stems; 'Brandywine', scarlet flowers on 3-foot stems; 'Pfitzer's Chinese Coral', rich coral pink blossoms; 'Pfitzer's Crimson Beauty', bright red flowers on 18-inch stems; 'Pfitzer's Primrose Yellow', soft yellow blooms; 'Pfitzer's Salmon',

Canna 'Brandywine'

unusually large salmon pink flowers; 'Pretoria', yellow-orange flowers above deep green leaves striped with cream.

Growing conditions and maintenance: In Zones 9 and 10, set cannas out as bedding plants in spring, planting the rhizomes 4 to 6 inches deep; space standard cultivars 2 feet apart, dwarf cultivars 1 foot apart. Provide ample moisture and high humidity during the growing season. Cannas can remain in the ground year round in frost-free areas; in Zone 8, provide a protective winter mulch. North of Zone 8, start cannas for beds or containers indoors 4 weeks before night temperatures reach 60°F; in fall, cut foliage back to 6 inches and lift rhizomes for winter storage. Pinch each container-grown rhizome back to a single shoot for largest flowers. Propagate cannas from seed, soaking seeds for 48 hours before planting to loosen their tough outer coats; or by division in spring, sectioning to allow no more than two buds per piece.

Cardiocrinum
(kar-dee-o-KREE-num)
GIANT LILY

Cardiocrinum giganteum

Hardiness: *Zones 6-8*

Type of bulb: *true bulb*

Flowering season: *summer*

Height: *8 to 12 feet*

Soil: *moist, well-drained, acid, fertile*

Light: *light shade*

Giant lilies produce clusters of fragrant, narrow flower trumpets as much as 6 inches long atop stout stems. Pencil-shaped buds open into drooping, flared funnels in tiers all around each stem. Glossy, heart-shaped leaves up to 18 inches long form a basal rosette and sparsely line each stem. Giant lilies grow best in filtered shade at the edges of moist woodlands.

Selected species and varieties: *C. giganteum* (heart lily)—up to 20 nodding white flowers suffused with green on the outside and striped maroon inside tipping stems to 12 feet tall.

Growing conditions and maintenance: Plant giant lily bulbs in spring or fall with their tops just at the soil line, spaced 18 inches apart. Giant lilies produce non-flowering shoots for several years before blossoming. Then bulbs die, leaving small bulblets, which will grow to flowering size in 3 to 4 years. Plant bulbs of different sizes to ensure blooms each year. Propagate by lifting and replanting bulblets after the main bulb flowers.

Chionodoxa
(kee-on-o-DOKS-a)
GLORY-OF-THE-SNOW

Chionodoxa luciliae 'Pink Giant'

Hardiness: *Zones 4-9*

Type of bulb: *true bulb*

Flowering season: *spring*

Height: *4 to 10 inches*

Soil: *moist, well-drained*

Light: *full sun to light shade*

Glory-of-the-snow is one of the earliest bulbs to appear in spring, often before snows have completely melted. Small clusters of open-faced flower stars with narrow, gracefully curved petals are carried above grassy leaves on short stems. Glory-of-the-snow naturalizes easily in rock or wildflower gardens to create carpets of color beneath taller spring bulbs or deciduous shrubs. The plant can also be forced for indoor winter bloom.

Selected species and varieties: *C. luciliae*—clusters of three or more 1-inch blue flowers with centers suffused with white on 4-inch stems; 'Alba' grows pure white; 'Pink Giant' produces bright pink flowers on 3- to 6-inch stems; 'Rosea' is pink. *C. sardensis*—deep blue flowers on stems to 6 inches.

Growing conditions and maintenance: Plant glory-of-the-snow in masses for best effect, setting bulbs 3 inches deep and 3 inches apart. For forcing, allow 12 to 18 bulbs per 8-inch bulb pan. Propagate from seed or by removing and replanting bulblets growing alongside older bulbs.

Chlidanthus
(klid-ANTH-us)
DELICATE LILY

Chlidanthus fragrans

Hardiness: *tender or Zones 9-11*

Type of bulb: *true bulb*

Flowering season: *summer*

Height: *8 to 10 inches*

Soil: *moist, well-drained, sandy*

Light: *full sun*

Lemon-scented flower funnels with six pointed petals layered like overlapping triangles grow in small clusters at the tips of the delicate lily's slender stalks. Narrow, strap-shaped, gray-green leaves appear after the flowers. Delicate lilies will slowly spread into small colonies when left in the ground in Zones 9-10 and make excellent potted plants for indoor use or patio specimens anywhere. They are also used as cut flowers.

Selected species and varieties: *C. fragrans* (perfumed fairy lily)—loose clusters of 3 to 4 yellow blossoms up to 3 inches across.

Growing conditions and maintenance: Plant outdoors in spring, setting bulbs 2 inches deep and 6 to 8 inches apart. North of Zone 8, lift bulbs in fall. In containers, allow one bulb per 6-inch pot, setting bulb tops at the soil line. Dry bulbs off in fall and repot in fresh soil the following spring. Propagate by removing and replanting small bulblets growing at the base of larger bulbs.

Clivia
(KLY-vee-a)
NATAL LILY

Clivia miniata

Hardiness: *tender or Zones 8-11*

Type of bulb: *tuber*

Flowering season: *spring or summer*

Height: *12 to 18 inches*

Soil: *moist, well-drained*

Light: *light shade*

A popular houseplant in Victorian times, clivias bear domed clusters of up to 20 trumpet-shaped 3-inch flowers in dramatic hues atop a single thick stalk flanked by pairs of broad, straplike evergreen leaves up to 18 inches long. Bulbs may produce their long-lasting flowers twice a year under ideal conditions, and inch-long red berries follow the blossoms. Clivias can be grown outdoors in warm zones but bloom best as rootbound houseplants.

Selected species and varieties: *C.* x *cyrtanthiflora*—deep salmon pink blooms. *C. miniata*—scarlet blossoms with yellow-splashed throats; 'Aurea' grows golden yellow; 'Flame', deep red-orange; 'Grandiflora' produces larger scarlet flowers.

Growing conditions and maintenance: Plant Natal lilies outdoors in fall, setting the top of the bulbous roots at the soil line and spacing them 18 to 24 inches apart. Indoors, plant roots in 9-inch pots and leave undisturbed. Propagate from seed or by dividing the fleshy rootstocks after flowering.

Colchicum
(KOL-chi-kum)
AUTUMN CROCUS

Colchicum autumnale

Hardiness: *Zones 4-9*

Type of bulb: *corm*

Flowering season: *fall or spring*

Height: *4 to 12 inches*

Soil: *moist, well-drained, fertile*

Light: *full sun to light shade*

Actually a member of the lily family, colchicum has the common name autumn crocus because of the resemblance of its cupped, star-shaped flowers to those of the spring-flowering crocus. With the exception of one species that blooms in spring, colchicum's bare flower stems appear in fall to provide 2 to 3 weeks of color. Each corm produces multiple blossoms, so flowers carpet the ground when bulbs are planted thickly. The coarse, shiny, strap-shaped foliage appears later in winter, long after the flowers have faded. Colchicum naturalizes easily in rock gardens and lawns. The corms, which are poisonous, can also be forced as houseplants.

Selected species and varieties: *C. agrippinum*—flowers checkered purple and rose. *C. atropurpureum*—deep mauve 4-inch blossoms. *C. autumnale* (common autumn crocus, mysteria)—4-inch pink to lilac flowers; 'Album' is white; 'Alboplenum', double-petaled. *C. bornmuelleri*—very large mauve blooms. *C. byzantinum*—a dozen or more pale lilac flowers followed by extremely broad foliage. *C. cilicicum* (Byzantine autumn crocus)—up to 25 bright rose 2½-inch flowers; 'Purpureum' is rosy violet. *C. giganteum*—large carmine red blossoms. *C. luteum* [also called *Synsiphon luteum*]—rare spring-flowering species with 2-inch yellow flowers. *C. speciosum* (showy autumn crocus)—4-inch rose to purple flowers with white throats; 'Dick Trotter' yields early blossoms; 'Lilac Wonder', 6-inch-wide amethyst flowers; 'The Giant', 6- to 8-inch-wide rich rose flowers with white throats; 'Violet Queen', large clumps of 6- to 8-inch violet flowers with white-striped throats; 'Waterlily', double-petaled 4- to 6-inch rich lavender flowers.

Colchicum 'The Giant'

Growing conditions and maintenance: Plant autumn crocus in summer, setting corms 3 to 4 inches deep and 6 to 9 inches apart. *C. luteum* is hardy only in Zones 7-9. *C. autumnale* and *C. byzantinum* tolerate light shade, but all other species prefer full sun. Where autumn crocus has naturalized in lawns, avoid mowing until foliage yellows and dies. To force as houseplants, set corms on pebbles just above water and keep the growing roots constantly moist; discard after flowering. Propagate autumn crocus by removing cormels growing alongside larger corms in early summer after foliage withers; or remove mature seed immediately when leaves wither and plant at once for corms that will reach blooming size in 3 to 4 years.

Convallaria
(kon-va-LAH-ree-a)
LILY OF THE VALLEY

Convallaria majalis 'Aureovariegata'

Hardiness: *Zones 2-7*

Type of bulb: *rhizome*

Flowering season: *spring*

Height: *8 to 10 inches*

Soil: *moist, acid, fertile*

Light: *full to light shade*

Lily of the valley's nodding flower bells line slender stalks nestled tightly within pairs of oval, pointed leaves that emerge from slender rhizomes called pips. The sweetly fragrant blossoms with furled edges make excellent cut flowers. Plant pips in woodland gardens or mass them to create a ground cover in shady areas. Lily of the valley can also be forced for indoor display.

Selected species and varieties: *C. majalis*—five to eight ¼-inch white flower bells for up to 2 weeks; 'Flore Pleno' produces ruffly, double-petaled flowers; 'Rosea' is light pink; 'Aureovariegata' grows variegated foliage.

Growing conditions and maintenance: Plant pips in spring or fall, setting them 1 inch deep and 4 to 6 inches apart. Lily of the valley competes well with shallow-rooted trees and shrubs. For forcing, buy prechilled pips or refrigerate bare pips 8 weeks or more in a plastic bag at 40°F, then pot with the top of pips just below the surface and keep in a warm room. Propagate by division in fall.

Corydalis
(ko-RID-a-lis)
CORYDALIS

Corydalis solida

Hardiness: *Zones 6-10*

Type of bulb: *tuber*

Flowering season: *spring*

Height: *6 to 8 inches*

Soil: *moist, well-drained, fertile*

Light: *light shade to full sun*

Corydalis produces spiky clusters of up to 20 curving, tubular flowers with flared lips and a single, tiny pointed spur that dangle from stems above tufts of delicate green or blue-green foliage that resembles flat parsley. Foliage remains attractive throughout the summer. Corydalis naturalizes easily in rock or woodland gardens or borders.

Selected species and varieties: *C. bulbosa*—clusters of rosy lavender flowers on 8-inch stems above green leaves; 'Albiflora' is white. *C. solida* (fumewort)—dense 2-inch clusters of light purple flowers on 6-inch stems above blue-green foliage.

Growing conditions and maintenance: Plant corydalis tubers 3 inches deep and 4 to 5 inches apart in summer or fall. Both species prefer shade, but *C. solida* will grow in full sun. Propagate by dividing tubers after foliage dies back in late summer or fall, or from seed, to reach blooming size in 2 to 3 years.

Crinodonna
(kree-no-DON-a)
CRINODONNA

X Crinodonna corsii

Hardiness: *tender or Zones 9-11*

Type of bulb: *true bulb*

Flowering season: *late summer to fall*

Height: *2½ to 3 feet*

Soil: *moist, well-drained*

Light: *full sun to light shade*

Crinodonna's dense heads of oval, pointed flower buds open into large funnels with gracefully curving stamens and prominent anthers to add color and interest. The fragrant flowers unfold at the tips of sturdy, erect flower stalks. Each stalk rises from a clump of evergreen arching, narrow leaves that remain attractive year round. Crinodonna can be grown as border specimens in frost-free areas but bloom best as root-bound container plants.

Selected species and varieties: X *C. corsii* [also called X *Amarcrinum memoria-corsii*]—4- to 5-inch-wide pink flowers on stalks to 3 feet.

Growing conditions and maintenance: Outdoors, plant crinodonna bulbs at the soil line and space them 8 to 12 inches apart. Indoors, plant one 4-inch bulb per 6- to 8-inch pot. Bulbs should be left undisturbed for several years, as they bloom best when roots are crowded. Propagate by removing offsets, which grow at the base of larger bulbs.

Crinum
(KREE-num)
SPIDER LILY

Crinum x powellii

Hardiness: *tender or Zones 7-11*

Type of bulb: *true bulb*

Flowering season: *spring, summer, fall*

Height: *2 to 4 feet*

Soil: *moist, well-drained, fertile*

Light: *full sun to light shade*

Crinums produce whorls of lilylike flowers with a spicy fragrance over a long season of bloom. Each cluster blooms atop a stout stem rising from a clump of deep green, sword-shaped, evergreen or deciduous leaves. The blossoms are either funnel shaped with thick, ridged petals curving backward, or lacy and spidery with narrow, straplike petals. Crinum's unusual bulbs, about the size of a grapefruit, have elongated necks up to a foot long and bloom best when they are crowded. In warmer areas, plant them where they can remain undisturbed for several years. They do especially well at the edges of ponds and streams where there is constant moisture, slowly naturalizing into large clumps. In northern areas, sink bulbs in tubs, which can be moved indoors to a greenhouse or conservatory for the winter.

Selected species and varieties: *C. americanum* (Florida swamp lily)—up to 6 white flower funnels in late spring or summer on 2-foot stems before leaves appear. *C. asiaticum* (grand crinum, poison bulb)—up to 50 heavily scented white flowers with straplike petals and

pink stamens in summer on stalks to 4 feet. *C. bulbispermum* (Orange River lily)—a dozen or more pink or white flower trumpets with rose-striped petals in fall on 3-foot stems above deciduous foliage. *C. moorei* (Cape Coast lily, long-neck swamp lily)—10 to 20 rose red flower funnels in summer on 4-foot stalks rising from bold evergreen leaves. *C.* x *powellii* (Powell's swamp lily)—six to eight red flower trumpets touched with green at their base on 2-foot stalks rising from evergreen leaves up to 4 feet long; 'Album' has white flowers. *C.* 'Cecil Houdyshel'—profuse pink flowers. *C.* 'Ellen Bosanquet'—wine red summer flowers above evergreen foliage.

Growing conditions and maintenance: Outdoors, plant crinums so that the necks of the bulbs remain above ground and the bulbs are 2 to 3 feet apart. Keep

Crinum moorei

constantly moist for best bloom. In tubs, allow no more than 1 or 2 inches of soil space between the sides of the bulbs and their container. With southern exposure and heavy mulching to protect them from frost, *C. bulbispermum* and *C.* x *powellii* sometimes thrive in Zones 7-8. *C. moorei* and *C.* 'Ellen Bosanquet' make excellent tub specimens. Propagate species from seeds, which sometimes begin forming roots while still on plants. Remove seeds as soon as they ripen and sow immediately to reach flowering-size bulbs in 3 years; hybrids may revert to their parent forms. Both species and hybrids can be propagated by removing and replanting the small offsets growing alongside mature bulbs in spring.

Crocosmia
(kro-KOS-mee-a)
MONTBRETIA

Crocosmia 'Lucifer'

Hardiness: *Zones 5-9*

Type of bulb: *corm*

Flowering season: *summer or fall*

Height: *2 to 4 feet*

Soil: *moist, well-drained, fertile*

Light: *full sun*

Crocosmia's wiry stems are lined with up to 50 or more tightly clasped, inch-long flower buds that unfurl in succession from bottom to top over a long season of bloom. The vividly colored tubular flowers flare into open stars as much as 2 inches across. Emerging on either side of the stems, the combination of unopened buds and open blossoms provides interesting visual texture in the flower border. Two or more flower stems rise from sparse fans of pleated, swordlike foliage and gracefully arch with the weight of developing buds and flowers. In areas with mild winters, crocosmias will slowly spread into large clumps. Elsewhere, they make excellent container plants or can be treated as tender bulbs. Crocosmias serve well as cut flowers, with sprays lasting up to a week in floral bouquets.

Selected species and varieties: *C. aurea* [also called *Tritonia aurea*] (golden coppertip)—branched spikes of orange-tinged yellow flowers on arching 3½-foot stems. *C.* x *crocosmiiflora*—sturdy hybrids with sprays of star-shaped flowers 2 to 4 feet long in yellow, salmon, red, ma-

roon, and bicolors. Large-flowered types produce 1½- to 3-inch blossoms; 'Citronella' is lemon yellow; 'Emily McKenzie', orange; 'James Coey', red; 'Lady Wilson', yellow-orange; 'Mars', red; 'Norwich Canary', yellow-tinged red. Small-flowered types yield 1-inch blooms; 'Bouquet Parfait' is orange to yellow; 'Venus', bicolored red and yellow. *C.* 'Lucifer'—deep red blooms. *C. masoniorum* (golden swan tritonia)—red flowers appearing very early on 2- to 4-foot stems; 'Firebird' produces orange blooms.

Crocosmia x crocosmiiflora 'Emily McKenzie'

Growing conditions and maintenance: Plant crocosmias in spring, setting corms 3 to 5 inches deep and 6 to 8 inches apart. Where conditions are particularly favorable, they can become invasive. In Zones 7-8, choose sites sheltered from wind and protect from frost with winter mulch. North of Zone 7, lift corms in fall, cutting foliage back to 6 inches and allowing corms to dry slightly before storing at approximately 50°F for replanting in spring. Propagate by removing and repotting the small cormels that grow alongside larger corms in spring or fall, or from seed sown as soon as it ripens in fall, to flower in 3 to 4 years.

Crocus
(KRO-kus)
CROCUS

Crocus chrysanthus 'Cream Beauty'

Hardiness: *Zones 3-8*

Type of bulb: *corm*

Flowering season: *winter, spring, fall*

Height: *2 to 8 inches*

Soil: *well-drained*

Light: *full sun*

Delicate bowls of color in an otherwise drab landscape, crocus flowers hug the ground on short stems from late winter through midspring. There are also fall-blooming species, not to be confused with the flowers commonly known as autumn crocus, which are actually *Colchicum*. Narrow, grassy crocus leaves are sometimes attractively banded down their centers in gray-green or white and may appear before, at the same time as, or after several flowers rise from each small corm. They last several weeks before dying back. Some are fragrant. Each flower has six wide petals that open into a deep, oval cup shape, then relax into a round, open bowl. Crocuses are available in a broad range of hues, and are often striped, streaked, or tinged with more than one color. Prominent yellow or orange stigmas decorate the center of each blossom. Those of *C. sativus* are the source of saffron for many culinary uses; it takes more than 4,000 flowers to produce an ounce of the precious herb. Mass crocuses for best effect in beds, borders, and rock gardens. They naturalize easily and are often planted as edgings and allowed to ramble in lawns. Force them for indoor winter display.

Selected species and varieties: *C. ancyrensis* 'Golden Bunch'—winter-to-spring-blooming flowers that are yellow outside, orange fading to yellow inside, on 2-inch stems above 12-inch leaves; Zones 6-8. *C. angustifolius* 'Minor' (cloth-of-gold crocus)—deep yellow flower cups flushed with mahogany outside on stems 2 inches or less in winter to spring; Zones 5-8. *C. biflorus* (Scotch crocus)—white or lilac flowers veined or tinged purple with yellow throats on 4-inch stems in winter to spring; ssp. *alexandri* is white feathered with purple; ssp. *weldenii* 'Fairy', white with purple blotches; Zones 5-8. *C. chrysanthus* (snow crocus)—late winter flowers

Crocus ancyrensis

bloom on 4-inch stems before the 12-inch leaves appear; 'Advance' produces peachy yellow flowers touched with violet; 'Ard Schenk', long-lasting white blooms; 'Blue Bird', blooms that are blue violet outside, creamy inside; 'Blue Pearl', petals that are lavender outside touched with bronze at their base, white inside blending to a yellow throat; 'Cream Beauty', long-lasting creamy yellow blooms; 'Dorothy', long-lasting yellow flowers feathered with bronze; 'Gipsy Girl', profuse, long-lasting yellow flowers streaked reddish brown; 'Ladykiller', petals violet-purple outside, creamy white inside; 'Miss Vain', pure white blossoms with lemon yellow throats; 'Prins Claus' is a dwarf cultivar with long-lasting white flowers blotched in blue; 'Snow Bunting' has white flowers with lilac streaking and yellow throats; 'Zwanenburg Bronze', reddish

brown petals striped with yellow; Zones 4-8. *C. etruscus* 'Zwanenburg'—lilac flowers veined with deep purple appearing the same time as the white-striped leaves in winter to spring; Zones 3-8. *C. flavus*—yellow to orange flowers appearing on 7-inch stems at the same time as the grassy foliage in winter to spring; 'Golden Yellow' [formerly *C. vernus* 'Yel-

Crocus chrysanthus 'Zwanenburg Bronze'

low Giant'] has rich yellow blossoms; Zones 4-8. *C. kotschyanus* [formerly *C. zonatus*]—rose-lilac flowers splashed with orange in fall; Zones 5-8. *C. medius*—lilac to purple flowers with deep purple veining on stems to 10 inches in fall; Zones 6-7. *C. minimus*—pale violet to white flowers with prominent red-orange stigmas on 2- to 3-inch stems in spring; Zones 5-8. *C. ochroleucus*—white to pale cream petals tinged with orange on 3- to 6-inch stems in fall; Zones 5-8. *C. pulchellus*—bright lilac blossoms with yellow interiors appearing the same time as the leaves in fall; 'Zephyr' is pure white; Zones 6-8. *C. sativus* (saffron crocus)—lilac or white fall flowers on 2-inch stems with prominent stamens that are dried and used for flavoring and coloring in cooking; Zones 6-8. *C. serotinus* ssp. *clusii*—fragrant, purple-veined pale lilac flowers with creamy throats on 3- to 4-inch stems appearing at the same time as sparse foliage in fall; ssp. *salzmannii* is similar but with sparser leaves and no fragrance; Zones 6-8. *C. sieberi* (Sieber crocus)—fragrant late-winter-to-spring flowers; ssp. *atticus* has white flowers streaked with purple on 2- to 3-inch stems; ssp. *sublimis* 'Tricolor', lilac blue flowers with white banding at the edge of a yellow

throat; 'Firefly', white flowers touched with violet; 'Hubert Edelsten', deep purple to soft lilac flowers on 4-inch stems; 'Violet Queen', deep violet blooms on 3-inch stems; Zones 7-8. *C. speciosus*—light blue fall flowers with darker blue veining and prominent orange stigmas on 3- to 6-inch stems; 'Artabir' grows fragrant light blue flowers with conspicuous veining; 'Cassiope', lavender-blue blooms with creamy yellow throats; 'Conqueror', clear blue flowers; var. *aitchisonii*, pale lilac flowers veined with deeper lilac, the largest of all crocus blossoms; Zones 5-8. *C. tomasinianus*—lilac to purple flowers appearing at the same time as leaves in late winter to spring, reputed to be rodent resistant; 'Barr's Purple' yields large royal purple flowers; 'Ruby Giant', large violet blooms; 'Whitewell Purple' is reddish purple; Zones 5-9. *C. vernus* (Dutch crocus, common crocus)—large flowers on stems to 8 inches tall appearing at the

Crocus tomasinianus

same time as leaves in late winter to spring; 'Flower Record' is deep purple; 'Jeanne d'Arc', white; 'Paulus Potter', shiny reddish purple; 'Pickwick', white striped with lilac and splashed with purple at its base; 'Remembrance', bluish purple; 'Striped Beauty', lilac striped with white. *C. versicolor* 'Picturatus'—white flowers striped in purple with yellow throats on 5½-inch stems in late winter to spring; Zones 5-8.

Growing conditions and maintenance: Plant corms 3 to 4 inches deep and 4 to 5 inches apart in groups. They are not fussy about soil, but good drainage is essential. Space more closely in pots for forcing, allowing six to eight corms per 6-inch pot or shallow bulb pan, and setting the corms 1 inch deep. Hold potted corms at 40°F until roots form, then bring indoors at 65°F for flowering. Crocuses can also be forced in colorful bulb vases designed especially for the purpose with a pinched

Crocus vernus 'Jeanne d'Arc'

waist to suspend the corm just above the water line; when roots fill the vase, bring the corm into sunlight in a warm room for blooming. After forcing, allow foliage to die back, then plant corms out in the garden for reflowering the following spring. Cultivars of Dutch crocus are especially recommended for forcing. *C. ancyrensis* 'Golden Bunch', *C. speciosus* cultivars, and *C. vernus* 'Pickwick' are among the easiest crocuses to naturalize. To plant crocuses in lawns, cut and lift small patches of grass, place the corms, then replace the sod. Plant spring-flowering varieties from September to November, fall-flowering ones no later than August. Where crocuses have established themselves in lawns, avoid mowing in spring until the foliage of spring-flowering crocuses dies back; in fall, postpone mowing once the buds of fall-blooming species have broken through the ground until their flowers fade and foliage withers. Crocuses are easily grown from seed and self-sow freely, a characteristic that somewhat offsets the attractiveness of the corms to mice, chipmunks, and squirrels. Otherwise, propagate by lifting and dividing crowded clumps after foliage dies back, removing and replanting the smaller cormels that develop alongside mature corms. Buy *C. kotschyanus* only from reputable dealers who propagate their own bulbs, as collection in the wild has endangered this species.

Cyclamen
(SIK-la-men)
PERSIAN VIOLET

Cyclamen persicum

Hardiness:	*Zones 6-9*
Type of bulb:	*tuber*
Flowering season:	*fall, winter, spring*
Height:	*3 to 12 inches*
Soil:	*moist, well-drained, fertile*
Light:	*light shade*

Cyclamen's unusual, sometimes fragrant, flowers have petals swept back from a prominent center or eye. The petals are sometimes twisted, double, ruffled, shredded, or ridged, giving the delicate, inch-long blossoms the appearance of exotic birds or butterflies. Each flower rises on a slender stem from a clump of long-lasting heart- or kidney-shaped leaves that are sometimes marbled green and gray above or reddish underneath. Multiple flower stalks appear over a long season of bloom. While the florist's cyclamen, popular as a houseplant, is a tender pot plant, other cyclamens are hardy species that will spread in wildflower gardens, rock gardens, and shady borders, naturalizing into low ground covers beneath both deciduous and evergreen plantings.

Selected species and varieties: *C. africanum*—rose to carmine fall flowers above large, fleshy 6-inch leaves with wavy edges; Zones 8-9. *C. cilicium* (Sicily cyclamen)—twisted pink or light rose blossoms with a dark rose eye on 3-inch stems in fall above leaves with silver centers; Zones 7-8. *C. coum*—white to carmine flowers with purple blotches blooming from winter to spring on 3- to 6-inch stems above green or marbled leaves with reddish undersides; 'Album' is white; 'Roseum', pale pink. *C. graecum*—fall-blooming rose flowers with a deep carmine eye, sometimes scented; Zones 7-9. *C. hederifolium* [also called *C. neopolitanum*] (baby cyclamen, ivy-leaved cyclamen)—pink or white, sometimes fragrant, flowers with a crimson eye on 3- to 6-inch stems blooming from summer to fall above marbled leaves; 'Album' is white; Zones 6-9. *C. persicum* (florist's cyclamen, common cyclamen)—rose, pink, or white, sometimes fragrant flowers, with dark eyes on 6- to 12-inch stems above marbled leaves with toothed edges in winter; Zone 9.

Cyclamen hederifolium

Growing conditions and maintenance: Plant cyclamen's flat, cormlike tubers in summer or fall, setting them ½-inch deep and 4 to 6 inches apart in soil that has a neutral to alkaline pH. Provide an annual top dressing of leaf mold. Pot florist's cyclamen's large tuber-corms individually in pots and maintain plants at temperatures of 60° to 65°F throughout the blooming period. Cyclamens do not produce offsets, but plants self-sow seed freely. Propagate from seed to reach blooming size in 3 years or by transplanting the self-sown seedlings in summer or fall.

Dahlia
(DAH-lee-a)
DAHLIA

Dahlia 'Tamjoh'

Hardiness: *tender or Zones 9-11*

Type of bulb: *tuber*

Flowering season: *summer to fall*

Height: *12 inches to 8 feet*

Soil: *moist, well-drained, fertile*

Light: *full sun*

Dahlias reliably brighten the flower border over a long season of bloom with highly diverse blossoms varying from flat-faced, single-petaled types to round, dense mounds of petals. Dahlia sizes are as variable as petal forms, with some flowers only a few inches across and others the diameter of a dinner plate. Related to daisies, dahlias have a central disk of tightly packed disk flowers surrounded by one or more rows of petal-like ray flowers that are sometimes doubled, curved inward, twisted, cupped, or rolled into tiny tubes. Colors range widely, and some dahlias are bicolored or variegated, with petals tipped, streaked, or backed with contrasting color. The more than 20,000 cultivars available to modern gardeners descend from a few wild species cultivated by Aztec botanists. For the garden trade, dahlias are classified by the shape and arrangement of their ray flowers and coded according to flower size. Dwarf dahlias are cultivated in sunny beds or borders as low-growing bushy edgings, standard dahlias as medium to tall fillers or as exhibition-size specimens. All dahlias make long-lasting cut flowers.

Selected species and varieties: *Single dahlias*—one or two rows of flat petals surrounding a flat, central disk; 'Bambino White' is a dwarf cultivar with 1-inch flowers on 14-inch bushes. *Anemone-flowered dahlias*—a central disk obscured by a fluffy ball of short, tubular petals and rimmed by one or more rows of longer, flat petals; 'Siemen Doorenbosch' has flat lavender petals surrounding a creamy central pincushion on 20-inch plants. *Collarette dahlias*—central disks surrounded by a collar of short, often ruffled or cupped petals, backed by a second collar of broader, flat petals; 'Jack O'Lantern' has an inner collar streaked yellow and orange and deep orange outer petals on 4-foot plants; 'Mickey' has a yellow inner collar backed by deep red outer ray flowers on 3-foot bushes. *Peony-flowered dahlias*—two or three overlapping layers of ray petals, often twisted or curled, surrounding a central

Dahlia 'Hullins Carnival'

disk; 'Japanese Bishop' grows dark orange flowers on 3-foot plants; 'Jescott Julie' has petals that are orange above, burgundy below, on 3-foot stems. *Formal decorative dahlias*—double rows of flat, evenly spaced petals covering the central disk; 'Duet' has crimson petals tipped with white on 3-foot plants; 'Orange Julius', orange petals edged in yellow on 4-foot stems. *Informal decorative dahlias*—double rows of randomly spaced flat petals hiding the central disk; 'Gay Princess' is pink with creamy centers on 4-foot plants. *Ball dahlias*—cupped, doubled petals crowding spirally into round domes or slightly flattened globes; 'Nijinsky' has purple flowers on 4-foot stems; 'Rothsay Superb', red

blooms on 3-foot plants. *Pompom dahlias*—small round balls of tightly rolled petals less than 2 inches in diameter; 'Amber Queen' is golden amber to bronze on 4-foot stems; 'Chick-a-dee', wine red touched with pink on 3-foot

Dahlia 'Nijinsky'

plants. *Cactus dahlias*—straight or twisted petals rolled like quills or straws over half their length to a pointed tip; 'Border Princess' is apricot-bronze to yellow on 2-foot stems; 'Brookside Cheri', salmon pink on 4-foot plants; 'Juanita', ruby red on 4-foot stems. *Semicactus dahlias*—flat petals curling over less than half their length into tubes at their tips; 'Amanda Jarvis' produces rose flowers on 3-foot stems; 'Bella Bimba', apricot pink blooms on 4-foot plants. *Star dahlias*—two or three rows of short petals curving inward. *Chrysanthemum-type dahlias*—double rows of petals curving inward and hiding the central disk. *Waterlily-flowered dahlias*—short petals tightly clasped over the central disk like a water lily bud, surrounded by several rows of broad, flat petals; 'Lauren Michelle' has petals that are rosy lavender above, purple below on 4½-foot stems; 'Gerry Hoek', shell pink flowers on 4-foot plants.

Within each of these classifications, dahlias are also coded by size: Giant or AA dahlias have flowers more than 10 inches wide; large or A, 8- to 10-inch flowers; medium or B, 6- to 8-inch flowers; small or BB, 4- to 6-inch blooms; miniature or M, flowers up to 4 inches across; pompom or P, blossoms under 2 inches.

Growing conditions and maintenance: Plant dahlia tubers in spring, placing those of taller cultivars in a hole 6 to 8 inches deep and covering them with 2 to 3 inches of soil. Space the holes 3 to 4 feet apart. As shoots develop and extend above ground level, remove all but one or two and add soil to fill the hole. Plant tubers of shorter cultivars 2 to 3 inches deep and 1 to 2 feet apart. In transplanting potted seedlings, position them 2 inches deeper than the depth of their pot. Stake all but dwarfs, pompoms, and miniatures. Dahlias bloom 2½ to 4

Dahlia 'Brookside Cheri'

months after planting. To keep plants blooming continuously, give them at least an inch of water weekly while blooming, and mulch with 2 to 3 inches of manure, compost, or ground peat moss to retain moisture and provide nutrients. To produce bushy plants, pinch out terminal leaf buds when leaves first appear and again when the first lateral branches emerge. To develop large, exhibition-size blossoms, prune all lateral side shoots and remove all but the center bud when flower buds appear. Remove faded flowers before they go to seed to prolong blooming period. For long-lasting cut flowers, pick dahlias while it is cool and stand cut stems in hot water, 100° to 160°F, in a cool, shaded location for several hours before arranging. Propagate dahlias from seed started indoors in very early spring to flower that season, from stem cuttings, or by dividing tubers in spring.

Dichelostemma
(di-kel-o-STEM-a)
DICHELOSTEMMA

Dichelostemma congestum

Hardiness: *Zones 5-7*

Type of bulb: *corm*

Flowering season: *spring*

Height: *1½ to 3 feet*

Soil: *very well drained, sandy*

Light: *full sun*

A native American wildflower, *Dichelostemma* produces loose, silver-dollar-size flower clusters. The flowers, which appear on slender stems above sparse, narrow, grassy leaves, are excellent in arrangements. Mass dichelostemmas in sunny borders and allow them to naturalize, or pot them in containers.

Selected species and varieties: *D. congestum* (ookow)—clusters of pale blue-violet flower trumpets decorated with long, split stamens.

Growing conditions and maintenance: Plant dichelostemma corms in fall, setting them 3½ to 5 inches deep and 3 inches apart. Dichelostemmas require excellent drainage, even dry conditions, in summer after blooming. In areas with wet summers, dig corms after foliage fades and replant in fall. Mulch bulbs for winter protection in northern zones. In containers, plant four or five bulbs per 6-inch container. Propagate by removing the small cormels that develop alongside mature bulbs for planting in fall.

Eranthis
(e-RAN-this)
WINTER ACONITE

Eranthis hyemalis

Hardiness: *Zones 4-7*

Type of bulb: *tuber*

Flowering season: *late winter to spring*

Height: *2 to 4 inches*

Soil: *moist, well-drained, fertile*

Light: *full sun to light shade*

Often blooming before the snow has melted, winter aconites produce cheery buttercup-like flowers composed of waxy, curved petals cradling a loose pompom of frilly stamens. Each almost stemless blossom opens above a tiny ruff of oval, pointed leaves. The blossoms close tightly to protect themselves during cold nights, then reopen the next day with the sun's warmth. Winter aconites readily naturalize into golden ground covers in woodland or rock gardens.

Selected species and varieties: *E. cilicica* (Cilician winter aconite)—1½-inch-deep yellow flowers on 2½-inch stems with bronzy foliage. *E. hyemalis*—inch-wide yellow flowers on 2- to 4-inch stems.

Growing conditions and maintenance: Plant winter aconite tubers in late summer or very early fall to allow roots time to establish themselves for late-winter blooming. Soak the brittle roots overnight, then set tubers 2 to 3 inches deep and 3 inches apart where they will receive sufficient moisture. Winter aconites self-sow readily. Propagate from seed or by dividing the tiny tubers in late summer.

Eremurus
(e-ray-MEW-rus)
DESERT-CANDLE

Eremurus 'Moneymaker'

Hardiness: *Zones 4-8*

Type of bulb: *tuber*

Flowering season: *spring to summer*

Height: *3 to 8 feet*

Soil: *well-drained, sandy, fertile*

Light: *full sun*

Desert-candles carry hundreds of tiny bell-shaped flowers in enormous, elongated spikes often 5 to 6 inches across and up to 4 feet long above rosettes of thick, fleshy leaves resembling those of yucca plants. Over a period of several weeks, the small flowers open from bottom to top along the stem so that each spike offers a range of textures and tones from lighter-colored mature flowers with prominent frothy anthers to more deeply colored, tight oval buds. Desert-candles are outstanding when grouped at the back of a border or in front of dark shrubbery. The spikes last up to 3 weeks when used as cut flowers.

Selected species and varieties: *E. himalaicus* (Himalayan desert-candle)—pure white flower spikes on 3- to 4-foot stems above clumps of 1-foot leaves; Zones 4-8. *E. robustus*—bright pink flowers and darker pink buds in 4-foot spikes on stems 6 to 10 feet tall above broad green foliage; 'Albus' is a white strain; Zones 7-9. *E. stenophyllus* (Afghan desert-candle)—yellow or golden yellow flowers covering the upper half or more of 2- to 3-foot stems; Zones

4-8. *E.* Ruiter and *E.* Shelford hybrids—spikes of 1-inch flowers in shades of white or cream to yellow, orange, peach pink, or rose on 3- to 4-foot stems with Ruiter hybrids flowering earlier than Shelford hybrids; 'Cleopatra' has orange flowers with a red stripe on the outside of each petal, orange anthers, and deep burnt orange buds; 'Moneymaker' is vivid yellow-orange; 'Pinokkio', softer orange; Zones 6-8.

Growing conditions and maintenance: Plant desert-candles in fall, choosing sites where plants can remain undisturbed for 10 years or more. Place the brittle, star-shaped clumps of tubers with egg-size buds at their centers on a mound of sand

Eremurus robustus

at the bottom of a hole 2 feet wide and deep enough to set the crowns 4 to 6 inches down. Once established, desert-candles are best left alone unless their crowns lift out of the soil. Support tall species by staking in windy sites, taking care not to disturb the tubers when setting the stakes. Foliage withers soon after blooms fade; some gardeners install stakes when they plant the tubers, not only to avoid disturbing the roots later but also to mark their location when digging other bulbs or perennials around them. Provide winter mulch in colder zones. Propagate by dividing tubers that are at least 3 years old; propagation from seed is possible but may require a wait of 5 or 6 years for bloom.

Erythronium
(eh-rith-RONE-ee-um)
DOGTOOTH VIOLET

Erythronium 'Kondo'

Hardiness: *Zones 3-8*

Type of bulb: *corm*

Flowering season: *spring*

Height: *6 inches to 2 feet*

Soil: *moist, well-drained, fertile*

Light: *partial to full shade*

Native woodland wildflowers, dogtooth violets produce delicate, nodding lilylike blooms with petals curved back to reveal prominent stamens and anthers either singly or in small clusters. The flowers rise from pairs of oval, pointed leaves that are often marbled or mottled in gray, brown, or bronze. Mass dogtooth violets in woodland gardens or as a spring ground cover beneath deciduous shrubs, where they will naturalize into colonies.

Selected species and varieties: *E. citrinum*—clusters of 1½-inch white or cream flowers with pale lemon throats on 10- to 12-inch stems; Zones 6-8. *E. dens-canis* (dogtooth fawn lily, European dogtooth violet)—single white to pink or purple flowers 2 inches across with blue or purple anthers on 6- to 12-inch stems above leaves marbled brown and bluish green; 'Charmer' produces pure white flowers touched with brown at their base above leaves mottled with brown; 'Frans Hals', royal purple blooms with a green throat; 'Lilac Wonder' is soft lilac with a brownish base; 'Pink Perfection', bright pink; 'Purple King', reddish purple with a white throat above brown-spotted leaves; 'Rose Queen', rosy pink; 'Snowflake', pure white; var. *japonicum* is a miniature only 4 to 6 inches tall with violet flowers tinged purple at the base; var. *niveus* is pale pink; Zones 3-8. *E. grandiflorum* (glacier lily, avalanche lily)—golden yellow flowers with red anthers in clusters on 1- to 2-foot stems. *E. revolutum* (mahogany fawn lily, coast fawn lily)—1½-inch white to pale lavender flowers aging to purple on 16-inch stems; 'White Beauty' is a dwarf producing 2- to 3-inch white flowers with yellow throats on 7-inch stems above leaves veined in white; Zones 3-8. *E. tuolumnense* (Tuolumne fawn lily)—1¼-inch

Erythronium grandiflorum

yellow flowers touched with green at the base on 12-inch stems above bright green 12-inch leaves; Zones 3-8. *E.* hybrids—'Citronella' yields lemon yellow flowers on 10-inch stems; 'Jeannine', sulfur yellow blooms; 'Kondo', greenish yellow blossoms touched with brown at the base; 'Pagoda', pale yellow flowers with a deeper yellow throat on 10-inch stems.

Growing conditions and maintenance: Plant dogtooth violets in summer or fall, placing the corms 2 to 3 inches deep and 4 to 6 inches apart. Dogtooth violets often take a year to become established before blooming. Provide adequate moisture in summer after flowers and foliage fade. Propagate from seed to bloom in 3 to 4 years or by removing and immediately replanting the small cormels that develop at the base of mature corms in late summer or fall.

Eucharis
(YEW-kar-is)
AMAZON LILY

Eucharis amazonica

Hardiness: *tender or Zones 9-11*

Type of bulb: *true bulb*

Flowering season: *spring, summer, or fall*

Height: *1 to 2 feet*

Soil: *moist, well-drained*

Light: *partial shade*

Amazon lilies bear clusters of highly fragrant flowers with six waxy, starlike petals and flat stamens joined to resemble the corona of a daffodil. The flowers rise from clumps of broad evergreen leaves with wavy edges. Amazon lilies can be grown in beds and borders in frost-free areas where summers are hot and humid and can be forced anytime for indoor use.

Selected species and varieties: *E. amazonica* (Eucharist lily, star-of-Bethlehem)—drooping white flowers up to 5 inches across above leaves a foot long and 6 inches wide.

Growing conditions and maintenance: Outdoors, set bulbs with their necks at the soil line, spacing the bulbs 8 to 10 inches apart. The plants need high humidity and temperatures above 60°F to thrive, and they bloom best when crowded or potbound. Indoors, space bulbs 3 inches apart in pots, allowing three or four bulbs to each pot. To force, maintain bulbs at 80°F or higher for 4 weeks, then lower temperatures 10°F for another 12 weeks. Raise temperatures again to induce blooming. Propagate by removing and planting the bulb offsets.

Eucomis
(yew-KOME-is)
PINEAPPLE LILY

Eucomis bicolor

Hardiness: *Zones 7-10*

Type of bulb: *true bulb*

Flowering season: *summer*

Height: *1 to 2 feet*

Soil: *well-drained, sandy*

Light: *full sun to light shade*

Pineapple lilies produce dense bottlebrush spikes of tiny flower stars topped by an arching tuft of leaflike bracts. The spikes rise from rosettes of strap-shaped leaves. Group pineapple lilies in borders, or grow them in containers as house or patio plants. They make long-lasting cut flowers.

Selected species and varieties: *E. autumnalis*—spikes of ¾-inch greenish white flowers fading to yellow-green on 1- to 2-foot stems; Zones 7-10. *E. bicolor*—greenish white flowers edged with purple on 2-foot stems; Zones 8-10. *E. comosa* (pineapple flower)—½-inch greenish white, sometimes pinkish, blossoms with purple throats on 2-foot stems; Zones 8-10.

Growing conditions and maintenance: Plant outdoors in fall, setting bulbs 5 to 6 inches deep and 1 foot apart. Mulch bulbs in Zones 7 and 8. North of Zone 7, grow pineapple lilies as container plants, setting bulbs just below the surface and allowing three to five bulbs per 12-inch pot. Propagate by removing bulb offsets that develop at the base of mature bulbs, or from seed to flower in 5 years.

Freesia
(FREEZ-ee-a)
FREESIA

Freesia 'Ballerina'

Hardiness: *tender or Zones 9-11*

Type of bulb: *corm*

Flowering season: *winter to spring*

Height: *1 to 2 feet*

Soil: *moist, well-drained, sandy*

Light: *full sun to light shade*

Freesias are renowned for their intense citrusy fragrance, which quickly pervades any room. Their crowded fans of flaring tubular flowers are held at right angles to branched, arching stems that rise from clumps of sword-shaped 6-inch leaves, which persist after flowers fade. The flowers open in sequence along each upright cluster for a long period of bloom. In warm zones, grow freesias in borders or rock gardens. Elsewhere, pot them for houseplants or greenhouse specimens. Freesias last 5 to 12 days as cut flowers.

Selected species and varieties: *F. refracta* (common freesia)—inch-wide flowers in white to greenish yellow to bright yellow, sometimes touched with mauve, on 12-inch stems. *F.* x hybrids—2-inch flowers on stems 18 to 24 inches tall; 'Ballerina' produces large white flowers touched with yellow at the throat; 'Diana', double white flowers; 'Fantasy', cream-colored doubled petals; 'Riande' is yellow-gold; 'Royal Gold', golden yellow; 'Princess Marijke', yellow-orange touched with bronze; 'Pimpernel', flaming scarlet; 'Rose Marie', double-petaled

dark pink; 'Stockholm', red with a yellow throat; 'Viking', pink; 'Romany', double-petaled bluish purple; 'Royal Blue', bright blue with a violet-striped throat.

Growing conditions and maintenance: Plant freesias outdoors in Zones 9 and 10, setting corms 2 inches deep and 2 to 4 inches apart. Corms take 10 to 12 weeks to bloom; plant in summer for winter bloom, in fall for spring bloom. Provide support for their weak stems. Left in the ground, freesias will revert to their normal late-winter to early-spring blooming cycle. North of Zone 9, plant freesias outdoors in spring for summer bloom, then dig corms for winter storage after foliage fades. Indoors, pot 6 to 8 corms per 6-inch bulb pan or 10 to 12 per 8-inch pan, setting corms barely below

Freesia 'Riande'

the surface. Water and feed freesias while growing and blooming, then withhold water after foliage fades to induce dormancy. Remove corms from pots and store in a cool, dark place for replanting. Propagate freesias from seed to bloom in 6 months to a year or by removing the tiny cormels that develop alongside mature corms.

Fritillaria
(fri-ti-LAH-ree-a)
FRITILLARY

Fritillaria imperialis

Hardiness: *Zones 3-8*

Type of bulb: *true bulb*

Flowering season: *spring*

Height: *6 inches to 2½ feet*

Soil: *moist, well-drained, sandy*

Light: *full sun to light shade*

From the imposing, musky-scented crown imperial bearing a garland of blossoms aloft on stout stalks to small, dainty woodland species with single blooms on wiry stems, fritillaries produce nodding flower bells in unusual colors and patterns in a variety of forms to accent spring gardens. The flowers have prominent, colorful stamens and are often striped, speckled, or checkered in a wide range of hues. Touching the petals sometimes produces a small "tear" from reservoirs of nectar at the base of each petal. The often glossy leaves are highly variable, sometimes appearing in whorls extending halfway up the flower stalk, sometimes alternating from one side of the stem to the other throughout its length, occasionally growing in a tuft at the stem's base. Mass fritillaries in wildflower gardens, rock gardens, or perennial borders where other plants will fill in when their foliage dies down in early summer.

Selected species and varieties: *F. acmopetala*—purple-striped olive green flower bells tinged lighter green inside on 18-inch stalks; Zones 3-8. *F. assyriaca*—lime green-and-violet blossoms on

12- to 20-inch stems; Zones 3-8. *F. bi-flora* 'Martha Roderick' (mission bells, black fritillary)—four to six brownish orange flower bells with white spots in their centers on 15-inch stems; Zones 3-8. *F. camschatcensis* (Kamchatka lily, black sarana)—one to six 1-inch purple-brown-and-black flower bells on wiry 2-

Fritillaria meleagris

foot stems; Zones 3-8. *F. davisii*—plum purple blossoms on dainty plants 6 to 10 inches tall; Zones 3-8. *F. imperialis* (crown imperial)—bold 30-inch stalks, the lower half lined with whorls of glossy, pointed leaves, the tip crowned by a tuft of shorter leaves with a ring of large, 2-inch flower bells with dangling yellow stamens below it; 'Maxima Lutea' is lemon yellow; 'Rubra Maxima', dark red; Zones 4-7. *F. meleagris* (snake's-head fritillary, checkered lily, guinea hen tulip, leper lily)—1½-inch flower bells checkered dark maroon and white on 8- to 10-inch stems; 'Alba' is pure white; Zones 3-8. *F. michailovskyi*—up to five deep purplish red-and-yellow flower bells with their tips flipped daintily outward on 4- to 8-inch stems; Zones 5-8. *F. pallidiflora*—up to a dozen pale yellow and green 1- to 1½-inch flower bells flecked with brown and red, borne in the upper leaf joints along arching 18-inch stems; Zones 3-8. *F. persica*—up to 30 velvety purple blossoms lining 30-inch stems; 'Adiyaman' yields inch-wide plum flowers; Zones 4-8. *F. pudica* (yellow fritillary, yellow bell)—¾-inch yellow-orange flowers tinged purple in clusters of three on 9-inch stems; Zones 4-8. *F. purdyi* 'Tinkerbell'—six or seven dainty white flower bells striped rusty brown on the outside and spotted red inside on 6-inch

stems above a low rosette of 6-inch leaves; Zones 5-8. *F. uva-vulpis*—solitary purplish gray flower bells edged in yellow on 12- to 18-inch stems; Zones 3-8. *F. verticillata*—1¼-inch cup-shaped pale yellow blossoms flecked with green outside and spotted purple inside lining 2-foot stems, the tips of the upper leaves elongating into tendrils; Zones 6-8.

Growing conditions and maintenance: Plant fritillaries in late summer or fall, setting large bulbs 4 inches deep and 12 inches apart, smaller bulbs 2 inches deep and 8 inches apart. Bulbs may take a year to become established in new locations before they flower. Most fritillaries like full sun and very well drained soil, but *F. camschatcensis, F. meleagris,* and *F. pallidiflora* prefer light shade and moist soil. For all fritillaries, avoid sites with cold, wet soils, and reduce watering once

Fritillaria pudica

foliage dies back. Both *F. imperialis* 'Rubra Maxima' and *F. persica* are endangered in the wild; buy bulbs from reputable growers selling stock propagated by themselves or other growers rather than purchased from collectors. The skunklike odor of crown imperial is said to repel mice, chipmunks, and other rodents. Propagate fritillaries by removing and replanting bulb offsets in late summer or early fall to reach flowering size in 3 to 4 years; or by removing and planting bulb scales to produce bulblets.

Galanthus
(ga-LANTH-us)
SNOWDROP

Galanthus nivalis

Hardiness: *Zones 3-8*

Type of bulb: *true bulb*

Flowering season: *winter to spring*

Height: *6 to 12 inches*

Soil: *moist, well-drained, sandy*

Light: *full sun to light shade*

Snowdrops produce small white flowers that often bloom before the last snow melts. Each winged blossom is composed of three longer petals almost concealing three shorter, inner petals tipped with green. A single flower dangles from a slender stem above two to three grassy leaves. Snowdrops rapidly naturalize under deciduous shrubs or on lawns, in rock gardens, and in woodland borders. They can also be potted as houseplants.

Selected species and varieties: *G. elwesii* (giant snowdrop)—1½-inch blossoms on flower stalks to 12 inches above blue-green leaves. *G. nivalis* (common snowdrop)—1-inch blooms on 4- to 6-inch stems; 'Flore Pleno' produces double flowers; 'Sam Arnott', large, fragrant blossoms; 'Viridi-apice' has both its outer and inner petals tipped with green.

Growing conditions and maintenance: Plant bulbs 3 inches deep and 3 inches apart in late summer or fall. For indoor bloom, pot bulbs in fall, placing four to six bulbs an inch deep in each 4-inch pot. Snowdrops self-sow readily and can be propagated from seed or by lifting and dividing the clumps of bulbs that form.

Galtonia
(gawl-TONE-ee-a)
SUMMER HYACINTH

Galtonia candicans

Hardiness: *Zones 6-10*

Type of bulb: *true bulb*

Flowering season: *summer to fall*

Height: *2 to 4 feet*

Soil: *well-drained, sandy, fertile*

Light: *full sun to light shade*

Summer hyacinth produces loose spires of fragrant, nodding flower bells that open from bottom to top on stout stems above clumps of fleshy, narrow, straplike leaves. The pale flowers are accented by dark stamens. Plant tall varieties at the back of flower borders where they will spread very slowly into larger clumps.

Selected species and varieties: *G. candicans* (giant summer hyacinth)—2-inch white blossoms tinged green along the upper third of erect stalks to 4 feet tall. *G. viridiflora*—green flowers on 2- to 3-foot stalks above broad leaves.

Growing conditions and maintenance: Plant summer hyacinths in spring or fall, placing bulbs 6 inches deep and 18 to 24 inches apart. Mulch bulbs in northern zones with 2 inches of leaf mold or compost in winter. North of Zone 6, lift bulbs in fall, allow to dry several hours, then remove tops and store for replanting the following spring. Propagate from seed to bloom in several years; or by removing and replanting the few bulblets that may develop alongside mature bulbs.

Gladiolus
(glad-ee-O-lus)
CORN FLAG

Gladiolus communis ssp. byzantinus

Hardiness: *tender or Zones 4-11*

Type of bulb: *corm*

Flowering season: *spring to fall*

Height: *1 to 7 feet*

Soil: *well-drained, fertile*

Light: *full sun*

Gladiolus produce showy spikes of 1½- to 5½-inch flowers above fans of stiff, sword-shaped leaves. The closely spaced flowers open from bottom to top on alternate sides of the stiff flower stems. Abundant, sometimes fragrant, flowers open one at a time to provide several weeks of bloom. Use tall gladiolus in groups at the back of a border, shorter species in rock gardens or mixed in borders with spring bulbs. Gladiolus make long-lasting cut flowers; shorter species can be forced for indoor bloom.

Selected species and varieties: *G. callianthus* [formerly classified as *Acidanthera bicolor*] 'Murielae'—fragrant 2- to 3-inch white flowers with purple throats on 2-foot stems in summer; Zones 7-11. *G. carneus* (painted lady)—white, cream, mauve, or pink blossoms flecked purple on 2-foot stems, blooming spring to summer; Zones 9-11. *G.* x *colvillei* (Coronado hybrid)—2-inch scarlet flowers blotched yellow on branching 2-foot stems in spring; Zones 7-11. *G. communis* ssp. *byzantinus* (Byzantine gladiolus)—white-streaked burgundy flowers on 2-foot stems in spring to summer;

Zones 5-11. *G.* hybrids—ruffled, waved, crimped, or frilled flowers in shades of white, yellow, red, purple, blue, or green, sometimes bicolored or multicolored, on stems to 7 feet in summer through fall; 'Nova Lux' is pure velvety yellow; 'Red Bird', flaming red; 'Priscilla', white-feathered pink with a yellow throat; 'Royal Blush' has deep rose red petals edged in white; 'White Knight' is pure white; tender. *G. nanus* [also classified as *Babiana nana*]—spring-to-summer-blooming dwarf plants 1 to 2 feet tall; 'Amanda Mahy' is salmon with violet splotches; 'Desire', cream; 'Guernsey Glory' has pink to purple petals with red edges and cream blotches; 'Impressive' is pinkish white

Gladiolus nanus 'Prince Carnival'

splotched deep rose; 'Prins Claus', ivory with purple spotting; Zones 4-11.

Growing conditions and maintenance: Work well-rotted manure or other organic matter deeply into the soil a year before planting. North of Zone 8, plant hardy gladiolus in fall, tender ones in spring. Set large corms 4 to 6 inches deep and 6 to 9 inches apart, smaller ones 3 to 4 inches deep and 4 to 6 inches apart. Provide ample water while growing and blooming. North of Zone 8, tender gladiolus should be dug in fall for replanting in spring. Early-blooming hybrids flower 90 days after planting, midseason varieties in 110 days, and late midseason ones in 120 days. To avoid fungus problems, do not plant gladiolus in the same location from year to year. Pick for cut flowers as the first bloom begins to open, leaving four to five leaves to feed the corm. Propagate by removing the cormels that develop around mature corms.

Gloriosa
(glo-ree-O-sa)
GLORIOSA LILY

Gloriosa superba 'Rothschildiana'

Hardiness: *tender or Zones 10-11*

Type of bulb: *tuber*

Flowering season: *year round or summer*

Height: *6 to 12 feet*

Soil: *moist, well-drained, fertile*

Light: *full sun to light shade*

Gloriosa lilies produce exotic flowers on climbing vines. Narrow petals with wavy or crimped edges rake backward to expose prominent stamens. The tips of the slender 4- to 6-inch-long leaves elongate into tendrils to enable the vine to scramble up fences or trellises at the back of a border. In northern zones, plant gloriosa lilies outdoors as annuals or grow them indoors as container plants. They make excellent cut flowers. Caution: All parts of these plants are poisonous.

Selected species and varieties: *G. superba* (Malabar gloriosa lily, crisped glory lily)—twisted yellow petals tipped with red, aging to dark red; 'Africana' has orange petals edged in yellow; 'Rothschildiana', wavy reddish purple petals edged in yellow.

Growing conditions and maintenance: In Zones 10 and 11, plant gloriosa lilies anytime, laying tubers on their sides 4 inches deep and 8 to 12 inches apart. North of Zone 10, plant in spring and lift in fall for winter storage. Indoors, pot tubers 1 to 2 inches deep in midwinter for blooms from late summer through fall. Propagate from seed or by dividing tubers.

Habranthus
(ha-BRANTH-us)
HABRANTHUS

Habranthus robustus

Hardiness: *tender or Zones 9-11*

Type of bulb: *true bulb*

Flowering season: *summer to fall*

Height: *9 to 12 inches*

Soil: *moist, well-drained*

Light: *full sun*

Habranthus produces funnel-shaped flowers composed of six pointed petals curved back to reveal prominent stamens above tufts of arching, grassy leaves. The upright or slightly pendent blossoms are short-lived in rock gardens or flower beds in warmer zones. Elsewhere they are grown indoors as potted plants.

Selected species and varieties: *H. brachyandrus* [formerly *Hippeastrum brachyandrum*]—3-inch pink flower funnels shading to burgundy throats on 12-inch stems. *H. robustus*—drooping rosy pink to red flowers with green throats on 9- to 12-inch stems. *H. tubispathus* [formerly *Hippeastrum robustus* and *Zephyranthus robusta*]—1-inch flowers with petals yellow inside, copper outside, on 9-inch stems.

Growing conditions and maintenance: Plant habranthus outdoors anytime, setting bulbs 4 to 5 inches deep and 6 inches apart. Indoors, plant bulbs singly in 6-inch pots in spring for summer blooms. Propagate from seed; may also be grown from the few bulblets that may develop at the base of mature bulbs.

Haemanthus
(heem-ANTH-us)
BLOOD LILY

Haemanthus katherinae

Hardiness: *tender or Zones 9-11*

Type of bulb: *true bulb*

Flowering season: *summer*

Height: *12 to 18 inches*

Soil: *moist, well-drained*

Light: *full sun to light shade*

Blood lilies produce frothy clusters of tubular flowers with colorful protruding stamens cradled within broad, petal-like bracts or in spherical clusters atop stout, leafless stems. While sometimes grown outdoors in warm zones, they bloom best as root-bound container specimens.

Selected species and varieties: *H. albiflos* (white paintbrush)—2-inch flower clusters with yellow-orange stamens within greenish white bracts on 12- to 18-inch stems. *H. coccineus* (Cape tulip)—3-inch clusters of 1-inch flowers with golden stamens within red bracts on 12-inch stems. *H. katherinae* [also known as *Scadoxus multiflorus* ssp. *katherinae*] (Catherine-wheel)—over 200 small 2½-inch pink-red flowers in 9-inch globes on 18-inch stems. *H. multiflorus* (salmon blood lily)—up to 200 inch-long coral red flowers with spiky stamens in 3- to 6-inch spheres on 18-inch stems.

Growing conditions and maintenance: Plant 6 to 8 inches apart outdoors or in pots, with the tip of the bulb at the soil surface. Start potted lilies in spring, then dry off and store over winter. Propagate from seed or from bulb offsets.

Hermodactylus
(her-mo-DAK-til-us)
HERMODACTYLUS

Hermodactylus tuberosus

Hardiness: *Zones 6-9*

Type of bulb: *tuber*

Flowering season: *spring*

Height: *to 18 inches*

Soil: *well-drained, fertile*

Light: *full sun*

Hermodactylus produces solitary, irislike flowers rising from unusual squared, blue-green leaves. The subtly colored blossoms have a fragrance reminiscent of roses. They are ideal in rock gardens or sunny borders, where they will slowly grow into large colonies. They can also be grown in containers.

Selected species and varieties: *H. tuberosus* (snake's-head iris, widow iris)—2-inch flowers with delicate lime green ruffled inner petals enclosed in broader, darker green outer petals tipped with purple, rising from 2-foot leaves.

Growing conditions and maintenance: Plant snake's-head iris tubers 3 inches deep and 6 to 8 inches apart in neutral to alkaline soil in late summer or fall. The tubers die after flowering but produce fingerlike offsets that will bloom the following year. Repot container-grown specimens annually while dormant in late summer or fall, discarding old tubers. Propagate from seed.

Hippeastrum
(hip-ee-AS-trum)
AMARYLLIS

Hippeastrum 'Bold Leader'

Hardiness: *tender or Zones 9-11*

Type of bulb: *true bulb*

Flowering season: *spring*

Height: *1 to 2 feet*

Soil: *moist, well-drained, sandy*

Light: *full sun*

Spectacular amaryllis, with its flowers that can be as large as 8 inches across, is sometimes grown in sunny borders in warmer zones but is most renowned as a pot plant for indoor forcing.

Selected species and varieties: *H.* hybrids—'Apple Blossom' is cherry pink flushed white; 'Bold Leader', signal red; 'Double Record' has double white flowers veined and tipped red; 'Lady Jane', deep salmon orange double flowers; 'Orange Sovereign', bright orange blooms; 'Picotee', white petals rimmed red; 'Red Lion', velvety red flowers; 'Scarlet Baby' is a red miniature with two to three flower stems; 'White Christmas' is white.

Growing conditions and maintenance: Outdoors in Zones 10-11, plant in fall or spring, setting bulbs 6 inches deep and 1 foot apart. Indoors, plant the bulb with its top third out of the soil in a pot 2 inches wider than the bulb. Pot from late fall through winter; blooms in 5 to 8 weeks. Keep bulb barely moist until growth starts. After flowering, remove stem and fertilize until foliage dies. Dry bulb off for repotting. Propagate by separating offsets after foliage dies or from seed.

Hyacinthoides
(hy-a-sin-THOY-deez)
HYACINTHOIDES

Hyacinthoides hispanica

Hardiness: *Zones 5-9*

Type of bulb: *true bulb*

Flowering season: *spring*

Height: *15 to 20 inches*

Soil: *moist, acid, fertile*

Light: *partial to bright full shade*

Tiny, sometimes fragrant flowers line the tips of hyacinthoides' erect stems above strap-shaped, fleshy leaves. Both Spanish and English bluebells naturalize in woodland gardens, borders, or rock gardens and are good for forcing.

Selected species and varieties: *H. hispanica* [formerly *Endymion hispanicus, Scilla hispanica,* and *Scilla campanulata*] (Spanish bluebell)—¾-inch bells on 20-inch stalks; 'Blue Queen' is pale blue; 'Dainty Maid', purple-pink; 'Danube', deep blue; 'Excelsior', blue-violet with deeper blue edges; 'Rosabella', violet pink; 'Rose Queen', pure pink; 'White City', snowy white; 'White Triumphator', white, vigorous. *H. non-scripta* [formerly *Endymion non-scripta, Scilla non-scripta,* and *Scilla nutans*] (English bluebell, wood hyacinth, harebell)—fragrant ½- to ¾-inch blue-violet to pink or white flowers lining one side of 15- to 18-inch stems.

Growing conditions and maintenance: Plant in fall, setting bulbs 3 inches deep and 3 to 6 inches apart. To force, place six or seven bulbs 1 inch deep in 6-inch pots. Propagate from seed or by dividing bulb offsets. Both species self-sow freely.

Hyacinthus
(hy-a-SIN-thus)
HYACINTH

Hyacinthus 'Blue Jacket'

Hardiness: *Zones 3-7*

Type of bulb: *true bulb*

Flowering season: *spring*

Height: *4 to 12 inches*

Soil: *well-drained, fertile*

Light: *full sun*

With their heady fragrance, hyacinths are a classic bulb in the spring border. When first planted, most produce a single stiff, cylindrical cluster of inch-wide flower stars crowded on all sides of formally erect stems. Petal tips curve backward gracefully, giving the dense clusters a frilly appearance, an effect that is heightened when flowers are shaded in two tones of the same color. In subsequent years, flower stems grow longer and clusters become looser and more informal. The blooms last up to 2 weeks in the garden above straplike leaves at the base of the flower stalks. There are doubled cultivars with whorls of petals in graduated sizes engulfing each tiny blossom, and multiflora cultivars that produce several flower stems with widely spaced blossoms from each bulb. Mingle hyacinths with other spring bulbs in beds and borders, or force them indoors in pots or special glass hyacinth vases. They last almost a week as cut flowers.

Selected species and varieties: *H. orientalis* (Dutch hyacinth, common hyacinth, garden hyacinth)—clusters of star-shaped blossoms in an array of colors above foot-long leaves; 'Anne Marie' is pastel pink aging to salmon; 'Blue Giant' has large pastel blue clusters; 'Blue Jacket' is deep purple with paler petal edges; 'Blue Magic', purple-blue with a white throat; 'Carnegie', elegant pure white; 'City of Harlem', pastel lemon yellow; 'Delft Blue', porcelain blue with paler edges; 'French Roman Blue' is a multiflora cultivar with blue blooms; 'Gipsy Queen', yellow-tinged clear orange; 'Hollyhock' has flowers with double red petals on 4-inch stalks; 'Jan Bos' is clear candy-apple red in slender spikes; 'Lady Derby', rosy pink; 'Lord Balfour' has loose clusters of rose-purple blossoms; 'Oranje Boven' is salmon; 'Pe-

Hyacinthus 'Anne Marie'

ter Stuyvesant', deep purple-blue; 'Pink Pearl', deep luminescent pink; 'Snow White' is a white multiflora variety; 'Violet Pearl' is lilac-rose aging to silver.

Growing conditions and maintenance: Outdoors, plant bulbs in fall, setting them 4 to 6 inches deep and 6 to 8 inches apart. Indoors, allow 4 or 5 bulbs per 6-inch pot. Plant indoor bulbs in fall as well; specially prechilled bulbs will bloom earlier than ordinary bulbs. Keep potted bulbs damp in a dark location below 50° F for about 12 weeks or until roots fill the pot and bulbs show 2 inches of leaf growth. Then move the pots into filtered sunlight at a temperature no higher than 65° F. If using special hyacinth vases, suspend bulb above (but not touching) the water and treat the same as potted bulbs. 'Anne Marie' and 'Blue Jacket' are particularly good cultivars for forcing. Hyacinths are hard to propagate but sometimes form offsets alongside mature bulbs that can take up to 6 years to reach blooming size.

Hymenocallis
(hy-men-o-KAL-is)
SPIDER LILY

Hymenocallis x festalis 'Zwanenburg'

Hardiness: *tender or Zones 9-11*

Type of bulb: *true bulb*

Flowering season: *summer*

Height: *10 inches to 3 feet*

Soil: *well-drained, fertile*

Light: *full sun*

Spider lilies bear clusters of fragrant flowers with a funnel-shaped corona surrounded by curled, ribbonlike outer petals. Whorls of flowers bloom atop stout stems above straplike leaves. Use spider lilies in borders in warm zones or as annuals and container plants elsewhere. They last a week as cut flowers.

Selected species and varieties: *H.* x *festalis*—6- to 8-inch white blossoms with curly outer petals on 2-foot stems; 'Zwanenburg' is especially vigorous. *H. harrisiana*—a 10-inch-tall dwarf with white blooms. *H. longipetala*—up to 10 large flowers on 3-foot stems. *H. narcissiflora* (basket flower)—4- to 8-inch-long white blooms striped green with a fringed corona on 2-foot stems; 'Advance' is pure white; 'Sulfur Queen', yellow.

Growing conditions and maintenance: Plant spider lilies outdoors in spring, setting bulbs 4 inches deep and 1 foot apart. North of Zone 9, lift bulbs in fall for replanting the next spring. In containers, allow one bulb per 8-inch pot with the tip just breaking the surface. Propagate spider lilies from seed; the plants also produce a small number of bulblets.

Incarvillea
(in-kar-VILL-ee-a)
HARDY GLOXINIA

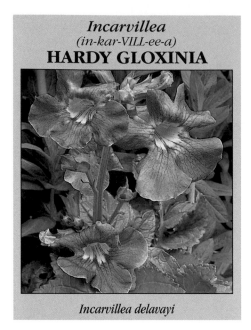

Incarvillea delavayi

Hardiness: *Zones 5-7*

Type of bulb: *tuber*

Flowering season: *summer*

Height: *1 to 2 feet*

Soil: *moist, well-drained*

Light: *full sun*

Hardy gloxinias bear funnel-shaped flowers flaring into wide, wavy-edged trumpets in clusters lining the tips of erect, leafless stems, which rise above clumps of ferny leaves. Plant them in rock gardens or sunny borders.

Selected species and varieties: *I. compacta*—purple flowers 2½ inches long and 1½ inches across on 1-foot stems above 8-inch leaves; 'Bee's Pink' has white to pink flowers. *I. delavayi*—purplish pink flower trumpets 3 inches long and as wide with yellow throats on 2-foot stems above 10-inch leaves.

Growing conditions and maintenance: Plant hardy gloxinias in spring, setting tubers 3 to 4 inches deep and 15 inches apart. Provide winter mulch in northern zones. Propagate from seed to bloom in 3 years or by division, although plants bloom best when undisturbed.

Ipheion
(IF-ee-on)
IPHEION

Ipheion uniflorum

Hardiness: *Zones 5-10*

Type of bulb: *true bulb*

Flowering season: *spring*

Height: *4 to 6 inches*

Soil: *acid well-drained loam*

Light: *full sun to light shade*

An ipheion bulb sends up several flowering stalks, each flower rising on a single stem from clumps of grassy leaves, for a long period of bloom. The flowers have tiny pointed petals surrounding a cluster of bright orange stamens. They are faintly mint scented, whereas the leaves give off an onion odor when bruised. The leaves appear in fall, and persist all winter and through the blooming period until the bulbs go dormant in summer. Plant ipheion in woodland or rock gardens, in meadows, or among paving stones, where it will rapidly naturalize. It can also be forced indoors for midwinter bloom.

Selected species and varieties: *I. uniflorum* [formerly *Brodiaea uniflora* and *Tritilea uniflora*] (spring starflower)—1-inch white flowers tinged blue; 'Wisley Blue' is light blue with a white center; 'Rolf Fiedler', deep electric blue.

Growing conditions and maintenance: Plant ipheion in late summer or fall, setting bulbs 3 inches deep and 3 to 6 inches apart. Provide winter mulch in Zones 5-6. Pot bulbs 1 inch deep for forcing. Propagate spring starflowers by dividing clumps of bulb offsets.

Iris
(EYE-ris)
FLAG, FLEUR-DE-LIS

Iris reticulata 'Harmony'

Hardiness: *Zones 5-9*

Type of bulb: *true bulb*

Flowering season: *spring or summer*

Height: *4 to 24 inches*

Soil: *well-drained, sandy*

Light: *full sun*

Bulbous irises are more delicate relatives of dramatic, tall bearded irises, which grow from rhizomes. Dwarf irises, which are sometimes scented, bloom on short stems before their grassy leaves have fully emerged. The leaves continue to grow to their full length after flowers fade. Bokara and Dutch iris emerge simultaneously with their leaves and produce their flowers on tall, erect stems. All irises have complex flowers composed of three drooping outer petals known as falls and three erect inner petals called standards. The falls are marked with contrasting color at their bases and are sometimes crested with a raised ridge or punctuated by a pair of small protrusions called horns. The shorter standards, appearing in a complementary or contrasting color, may be curved, frilled, or wavy. Flowers last 1 to 3 weeks in the garden. Dwarf irises are ideal in rock gardens and at the edge of borders. Dutch irises, some of which are fragrant, naturalize easily, rapidly forming large clumps in sunny beds. Both Bokara and Dutch irises make excellent cut flowers lasting up to 2 weeks. Irises can also be forced for indoor bloom.

Selected species and varieties: *I. bucharica* (Bokara iris)—2- to 2½-inch-wide spring flowers with yellow falls touched with white on 18-inch stems; Zones 5-9. *I. danfordiae* (Danford iris)—a dwarf iris producing fragrant, spring-blooming, 4-

Iris hollandica 'Blue Ideal'

inch single flowers with bristlelike canary yellow standards, falls splotched green and orange, and leaves growing to 12 inches; Zones 5-9. *I. histroides*—dwarfs to 9 inches tall with blue spring flowers and leaves up to 20 inches long; 'George' has plum purple falls touched with white; Zones 5-9. *I. hollandica* (Dutch iris)—fragrant 4-inch spring-to-summer flowers growing singly or in pairs on 15- to 24-inch stems; 'Angel's Wings' has pale blue standards and royal blue falls with white-rimmed yellow blotches; 'Blue Ideal', sky blue blooms on 20-inch stems; 'Blue Magic', deep blue-purple falls; 'Golden Harvest' is golden yellow shading to orange; 'Ideal' has dusty gray-blue falls blotched orange; 'Purple Sensation', deep violet falls with yellow blotches rimmed by royal blue; 'White Wedgewood' is pure white; Zones 6-9. *I. reticulata*—very fragrant, spring-blooming 3- to 9-inch dwarf plants, violet purple with white-bordered orange crests on falls and leaves to 18 inches; 'Cantab' is pale turquoise blue with white-rimmed orange blotches on its falls; 'Edward', dark blue spotted in orange; 'Gordon', medium blue with yellow-ridged falls; 'Harmony' has pale blue standards and royal blue falls with white-rimmed yellow splotches; 'Ida', light blue falls marked in yellow; 'Joyce', lavender-blue standards and deep sky blue falls touched with yellow and green; 'J. S.

Dijt', highly scented, rich purple standards and blue falls marked with yellow; 'Natashcha' is snow white tinged blue with orange splashes on its falls; 'Pauline' has violet standards and dark purple falls marked with a blue-and-white variegated blotch; 'Purple Gem', deep violet standards and rich plum purple falls; 'Spring Time', pale blue standards and deep violet falls spotted purple and yellow and tipped with white; Zones 5-9.

Growing conditions and maintenance: Plant dwarf irises in spring, Dutch irises in spring or fall, setting bulbs 4 inches deep and 3 to 6 inches apart and massing them

Iris hollandica 'Purple Sensation'

for best effect. Planted too shallowly, dwarf irises produce many nonflowering bulblets. *I. reticulata* prefers slightly alkaline soil. North of Zone 8, place Dutch irises in sites protected from wind and cover with winter mulch. Allow foliage to mature through summer. For indoor bloom, pot bulbous irises 1 inch deep, placing several bulbs in each 6-inch pot; all species listed here force readily, but *I. reticulata* 'Cantab' and 'Harmony' are particularly recommended. Outdoors, both dwarf and Dutch irises do best when allowed to form thick clumps over 3 to 5 years, after which flowering will probably diminish. Lift while dormant and propagate by removing and replanting the quantities of small offsets that form alongside mature bulbs in fall.

Ixia
(IKS-ee-a)
CORN LILY

Ixia viridiflora

Hardiness:	*tender or Zones 8-10*
Type of bulb:	*corm*
Flowering season:	*spring to summer*
Height:	*18 inches*
Soil:	*well-drained, sandy, fertile*
Light:	*full sun*

Corn lilies produce clusters of cup- or star-shaped flowers at the tips of wiry or wandlike stems rising from clumps of sparse, grassy leaves. In warm, dry climates, their multicolored blossoms can be used to decorate beds or borders. Elsewhere, force them as indoor plants.

Selected species and varieties: *I. viridiflora* (green ixia)—1-inch pale green flowers with black throats and black anthers at the tips of their stamens. *I.* hybrids—flower bells in shades of white, yellow, orange, pink, red, or blue; 'Bluebird' has violet petals streaked purple outside and white inside and a black throat; 'Marquette', yellow purple-tipped blossoms.

Growing conditions and maintenance: In Zones 8-10, plant outdoors in late fall, setting corms 3 inches deep and 6 inches apart in neutral soil. North of Zone 8, plant them in late spring or early summer and lift corms in fall for storage over winter. Corms must dry out while dormant in summer. Blossoms close in any degree of shade. Indoors, plant five or six corms 1 inch deep in 6-inch pots in fall for winter-to-spring bloom. Propagate by removing cormels growing around mature bulbs.

Ixiolirion
(iks-ee-o-LIR-ee-on)
SIBERIAN LILY

Ixiolirion tataricum

Hardiness: *Zones 7-10*

Type of bulb: *true bulb*

Flowering season: *spring to summer*

Height: *12 to 16 inches*

Soil: *well-drained, sandy*

Light: *full sun*

Siberian lilies produce small lilylike flower stars with petals curved gracefully back to reveal prominent short yellow stamens. The flowers cluster atop slender stems lined with narrow, grassy leaves. They will slowly naturalize in rock gardens where summers are hot and dry and can be grown as annuals or container plants in northern zones. Siberian lilies make excellent cut flowers.

Selected species and varieties: *I. tataricum*—bears up to 15 clear blue to lilac, slightly fragrant 2-inch flowers with narrow petals.

Growing conditions and maintenance: Plant Siberian lilies outdoors in fall, setting bulbs 3 inches deep and 2 to 6 inches apart. Provide winter mulch in Zone 7. In Zone 6 and north, plant bulbs in spring and lift in fall. Bulbs need hot, dry weather in summer and fall to ripen. Indoors, plant 5 to 6 bulbs per 6-inch pot. Propagate from seed.

Lachenalia
(lab-shen-AHL-ee-a)
CAPE COWSLIP

Lachenalia aloides

Hardiness: *tender or Zones 9-10*

Type of bulb: *true bulb*

Flowering season: *spring*

Height: *6 to 12 inches*

Soil: *moist, well-drained, sandy*

Light: *full sun*

Cape cowslips bear long spikes of drooping, tubular flowers above broad, oval, pointed leaves. The waxy, inch-long flowers are often tinged and tipped in multiple colors, and the fleshy leaves and stems are marbled purple. Cape cowslips are rock-garden plants where winters are warm and are grown as container specimens elsewhere. They make long-lasting cut flowers.

Selected species and varieties: *L. aloides* (tricolored Cape cowslip)—yellow petals tinged green and touched with red; 'Pearsonii' is golden yellow with maroon tips; 'Aurea', bright yellow-orange. *L. bulbifera* (nodding Cape cowslip)—coral pink to red, tipped with green and purple.

Growing conditions and maintenance: Plant Cape cowslips outdoors in fall, setting bulbs 1 inch deep and 2 inches apart. Indoors, set five to six bulbs 1 inch deep in a 6-inch pot. Propagate by removing the bulblets that grow alongside mature bulbs or, for *L. bulbifera,* potting the small bulbils that develop in the plant's leaf joints.

Leucocoryne
(loo-ko-KO-rin-ay)
LEUCOCORYNE

Leucocoryne ixioides

Hardiness: *tender or Zones 9-11*

Type of bulb: *true bulb*

Flowering season: *spring*

Height: *10 to 20 inches*

Soil: *well-drained*

Light: *full sun*

Leucocoryne produces small clusters of fragrant, star-shaped flowers on slender stems above clumps of grassy foot-long leaves. Making dainty accents in rock gardens or borders where winters are mild and summers hot and dry, they are grown as container specimens in other regions. They also make long-lasting cut flowers.

Selected species and varieties: *L. ixioides* (glory-of-the-sun)—up to a half-dozen white to pale blue blossoms ½ inch long and ¾ inch across.

Growing conditions and maintenance: Outdoors, plant glory-of-the-sun in fall, setting bulbs 4 to 6 inches deep and 6 to 8 inches apart. Bulbs must stay dry after foliage withers in early summer. Indoors, set bulbs 1 inch deep, allowing two to three bulbs per 6-inch pot. Propagate from seed or from offsets that develop at the base of mature bulbs.

Leucojum
(loo-KO-jum)
SNOWFLAKE

Leucojum aestivum 'Gravetye Giant'

Hardiness: *Zones 3-9*

Type of bulb: *true bulb*

Flowering season: *spring*

Height: *6 to 18 inches*

Soil: *moist, well-drained, sandy*

Light: *full sun to light shade*

Snowflakes are delicately spotted with contrasting color in the center of each of the pointed petal tips that unite to form dainty bells. Tips are flipped gaily outward. Sometimes fragrant, the flowers dangle from thin, arching stalks fanning out from the tip of erect, hollow stems above grassy leaves. Allow snowflakes to naturalize in woodland or rock gardens.

Selected species and varieties: *L. aestivum* (summer snowflake, giant snowflake, Loddon lily)—small clusters of ¾-inch green-spotted white bells on 12- to 18-inch stems; 'Gravetye Giant' produces 1½-inch flowers on stems to 24 inches. *L. vernum* (spring snowflake)—green- or yellow-spotted 1-inch white flowers growing singly or in pairs on 5- to 14-inch stems.

Growing conditions and maintenance: Plant spring and summer snowflakes in fall, setting bulbs 4 inches deep and 4 inches apart. They do best when left undisturbed to form large clumps. Propagate from seed to bloom in 3 years or by removing small bulblets growing alongside mature bulbs.

Liatris
(ly-AY-tris)
GAY-FEATHER

Liatris spicata 'Kobold'

Hardiness: *Zones 3-10*

Type of bulb: *corm*

Flowering season: *fall*

Height: *2 to 3 feet*

Soil: *moist, well-drained, poor*

Light: *full sun*

Gay-feather raises huge bottle-brush spires of tiny flowers with narrow, frilly petals crowded along the upper half of tall stems. The fat flower buds, resembling small balloons, open from top to bottom above a thick tuft of spiky, grasslike leaves that emerge in spring. Use gay-feather as a specimen planting in borders and wild gardens.

Selected species and varieties: *L. spicata* (spike gay-feather, button snakewort)—1- to 3-foot plants with deep purple flowers; 'Alba' is pure white; 'Kobold', a 2-foot dwarf.

Growing conditions and maintenance: Plant spike gay-feather corms in spring, setting them 3 to 4 inches deep and 18 to 24 inches apart. All except *L. spicata* 'Kobold' require staking, especially in fertile soils. Propagate from seed or by removing cormels growing around mature bulbs in spring.

Lilium
(LIL-ee-um)
LILY

Lilium 'Star Gazer'

Hardiness: *Zones 3-9*

Type of bulb: *true bulb*

Flowering season: *late spring to fall*

Height: *2 to 8 feet*

Soil: *moist, well-drained, fertile*

Light: *full sun to light shade*

Funnel-shaped lily flowers are composed of six overlapping pointed petals called tepals. Sometimes smooth, sometimes wavy or frilled, the tepals are flecked with raised spots, often in a contrasting shade. The flowers curve backward to varying degrees from almost flat or bowl-shaped faces to flaring trumpets to tightly rolled tiny turbans. Curling stamens carry anthers dusted with pollen in vivid colors. Lilies offer a wide range of colors and color combinations, with tepals flushed or striped in contrasting hues in addition to their spots. They bloom on flower stalks, either singly or in clusters, at the tips of stiff, erect stems lined with short, grassy leaves. Flowers may face upward or outward or may nod from arching stalks. Up to 50 often highly fragrant flowers may appear on a single stem. The wide range of choices allows fanciers to plant lilies for continuous bloom throughout the summer. Lilies attract attention when planted in borders, where they quickly develop into spreading clumps. They can also be grown in patio containers, forced for indoor bloom, or used as long-lasting cut flowers.

Selected species and varieties: *L.* hybrids—thousands of hybrids grouped into divisions of plants with similar flower size, height, form, and bloom time. *Division 1. Asiatic hybrids:* Early-summer-flowering compact lilies, usually 2 to 4 feet tall, divided into up-facing, outward-facing, and pendent subgroups based on the form of their 4- to 6-inch flowers, which are borne singly or in clusters; 'Avignon' is mellow orange; 'Connecticut

Lilium 'Avignon'

King' has flat-faced, upright yellow blossoms with gold throats; 'Enchantment King', upright red-orange blooms with black spotting; 'Grand Cru' is yellow with tepal centers flushed maroon; 'Melon Time' has apricot-orange upright flowers; 'Mona' is clear yellow with yellow spots; 'Montreux', lightly spotted dusty rose; 'Roma', deep cream with few spots; 'Rosefire', clear reddish gold without spotting. *Division 2. Martagon hybrids:* Late-spring-flowering plants 3 to 6 feet tall with 3- to 4-inch nodding flowers like tiny turbans; 'Mrs. R. O. Backhouse' produces yellow-orange flowers flushed with rose; 'Paisley hybrids' are yellow-orange spotted maroon. *Division 3. Candidum hybrids:* 3- to 4-foot-tall or taller plants flowering from late spring to early summer with tiered clusters of 3- to 4-inch tiny turbans; 'Cascade Strain' produces fragrant pure white flowers. *Division 4. American hybrids:* Lilies to 7 or 8 feet, flowering from late spring to midsummer with tiers of up to 30 or more tiny Turk's caps; 'Bellingham Hybrids' are 3- to 4-inch midsummer-blooming flowers in shades of yellow, orange, and red. *Division 5. Longiflorum hybrids:* Fragrant, outward-facing flower trumpets bloom-

ing in midsummer, though the familiar Easter lily is often forced for earlier bloom; 'Casa Rosa' has 6-inch pink blossoms. *Division 6. Trumpet hybrids* [also called *Aurelian hybrids*]: Summer-flowering lilies 4 to 6 feet tall with large 6- to 10-inch flowers that are either trumpet shaped, sunburst shaped, bowl shaped, or nodding; 'Black Dragon' yields creamy 6-inch white flower trumpets flushed with purple on the outside; 'Golden Splendor', fragrant golden yellow trumpets flushed copper outside; 'Pink Perfection', large deep pink trumpets. *Division 7. Oriental hybrids:* Mid- to late-summer-blooming garden favorites from 2 to 8 feet tall bearing trumpet-shaped, flat-faced, or bowl-shaped flowers up to 12 inches across or trusses of smaller turban-shaped flowers; 'Casa Blanca' has pure white trumpets with orange anthers; 'Imperial Crimson', fragrant flat-faced white flowers blushed with pink; 'Imperial Gold', fragrant, flat-faced white flowers banded with yellow and spotted in crimson; 'Star Gazer', erect, deep carmine flowers up to 8 inches across with wavy tepals spotted dark red and rimmed in white on compact stems; 'White Mountain', upward-facing white trumpets with golden throats.

Lilium 'Rosefire'

Division 8. Miscellaneous hybrids: Reserved for future hybrids not fitting any previous division. *Division 9. Species lilies:* L. auratum (gold-banded lily, gold-rayed lily, mountain lily)—up to 30 bowl-shaped, fragrant 10-inch-wide white flowers with tepals banded in gold down their centers and spotted with crimson on 4- to 6-foot stems blooming in mid- to late summer. *L. canadense* (Canada lily,

meadow lily, yellow lily)—3-inch dangling, bowl-shaped yellow to red-orange flowers spotted with crimson on stems to 6 feet in early to midsummer. *L. candidum* (Madonna lily, white lily)—fragrant trusses of shimmering white trum-

Lilium candidum

pets with yellow throats on 2- to 4-foot stems in early summer. *L. columbianum* (Columbia lily, Columbia tiger lily, Oregon lily)—tiered clusters of nodding 2-inch yellow to red turbans spotted maroon on 5-foot stalks in summer. *L. hansonii* (Japanese Turk's-cap)—loose spikes of 2½-inch yellow-orange turbans spotted purple on 2- to 5-foot stems in early summer. *L. henryi*—20 or more dangling light orange turbans with green throats on stems to 8 feet in late summer. *L. lancifolium* [also called *L. tigrinum*] (devil lily, tiger lily)—up to 25 nodding 5-inch orange or red Turk's caps spotted with purple on 6-foot plants in midsummer. *L. martagon* (Martagon lily, Turk's-cap lily, turban lily)—tiered clusters of up to 50 nodding light purple-rose flower turbans spotted with dark purple and unpleasantly scented on stems to 6 feet in midsummer; 'Album' is a pure ivory. *L. monadelphum* (Caucasian lily)—bell-shaped 5-inch yellow flowers tinged and spotted purple on 4- to 5-foot stems in early summer. *L. pumilum* (coral lily)—up to two dozen inch-wide, lacquer red nodding Turk's caps on compact 1- to 2-foot plants in early summer. *L. regale* (regal lily, royal lily)—fragrant, outward-facing white flower trumpets flushed purple outside with gold throats inside, clustered like a crown atop 3- to 5-foot stems in midsummer. *L. speciosum* (showy Japanese lily)—fragrant, nodding Turk's-caps rimmed in white on 4- to 5-foot stems in late summer to early fall; 'Album' is pure white; 'Rubrum', white blushed and spotted with crimson; 'Uchida', deep reddish pink with a white throat and crimson spots. *L. superbum* (American Turk's-cap lily, swamp lily, lily royal)— deep yellow-orange 3-inch flowers with maroon spots nodding in trusses on 5- to 8-foot stems in midsummer. *L.* x *testaceum* (Nankeen lily)—nodding 3-inch apricot turbans spotted red on 4- to 6-foot plants in midsummer.

Growing conditions and maintenance: With the exception of *L. candidum* and its *Division 3* hybrids, plant lilies in spring or fall, setting bulbs 2 to 3 times

Lilium columbianum

deeper than their diameter. Space bulbs 1 foot apart. Plant *L. candidum* and its hybrids with bulb tips an inch below the surface in fall. Mulch lilies to keep roots cool and moist in summer, protected from frost in winter. *L. auratum* and *L. speciosum* will not tolerate lime in the soil. *L. auratum, L. canadense,* and *L. speciosum* are susceptible to the lily mosaic virus. *L. lancifolium* is a carrier of the virus, which does not harm it but is spread to other lilies by aphids; buy only disease-free stock and plant far from other lilies. Stake taller lilies for support. For pots and patio containers, choose compact lilies and set bulbs deep enough to allow space for stem roots. Propagate lilies by removing and replanting the small bulblets that grow along the underground stem or by removing and potting the tiny black bulbils that appear in the leaf joints of some species.

Lycoris
(ly-KOR-is)
SPIDER LILY

Lycoris radiata

Hardiness: *tender or Zones 7-10*	
Type of bulb: *true bulb*	
Flowering season: *summer to fall*	
Height: *18 to 24 inches*	
Soil: *well-drained, fertile*	
Light: *full sun to light shade*	

Lycoris produces whorls of frilly blossoms from late summer to fall atop stout bare stems. These are followed by clumps of narrow, strap-shaped leaves like those of narcissus, which emerge in late winter to early spring, fading as the plants enter summer dormancy. In most species, the blooms consist of ribbonlike petals that are curled or crisped, with abundant thready stamen filaments arching out beyond them in a froth of color. The flowers are less ornate in other species, forming into small funnels or trumpets of overlapping petals with stamen filaments the same length as the petals. Use lycoris in borders, woodland gardens, or rock gardens. They make good indoor container plants and excellent cut flowers.

Selected species and varieties: *L. albiflora*—2-inch ivory flowers with prominent filaments on 24-inch-tall stems in early fall; Zones 7-10. *L. aurea* [also called *L. africana* and *Amaryllis aurea*] (golden hurricane lily, golden spider lily)— highly crisped golden yellow petals and filaments on 12- to 24-inch stems in late summer to early fall; Zones 7-10. *L. radi-*

ata (red spider lily)—1½-inch pink to deep red extremely crimped and frilled petals and abundant filaments on 18-inch flower stalks in early fall; Zones 7-10. *L. sanguinea*—2-inch erect, blood red frilled blossoms on 12- to 18-inch stems in late summer; Zones 7-10. *L. sprengeri*—vivid red to purple, blue, or rose 2- to 3-inch trumpets on 18-inch stems in late summer. *L. squamigera* (resurrection lily, magic lily)— extremely fragrant late-summer-blooming 3-inch rose to lilac trumpets on 2-foot

Lycoris squamigera

stalks, differing from the other species by appearing after the foliage has died back; Zones 5-10.

Growing conditions and maintenance: Plant lycoris bulbs 3 to 5 inches deep depending on their size and 6 inches apart. They do best in areas where winters are moist while bulbs are growing and summers dry while they are dormant. North of Zone 7, treat lycoris as a container plant, placing bulb tips just at the soil surface and allowing one bulb per 6-inch pot. Pot bulbs in late summer for fall flowers, then allow foliage to develop through spring. Dry bulbs off in early summer, then resume watering in late summer for rebloom. Propagate lycoris by removing the small bulblets that grow alongside mature bulbs. Disturbing established clumps may delay rebloom for a year or more.

Mertensia
(mer-TENZ-ee-a)
BLUEBELLS, LUNGWORT

Mertensia virginica

Hardiness: *Zones 3-8*

Type of bulb: *rhizome*

Flowering season: *spring*

Height: *18 to 24 inches*

Soil: *moist, well-drained, fertile*

Light: *light shade to full sun*

Mertensia produces loose clusters of nodding flower bells over several weeks. The blossoms dangle near the top of stems lined with oval, pointed, soft green leaves. Foliage dies back by midsummer. Bluebells will slowly grow into large clumps in woodland borders, rock gardens, and wildflower gardens, and provide textural contrast when interplanted with spring bulbs such as narcissus and tulip.

Selected species and varieties: *M. virginica*—(Virginia bluebells, Virginia cowslip, Roanoke bells)—inch-long pale dusty blue flowers with tiny curling crests at the tip of each petal.

Growing conditions and maintenance: Plant Virginia bluebells in fall, setting the tips of crowns just at the soil surface with buds facing up. Space crown sections 1½ to 3 feet apart. When purchasing Virginia bluebells, look for nursery-propagated crowns; refuse plants collected in the wild. To propagate, divide crowns in fall, making sure each section has at least one bud.

Muscari
(mus-KAH-ree)
GRAPE HYACINTH

Muscari armeniacum 'Blue Spike'

Hardiness: *Zones 4-8*

Type of bulb: *true bulb*

Flowering season: *late winter to spring*

Height: *6 to 12 inches*

Soil: *moist, well-drained*

Light: *full sun to light shade*

Among the earliest of spring bulbs to brighten the garden, low-growing grape hyacinths rapidly spread into carpets of color. Their tiny flowers, less than ½ inch long, cluster in pyramidal tiers at the tips of slender stems above narrow, grasslike leaves. The flowers are usually tubular, with their lips turned inward so that clusters resemble small bunches of grapes, or flipped outward like those of hyacinths. The fragrant blossoms are often attractively rimmed in contrasting color. Usually nodding, the flowers are occasionally so tightly crowded that lower blossoms hold upper ones facing out or up, giving the flowers a distinctive texture. Use grape hyacinths as edging plants, in beds or borders, or in wildflower or rock gardens, where they will naturalize quickly. They can also be forced for indoor bloom or used as cut flowers.

Selected species and varieties: *M. armeniacum* (Armenian grape hyacinth) —dense clusters of 20 to 30 spring-blooming blue flowers with flipped, white-rimmed edges nodding in overlapping tiers on 8- to 10-inch stems; 'Blue Spike' produces double-petaled, long

lasting flowers; 'Cantab', pale blue flowers blooming later than the species; 'Christmas Pearl', violet blooms; 'Fantasy Creation', soft blue double flowers; 'Saphir', long-lasting deep blue flowers rimmed with white. *M. aucheri* 'Tubergenianium'—a 6-inch dwarf with dense spikes of clear light blue blossoms at the top shading to deep blue rimmed in white at the bottom. *M. azureum* [also called *Pseudomuscari azurea*]—20 to 40 cylindrical, open blue bells facing out

Muscari botryoides 'Album'

and up on 8-inch stems; 'Album' is white. *M. botryoides* (common grape hyacinth, starch hyacinth)—overlapping tiers of nodding white, pink, violet, or blue flowers with white rims on 12-inch stems; 'Album' (Italian grape hyacinth) is a slightly shorter white cultivar. *M. comosum* [also called *Leopoldia comosa*] 'Plumosum' (feather hyacinth, tassel hyacinth)— dense clusters of light blue, violet, or fuchsia flowers with frilled, threadlike petals on 4- to 6-inch stems. *M. latifolium*—loose clusters of 10 to 20 flowers with flipped petals in spikes shading from light to dark blue on 12-inch stems. *M. neglectum*—dense clusters of 30 to 40 flowers with frilled white rims in spires shading from light to dark blue on 6-inch stems; 'Dark Eyes' is very dark blue; 'White Beauty', white tinged pink.

Growing conditions and maintenance: Plant grape hyacinths from late summer to fall, setting bulbs 2 to 3 inches deep and 3 to 4 inches apart. For indoor forcing, set bulbs 1 inch deep allowing 10 to 12 bulbs per 6-inch pot. Grape hyacinths self-sow freely. Propagate by removing bulblets that grow around mature bulbs or from seed.

Narcissus
(nar-SIS-us)
DAFFODIL

Narcissus 'Dutch Master'

Hardiness: *Zones 3-10*

Type of bulb: *true bulb*

Flowering season: *late winter to late spring*

Height: *4 to 18 inches*

Soil: *well-drained*

Light: *full sun to shade*

Daffodil flowers, growing either singly or in small clusters, bloom atop stout, hollow stems above clumps of narrow, glossy, grasslike leaves. Mature bulbs produce two or more stems. The 1- to 4-inch-wide flowers sometimes face upward or arch downward but most often face out. Each bloom consists of an outer ring of six petals called the perianth and a raised center called a corona, which may be an almost flat small cup, a large cup of medium length, or, when it is very long, a trumpet. The edges of the corona may be ruffled, fringed, flared, frilled, or split. The petals of the perianth may be pointed or round, overlapping or separate. Colors range the spectrum. Species narcissus are renowned for their sweet, intense fragrance. Hybrids of the species number in the thousands, and the genus is grouped into 12 divisions for identification. There are miniature cultivars within almost every division. Group them in borders, beds, and woodland or rock gardens, or scatter them to naturalize on lawns and in meadows. All narcissus make excellent cut flowers, and all, particularly some of the species, are excellent for forcing. All parts of narcissus are poisonous.

Selected species and varieties: The 12 divisions are based on the shape of the corona, its size relationship to the perianth, and, sometimes, the species from which the plants originated. *Division 1. Trumpet daffodils:* One flower per 16- to 20-inch stem, with the corona a trumpet as long as or longer than the perianth petals; 'Arctic Gold' is deep yellow; 'Bravoure' has white petals and a yellow cup; 'Dutch Master' is all yellow, good for forcing; 'Las Vegas' has giant white petals and a yellow corona; 'Little Beauty' is a 6-inch miniature with white petals and a golden yellow trumpet; 'Little Gem' is an all-yellow miniature; 'Lunar Sea' has soft yellow petals and a white cup; 'Mount

Narcissus 'Gigantic Star'

Hood', white petals with a cream trumpet; 'Spellbinder', yellow-green flowers with a corona aging white; 'Unsurpassable' is golden yellow with extremely large trumpets. *Division 2. Large-cup daffodils:* One flower on each 12- to 20-inch stem, the corona ranging in size from one-third the length of the petals to almost their length; 'Accent' has white petals and a pink corona; 'Ambergate', red corona and orange petals blushed red; 'Camelot' is a long-lasting golden yellow bloom; 'Carlton' has two shades of yellow and is vanilla scented; 'Ceylon' has yellow petals and an orange cup and grows vigorously; 'Daydream' is translucent yellow with a cup maturing to white; 'Flower Record' has white petals and a yellow corona rimmed red; 'Gigantic Star' is an extremely large pale yellow orange bloom with a vanilla scent; 'Ice Follies' has creamy white petals and a flat yellow cup aging white; 'Kissproof', copper yellow petals, a red-orange cup; 'Pink Charm', white petals, a corona banded salmon; 'Redhill', ivory petals, a deep red-orange corona; 'Salome', ivory petals, a pale yellow corona aging to salmon pink;

Narcissus 'Ice Follies'

'St. Keverne' is all yellow; 'St. Patrick's Day', bright yellow with a flat white corona; 'White Plume', pure white. *Division 3. Small-cup daffodils:* One flower per 10- to 20-inch stem, with the corona less than a third the length of the perianth petals; 'Barrett Browning' is early flowering with a white perianth and an orange to red corona; 'Birma' has deep yellow petals with a red cup. *Division 4. Double daffodils:* One or more flowers per 12- to 16-inch stem, with either the perianth petals or the corona or both doubled, the corona sometimes a tuft of tousled petals almost as wide as the perianth instead of a cup; 'Bridal Crown' has cream petals, deep red-orange centers; 'Cheerfulness' is a single white bloom flecked yellow; 'Erlicheer' yields eight or more fragrant, white-petaled flowers with yellow-tinged centers on each stem; 'Flower Drift' is ivory with a ruffled yellow-orange center; 'Pencrebar' is a bright orange miniature cultivar less than 6 inches tall; 'Sir Winston Churchill' has fragrant white petals with orange centers; 'Tahiti' is deep yellow with a red center; 'Unique', ivory white with an extremely frilled golden center. *Division 5. Triandus hybrid daffodils:* Two or more drooping flowers per 10- to 12-inch stem, with the perianth petals flared backwards; 'Hawera' is less than 6 inches tall with clusters of tiny yellow bells; 'Liberty Bells' is soft yellow; 'Petrel' produces up to 7 fragrant white flowers per stem; 'Thalia' grows two or more fragrant white flowers resembling orchids per stem. *Division 6. Cyclamineus hybrid daffodils:* One flower on each short stem—under 8 inches—with a trumpet-shaped corona and perianth petals swept backwards; 'February Gold' is yellow; 'Jack Snipe' has rounded white petals and a fringed yellow cup; 'Jenny' is pure white; 'Jet Fire' has red-orange petals with yellow cups; 'Jumblie' is a miniature, under 6 inches, with yellow petals swept back from a pencil-thin yellow-orange corolla; 'Peeping Tom' is lemon yellow; 'Tête-à-Tête' is a miniature under 6 inches with buttery yellow petals and a corona flushed orange. *Division 7.*

Narcissus 'Jack Snipe'

Jonquilla hybrid daffodils: Three to 6 fragrant flowers on a round 10- to 14-inch stem with small cups; 'Baby Moon' is a miniature, under 6 inches, with fragrant yellow blooms; 'Bell Song' is fragrant, with white petals and a pink corona; 'Pip-it', fragrant, with pale yellow petals and a white corona; 'Quail' is orangey yellow; 'Sun Disk', a yellow miniature, under 6 inches, with very rounded petals; 'Suzy' is fragrant, with yellow petals and a deep red-orange corona; 'Trevithian' has curled yellow petals and a frilled corona and is very fragrant. *Division 8. Tazetta hybrid daffodils:* Three to 20 fragrant flowers with almost flat coronas per 6- to 14-inch stem; 'Avalanche' has a perianth crowded with doubled white petals and a yellow corona; 'Geranium', fragrant white petals and a yellow-orange cup; 'Minnow', a miniature under 6 inches, has white petals and a bright yellow cup; 'Scarlet Gem', yellow-orange petals enfolding a deep red-orange corona with

frilled edges. *Division 9. Poeticus hybrid daffodils:* One fragrant flower per 12- to 16-inch stem with rounded pure white perianth petals and a tiny, brilliantly colored, disk-shaped, flat corona; 'Actaea' has brilliant white petals with deep green

Narcissus 'Minnow'

stamens tucked within a deep orange disk rimmed red. *Division 10. Species and wild forms:* N. bulbocodium var. conspicuus (hoop-petticoat daffodil)—petals reduced to tiny pointed projections around smooth, flaring yellow coronas like ladies' hoop skirts on 6- to 10-inch stems. N. jonquilla (jonquil)—2-inch golden yellow flowers with flat coronas in clusters on 12-inch stems. N. papyraceus (paper-white narcissus)—clusters of up to a dozen very fragrant flowers on 16-inch stems, excellent for forcing; 'Galilee' has pure white late blooms; 'Israel', creamy yellow petals and a deep yellow corona; 'Jerusalem' is pure white; 'Ziva', a very early white. N. poeticus var. recurvus (pheasant's-eye narcissus)—1½- to 3-inch blossoms with backswept white petals and a flat, disk-shaped yellow to red corona on 8- to 16-inch stems. N. pseudonarcissus ssp. obvallaris (Tenby daffodil)—rich deep yellow 2- to 3-inch flowers with ruffled and flared trumpets on 10-inch stems. N. tazetta (bunch-flowered narcissus, polyanthus narcissus)—4 to 8 fragrant blooms with a white perianth and yellow corona; 'Canaliculatus' has very fragrant blossoms with backswept white petals ringing a yellow cup on 6-inch stems; 'Grand Soleil d'Or', a deep yellow perianth and bright orange cup on 12-inch stems. *Division 11. Split-corona daffodils:* One upward-facing flower with a flattened corona split

one-third or more of its length on each 14- to 20-inch stem; 'Cassata' has white petals and a ruffled lemon yellow cup aging to white; 'Colbanc' is pure white with an "eye" of deep green stamens; 'Mondragon' is golden yellow and deep orange; 'Palmares' has white petals and pink ruffled centers; 'Tricollet', white petals around an orange corolla. Plants in the Division 11 subdivision *Papillion daffodils* resemble floral butterflies; 'Sorbet' is an ivory butterfly type with a sunny yellow center. *Division 12. Miscellaneous daffodils:* All daffodils not belonging to any of the previous divisions.

Growing conditions and maintenance: Plant narcissus in fall, setting the bulbs, which can range from ¼ to 2 inches in diameter, into the ground at a depth three

Narcissus bulbocodium

times the width of the bulb and spacing them 1 to 3 inches apart, depending on their size and the effect desired in the garden. Allow foliage to sprawl and to die back for at least 6 weeks in early summer before removing it. Fragrant N. tazetta and its hybrids are hardy only in Zones 9 and 10 but are among the choicest daffodils for forcing because they require no chilling. To force plants into bloom, buy prechilled bulbs or chill all daffodil bulbs except those of N. tazetta and its hybrids before potting them 1 inch deep in containers. Propagate narcissus by removing and immediately replanting the small bulblets that develop at the base of mature bulbs as soon as foliage withers, or dry the bulbs and hold them for replanting in fall. Bulblets take several years to grow to blooming size.

Nectaroscordum
(nek-ta-ro-SKOR-dum)
NECTAROSCORDUM

Nectaroscordum siculum

Hardiness: *Zones 6-10*

Type of bulb: *true bulb*

Flowering season: *spring*

Height: *4 feet*

Soil: *moist, well-drained*

Light: *full sun*

Nectaroscordum produces large, loose clusters of open flower bells atop tall stems clasped by strap-shaped 2-foot leaves at their base. Pendulous in flower, the stem tips become erect as seeds form. The odor of crushed or bruised leaves confirms nectaroscordum's membership in the onion family. The plant grows slowly into clumps in borders or sunny wildflower gardens. The dried seed pods are attractive in arrangements.

Selected species and varieties: *N. siculum* (Sicilian honey garlic)—½-inch flowers composed of six rounded petals, overlapping at their bases and flared open at their tips, each dull buff petal tinged green to purple-green with a darker purple stripe down its center.

Growing conditions and maintenance: Plant nectaroscordum in fall, setting bulbs 2 inches deep and 18 inches apart. They bloom best when clumps are undisturbed, and they will self-sow. Propagate from seed to grow bulbs of blooming size in 2 years or by dividing clumps in fall after leaves wither.

Nerine
(ne-RYE-nee)
NERINE

Nerine bowdenii

Hardiness: *tender or Zones 9-11*

Type of bulb: *true bulb*

Flowering season: *fall*

Height: *8 to 24 inches*

Soil: *well-drained, sandy*

Light: *full sun*

Nerines bear large clusters of star-shaped flowers with prominent stamens. The flowers appear on leafless stems in fall, followed by narrow, strap-shaped, glossy leaves from late winter to early spring. In warmer zones, use nerines in beds or borders; elsewhere, grow them as indoor plants. They make striking cut flowers.

Selected species and varieties: *N. bowdenii*—rose pink tufted flowers in 9-inch clusters on stems to 2 feet, appearing the same time as leaves; 'Pink Triumph' is iridescent pink; Zones 8-10. *N. sarniensis* (Guernsey lily)—10-inch clusters of iridescent white to deep scarlet flowers on 18-inch stems; 'Cherry Ripe' is rosy red; 'Early Snow', pure white; 'Radiant Queen', rosy pink; 'Salmon Supreme', salmon pink; Zones 9-10. *N. undulata* (Kalahari nerine)—2-inch flowers clustered on 8- to 18-inch stems; Zones 9-10.

Growing conditions and maintenance: Plant nerine bulbs in late summer, setting them 3 to 6 inches deep and 8 inches apart. Pot with the upper half of the bulb out of the soil. Keep bulbs dry during summer dormancy. Propagate from seed or by removing bulb offsets.

Ornithogalum
(or-nith-AH-ga-lum)
ORNITHOGALUM

Ornithogalum nutans

Hardiness: *Zones 5-10*

Type of bulb: *true bulb*

Flowering season: *spring or summer*

Height: *6 to 24 inches*

Soil: *moist, well-drained*

Light: *full sun to light shade*

Ornithogalum bears star-shaped, often fragrant, flowers with a distinctive tight "eye" of pistils at their centers. Usually white with a green stripe down the outside of each petal, some are yellow to orange. The flowers are carried in large clusters that are sometimes pendent but more often are facing upward in flat-topped bouquets above neat clumps of shimmering green, ribbonlike leaves. Ornithogalum species vary considerably in hardiness. Allow frost-resistant species to naturalize in borders, beds, and rock gardens, where they will self-sow. Tender species can be grown outdoors in warm zones or indoors as pot plants. Some species are used for long-lasting cut flowers.

Selected species and varieties: *O. arabicum* (Arabian starflower)—fragrant, pure white 1-inch flowers with black centers on 1½- to 2-foot stems in spring; Zones 8-10. *O. dubium*—enormous clusters of yellow flowers tinged orange with black centers on 8- to 12-inch stems; Zones 8-10. *O. nutans* (nodding star-of-Bethlehem)—fragrant greenish white 2-inch flowers nodding along one side of

12- to 18-inch stems from late spring to early summer; Zones 5-9. *O. saundersiae* (giant chincherinchee)—flat spikes of 1-inch white flowers with a greenish black eye on stems 3 feet or more tall above clumps of broad leaves in late

Ornithogalum umbellatum

spring; Zones 7-10. *O. thyrsoides* (wonder flower, chincherinchee)—¾-inch cream flowers with a greenish brown eye on 6- to 18-inch stems from late spring to summer; excellent for cutting, but all parts of the plant are poisonous; Zones 7-9. *O. umbellatum* (star-of-Bethlehem, nap-at-noon, summer snowflake)—1-inch flowers prominently striped green on the outside opening in the afternoon on 8- to 12-inch stems in spring; an aggressive naturalizer; Zones 5-9.

Growing conditions and maintenance: Outdoors, plant ornithogalum bulbs 4 inches deep and 2 to 5 inches apart. Nodding star-of-Bethlehem prefers shade; other species will grow in sun or shade, although *O. umbellatum* only opens fully in sun. North of Zone 8, treat tender species as annuals, lifting bulbs in fall for replanting in spring, or grow as container plants. Indoors, pot 5 to 6 bulbs 1 inch deep in a 6-inch pot. Propagate from seed sown in spring or by dividing bulbs and offsets in fall.

Oxalis
(oks-AH-lis)
WOOD SORREL

Oxalis deppei 'Iron Cross'

Hardiness:	*Zones 5-9*
Type of bulb:	*tuber or true bulb*
Flowering season:	*summer*
Height:	*2 to 12 inches*
Soil:	*well-drained*
Light:	*full sun to light shade*

Oxalis bears dainty, flat-faced flowers either singly or in clusters above lobed, cloverlike leaflets. The tiny leaves fold at night or on overcast days. Oxalis naturalizes easily, forming perfect carpets in rockeries and woodland gardens and makes fast-growing houseplants.

Selected species and varieties: *O. adenophylla* (Chilean oxalis)—a dwarf only 2 to 6 inches tall with tight rosettes of 1-inch pink flowers veined deeper pink above blue-green leaflets. *O. deppei* [also classified as *O. tetraphylla*] 'Iron Cross' (lucky clover, good-luck leaf)—clusters of rosy red-violet 1-inch flowers on 1-foot stems, above leaves with four leaflets arranged symmetrically and marked with deep purple to resemble an iron cross. *O. triangularis* ssp. *papilionacea*—white flowers above green leaflets.

Growing conditions and maintenance: Plant Chilean oxalis tubers in fall, 'Iron Cross' bulbs in spring, setting them 2 inches deep and 4 to 6 inches apart. To control invasiveness, plant in confined areas, such as between paving stones or in pots sunk into the garden. Propagate from seed or by dividing offsets.

Pancratium
(pan-KRAT-ee-um)
PANCRATIUM

Pancratium maritimum

Hardiness:	*tender or Zones 9-11*
Type of bulb:	*true bulb*
Flowering season:	*summer to fall*
Height:	*1 to 2 feet*
Soil:	*well-drained, sandy*
Light:	*full sun*

Pancratium produces extremely fragrant flowers reminiscent of frilled daffodils above gray-green sword-shaped leaves. Where climates are reliably frost free they can be grown in borders and rock gardens. North of Zone 9, plant them in containers for patio display or indoor use.

Selected species and varieties: *P. maritimum* (sea daffodil, sea lily)—pure white 3-inch flowers with a deeply toothed, trumpet-shaped corona surrounded by six narrow, pointed petals in clusters at the tip of each stem.

Growing conditions and maintenance: Plant sea daffodil bulbs where they can remain undisturbed for several years, setting them 3 inches deep and 10 to 12 inches apart. Allow one large bulb per 12-inch pot to allow room for bulb offsets to develop; set the tip of the bulb level with the soil surface. Repotting or division may reduce flowering the following season. Propagate from seed to blooming-size bulbs in 5 years or by carefully removing the offsets from around mature bulbs, which are fragile.

Polianthes
(pol-ee-AN-theez)
POLIANTHES

Polianthes tuberosa 'The Pearl'

Hardiness: *tender or Zones 9-10*

Type of bulb: *tuber*

Flowering season: *summer to fall*

Height: *2 to 4 feet*

Soil: *moist, well-drained*

Light: *full sun*

The long, curving buds of polianthes open into clusters of waxy flowers with a heavy, sweet fragrance above grassy, gray-green leaves. Each bud forms a narrow trumpet whose petal ends depict a tiny star. Use polianthes outdoors in beds and borders or indoors in containers. As cut flowers, they last as long as 2 weeks.

Selected species and varieties: *P. tuberosa* (tuberose)—white, 2½-inch-long flowers above 12- to 18-inch leaves; 'The Pearl' has double-petaled blossoms on 2-foot stems; 'Single Mexican', single flowers on 3- to 4-foot stems.

Growing conditions and maintenance: Plant tuberoses outdoors in spring, setting the tubers 3 inches deep and 6 inches apart. Mature tubers bloom, then die, leaving behind many small offsets that reach blooming size in 1 or 2 years. North of Zones 9, start tubers indoors 4 to 6 weeks before night temperatures reach 60° F and lift for winter storage. For pot plants, allow 1 tuber per 6-inch pot, setting bulbs 1 inch deep. Propagate by removing offsets that develop around mature tubers.

Puschkinia
(push-KIN-ee-a)
PUSCHKINIA

Puschkinia scilloides var. libanotica 'Alba'

Hardiness: *Zones 4-9*

Type of bulb: *true bulb*

Flowering season: *spring*

Height: *4 to 6 inches*

Soil: *moist, well-drained*

Light: *full sun to light shade*

Puschkinia's wands of tight, oval buds open first into loose clusters of tiny flower bells and finally into small stars on slender stems rising from tufts of narrow leaves like those of daffodils. The plants naturalize easily into drifts of blooms to carpet rockeries or beds and make an attractive border edging.

Selected species and varieties: *P. scilloides* var. *libanotica* (striped squill)—½-inch bluish white flowers striped darker blue above 6-inch leaves; 'Alba' is pure white.

Growing conditions and maintenance: Plant bulbs in fall, setting them 2 inches deep and 6 inches apart. Group them in small colonies for best effect. They bloom best when left undisturbed. Propagate by removing the small bulblets that grow alongside mature bulbs.

Ranunculus
(ra-NUN-kew-lus)
BUTTERCUP, CROWFOOT

Ranunculus asiaticus

Hardiness: *tender or Zones 9-11*

Type of bulb: *tuber*

Flowering season: *spring and summer*

Height: *10 to 18 inches*

Soil: *moist, very well drained, sandy*

Light: *full sun*

Buttercups produce quantities of saucer-shaped flowers over a long season of bloom. There are many hybrids, so thickly doubled that flowers become colorful domes of whorled overlapping petals. Each tuber may produce five or six dozen flowers up to four at a time throughout the season on stems lined with ferny leaflets. Buttercups can be used in borders and rock gardens, and they excel as cut flowers.

Selected species and varieties: *R. asiaticus* 'Tecolote Giants' (Persian buttercup)—flowers up to 5 inches across in pastel shades of pink, rose, yellow, tangerine, and white, with bi- and tricolors.

Growing conditions and maintenance: Plant Persian buttercups in fall, soaking the tubers overnight then setting them in the soil with the claws down with the tops 1½ inches deep. Space them 8 inches apart. Crowns are subject to rot, so sites with fast drainage are essential for success. Tubers go dormant in summer. North of Zone 9, treat plants as annuals, setting them out in spring and lifting them in fall for winter storage. Propagate from seed or by dividing tubers.

Rhodohypoxis
(ro-do-hi-POKS-is)
RHODOHYPOXIS

Rhodohypoxis baurii

Hardiness: *Zones 6-10*

Type of bulb: *rhizome*

Flowering season: *summer*

Height: *3 to 4 inches*

Soil: *well-drained, sandy*

Light: *full sun*

Rhodohypoxis sends up tufts of 3-inch, stiff, grassy leaves covered with downy hairs in spring, followed by dainty, flat-faced blossoms that appear throughout the season. Each blossom sits atop a slender stem; the plants produce several flowering stems at a time. Dwarf rhodohypoxis are excellent planted among paving stones and will form colonies in rock gardens or borders. They can also be grown as container specimens.

Selected species and varieties: *R. baurii* (red star)—1- to 1½-inch white, pink, rose, or red flowers with petals crowded closely together at the center, obscuring the stamens.

Growing conditions and maintenance: Plant rhodohypoxis in fall, setting rhizomes 1 to 2 inches deep and 2 to 3 inches apart. Protect rhizomes with winter mulch in Zones 5 and 6. North of Zone 6, treat rhodohypoxis as an annual, planting in spring and lifting in fall, or grow it in shallow containers, allowing 4 or 5 rhizomes per 6-inch bulb pan. They are best left undisturbed, but clumps of rhizomes can be lifted and separated for propagation in spring as leaves begin to show.

Sandersonia
(sahn-der-SONE-ee-a)
SANDERSONIA

Sandersonia aurantiaca

Hardiness: *tender or Zones 9-11*

Type of bulb: *tuber*

Flowering season: *summer*

Height: *2 to 3 feet*

Soil: *well-drained, sandy*

Light: *full sun*

The petals of sandersonia fuse into tiny, balloon-shaped flowers that dangle from thin stalks growing in the upper leaf joints along semierect, climbing stems. Soft green, narrow pointed leaves line the stems, sometimes tapering into tendrils. Plant sandersonias along fences or walls, or grow them in containers as patio specimens. Sandersonias make excellent cut flowers.

Selected species and varieties: *S. aurantiaca* (Chinese lantern lily, Christmas-bells)—inch-long, golden orange, puffy blossoms resembling chubby, upside-down urns, with threadlike green spurs.

Growing conditions and maintenance: Plant Chinese lantern lilies in spring, setting the brittle tubers 4 inches deep and 8 to 12 inches apart. North of Zone 9, lift tubers in fall or grow them in containers to bring indoors in winter. Propagate from seed to bloom in 2 years or by dividing tubers in spring.

Sauromatum
(sow-RO-ma-tum)
SAUROMATUM

Sauromatum venosum

Hardiness: *tender or Zones 10-11*

Type of bulb: *tuber*

Flowering season: *summer*

Height: *1 to 2 feet*

Soil: *moist, well-drained*

Light: *full sun*

Sauromatum's tiny, inconspicuous true flowers are carried on a pencil-shaped spadix that emerges from an exotically shaped and colored hood or spathe. The oval, pointed, curled spathe rises out of a thick, bottle-shaped stem. Blooming flowers give off a putrid odor. After the spathe withers, a finely divided leaf resembling a miniature palm tree appears. Sauromatums can be grown in beds or in containers as specimen plants.

Selected species and varieties: *S. venosum* [formerly *S. guttatum*] (voodoo lily, monarch-of-the-East, red calla)—12- to 20-inch spathe mottled and flecked purple, brown, green, and yellow, followed by 20- to 24-inch foliage.

Growing conditions and maintenance: In Zones 10-11 where air is humid and temperatures remain above 68° F, set tubers in a saucer of water on a sunny window sill, where they will grow without soil. Otherwise, plant them outdoors, setting tubers 4 to 6 inches deep and 12 inches apart. North of Zone 10, grow them as container plants, with the tubers set 2 inches deep in pots. Propagate by dividing offsets from the main tuber.

Schizostylis
(ski-zo-STI-lis)
CRIMSON FLAG

Schizostylis coccinea 'Mrs. Hegarty'

Hardiness: *tender or Zones 6-10*

Type of bulb: *rhizome*

Flowering season: *fall*

Height: *1½ to 2 feet*

Soil: *moist, fertile*

Light: *full sun*

Crimson flag produces flowers with satiny pointed petals rimming curled stamens. A slender stem carries multiple blossoms above a clump of narrow, sometimes evergreen, leaves. In warm climates, crimson flag may produce sparse flowers in spring and summer as well as a full burst of fall bloom. Crimson flag thrives in bog gardens or alongside streams and ponds. In colder areas, grow crimson flag indoors in containers. It produces excellent cut flowers.

Selected species and varieties: *S. coccinea* (river lily)—1- to 2-inch-deep crimson flower stars; 'Major' produces larger flowers than the species; 'Mrs. Hegarty' is rose pink.

Growing conditions and maintenance: Plant crimson flag outdoors in spring or fall, setting roots 2 inches deep and 9 to 12 inches apart. For containers, start roots outdoors in spring after threat of frost has passed, then pot them to bring indoors for late-fall-to-winter bloom. Propagate by division in spring or fall, although disturbed roots may take a year or more to resume flowering.

Scilla
(SIL-la)
SQUILL

Scilla peruviana

Hardiness: *tender or Zones 3-10*

Type of bulb: *true bulb*

Flowering season: *winter, spring, summer*

Height: *6 to 28 inches*

Soil: *moist, well-drained, fertile*

Light: *full sun to partial shade*

Squills are one of spring's classic bulbs, carpeting the ground beneath taller bulb plants and shrubbery with a haze of tiny bells that open into dainty stars. Sometimes facing upward, sometimes dangling, the blossoms appear in clusters on slender stems clasped at the base by a few narrow, ribbonlike leaves. Mass squill at the edge of borders, in rockeries, or in woodland gardens, where it will naturalize rapidly. Squill can also be forced for indoor bloom.

Selected species and varieties: *S. bifolia* (twinleaf squill)—loose, upright clusters of up to eight tiny ½-inch pale blue flowers on 6-inch stems above two or three leaves in early spring; 'Rosea' is rosy pink; Zones 4-8. *S. litardierei* (meadow squill)—up to 30 tiny ³⁄₁₆-inch blue flowers in a dense tuft on 8-inch stems in spring; Zones 5-8. *S. mischtschenkoana* [formerly *S. tubergeniana*] (Persian bluebell)—multiple 4- to 5-inch stems with sparse clusters of upturned 1½-inch pale blue flowers striped darker blue, and blooming late winter to early spring; Zones 5-8. *S. peruviana* (Peruvian lily, Peruvian jacinth, Cuban lily)—dense, domed 6-

inch clusters of deep violet ½-inch flowers above evergreen leaves on 18-inch stems in summer; Zones 9-10. *S. scilloides* (Chinese squill, Japanese jacinth)—12- to 18-inch leafless stems with clusters of up to 60 deep pink blossoms in summer followed by leaves in fall, sometimes persisting into spring; Zones 5-8. *S. siberica* (Siberian squill)—sparse clusters of nodding ½-inch gentian blue flowers on 4- to 6-inch stems in early spring; 'Alba' is white; 'Spring Beauty' has large, deep blue flower stars; Zones 3-8.

Growing conditions and maintenance: Select squills from reputable breeders who propagate their own bulbs, as collection has endangered many species in the wild. Plant tender Peruvian lilies outdoors in spring, setting bulbs with their necks at the soil line and 8 to 10 inches

Scilla bifolia 'Rosea'

apart. North of Zone 9, grow them as container plants, starting bulbs indoors in late winter for summer bloom. Plant all other squills outdoors in fall, setting bulbs 2 to 3 inches deep and 3 to 6 inches apart. Siberian squill even succeeds under evergreens, where other bulbs fail. Squills, particularly Siberian squill, self-sow easily. They can be propagated from seed to reach blooming-size bulbs in 3 years or by dividing small bulblets produced by mature bulbs in fall.

Sparaxis
(spa-RAKS-is)
WAND FLOWER

Sparaxis grandiflora

Hardiness: *tender or Zones 8-10*

Type of bulb: *corm*

Flowering season: *spring to summer*

Height: *12 inches*

Soil: *well-drained, fertile*

Light: *full sun*

Highly decorative wand flowers produce arching stems of up to five flowers each blooming in bold, splashy color combinations. Pointed petals form shallow saucers above stiff fans of narrow, pointed leaves. In warmer climates, wand flowers naturalize, spreading rapidly in beds, borders, or rock gardens. Elsewhere, they are grown as annuals or container specimens. Wand flowers are prized as cut flowers.

Selected species and varieties: *S. grandiflora*—3-inch flowers in shades of white, rose, and purple, often two-toned. *S. tricolor* (harlequin flower)—2-inch flowers with bright yellow throats rimmed with black or purple, the outer portion of the petals yellow, rose, red, or purple, and sometimes tinged brown.

Growing conditions and maintenance: Plant wand flowers in spring or fall, setting corms 2 to 3 inches deep and 1 to 1½ feet apart. North of Zone 8, plant corms in early spring and lift in fall or plant in containers for indoor forcing. Propagate from seed or by removing small cormels around the base of mature corms.

Sprekelia
(sprek-KEE-lee-a)
SPREKELIA

Sprekelia formosissima

Hardiness: *tender or Zones 9-11*

Type of bulb: *true bulb*

Flowering season: *summer*

Height: *to 12 inches*

Soil: *well-drained, sandy, fertile*

Light: *full sun*

Sprekelia produces orchidlike flowers with six velvety petals, the upper petals erect, the lower ones pinched together at their bases to form a channel for long, curving stamens. Flowers grow singly on leafless stems before a sparse clump of narrow, straplike leaves appear. In warm zones, sprekelia can be grown in the border. Elsewhere, it is grown as an annual or a pot plant.

Selected species and varieties: *S. formosissima* (Jacobean lily, Aztec lily, St. James's lily, orchid amaryllis)—4- to 6-inch deep red-orange or deep crimson flowers with bright yellow stamens and leaves to 12 inches.

Growing conditions and maintenance: Outdoors in Zones 9 and 10, plant Jacobean lilies in any season, setting bulbs 3 to 4 inches deep and 8 to 12 inches apart for blooms in 6 weeks. North of Zone 9, plant the bulbs outdoors in spring and lift in fall for winter storage. Indoors, plant with half the bulb above the soil surface, allowing one bulb per 4-inch pot or three bulbs per 6-inch pot. Propagate by removing bulblets that develop around the base of mature bulbs.

Sternbergia
(stern-BERG-ee-a)
AUTUMN DAFFODIL

Sternbergia lutea

Hardiness: *tender or Zones 6-10*

Type of bulb: *true bulb*

Flowering season: *fall*

Height: *6 to 12 inches*

Soil: *dry, well-drained, sandy*

Light: *full sun*

Autumn daffodils' egg-shaped buds open into deep goblets of shimmering, waxy petals reminiscent of crocuses. The flowers appear on slender stems shorter than the grassy ribbons of the foliage; each bulb commonly produces four or five flowers. Use autumn daffodils in rock gardens, tucked against walls, and in any other hot, dry location. They can also be potted for indoor forcing.

Selected species and varieties: *S. lutea*—1½- to 2-inch golden yellow blossoms on 4-inch stems among 6- to 12-inch leaves.

Growing conditions and maintenance: Plant autumn daffodils in summer, setting bulbs 4 inches deep and 4 to 6 inches apart. Provide a protective coat of winter mulch in Zone 6. North of Zone 6, grow as annuals or in bulb pans, placing five or six bulbs 2 inches deep in each 6-inch pan. Autumn daffodils can be propagated by removing the small bulb offsets from large clumps when flowering diminishes, but they do best when left undisturbed.

Tigridia
(tye-GRID-ee-a)
PEACOCK FLOWER

Tigridia pavonia

Hardiness: *tender or Zones 7-10*

Type of bulb: *corm*

Flowering season: *summer*

Height: *1 to 2 feet*

Soil: *moist, well-drained, fertile*

Light: *full sun*

Peacock flower's unique blossoms are composed of three large outer petals forming a broad triangle enfolding three gaily spotted inner petals united to form a deep cup. The blossoms appear singly on erect stems rising from stiff fans of swordlike leaves. Each flower lasts only a day, but the corms produce a succession of stems over 6 to 8 weeks. Mass peacock flowers for a long show of color in borders and beds, where they will slowly naturalize, or use small clumps as accents.

Selected species and varieties: *T. pavonia* (tiger flower)—white or buff to yellow, orange, purple, or pink 3- to 6-inch flowers with conspicuously spotted and mottled centers; 'Alba' has white outer petals; 'Aurea' is yellow; 'Rosea', rosy pink.

Growing conditions and maintenance: Plant peacock flowers in spring, setting corms 3 to 4 inches deep and 6 to 9 inches apart. Provide a protective winter mulch in Zone 7. North of Zone 7, plant bulbs in spring and lift in fall. Propagate from seed to bloom the first year or by removing the small cormels that develop at the base of mature corms.

Triteleia
(try-TEL-ee-a)
TRITELEIA

Triteleia laxa

Hardiness: *Zones 7-10*

Type of bulb: *corm*

Flowering season: *spring to summer*

Height: *18 to 30 inches*

Soil: *well-drained, sandy*

Light: *full*

Triteleias produce loose clusters of dainty flower stars on tall stems above sparse clumps of grassy leaves. They make good cut flowers and will naturalize in sunny beds, borders, or rock gardens when conditions suit them.

Selected species and varieties: *T. hyacinthina* (wild hyacinth)—flat-topped clusters of up to 30 tiny white, sometimes blue or lilac, ½-inch flower stars blooming late spring to summer on 1- to 2-foot stems. *T. laxa* (grass nut, triplet lily)—loose, open spheres of 1¾-inch blue to violet, sometimes white, flowers on 30-inch stems in spring; 'Queen Fabiola' has dense spheres of pale blue blossoms.

Growing conditions and maintenance: Plant triteleias in fall, setting corms 3 inches deep and 2 to 3 inches apart. They grow best where summers are completely dry, as in the western portions of Zones 8-10. Elsewhere, lift corms after foliage withers to dry for the summer and replant in fall. Provide a protective winter mulch in Zone 7. Propagate from seed to bloom in 2 years or by removing and replanting small cormels that develop around mature bulbs.

Tritonia
(try-TONE-ee-a)
BLAZING STAR

Tritonia crocata

Hardiness: *tender or Zones 7-10*

Type of bulb: *corm*

Flowering season: *spring to summer*

Height: *18 inches*

Soil: *moist, well-drained*

Light: *full sun*

Forming small bowls of pointed petals, tritonia's flowers open along one side of arching flower spikes in a way reminiscent of freesias. Flower stems rise from small fans of narrow pointed leaves. Use tritonia in beds, borders, or rock gardens. The stems make long-lasting cut flowers.

Selected species and varieties: *T. crocata* (flame freesia)—2-inch-wide flowers in a wide range of colors; 'Baby Doll' is salmon; 'Bridal Veil', white; 'Pink Sensation', pink; 'Serendipity', red; 'Tangerine', orange.

Growing conditions and maintenance: Plant tritonia in fall, setting corms 3 to 4 inches deep and 6 inches apart. From Zone 7 north, treat tritonia as an annual, planting in spring and lifting corms in fall for winter storage. Propagate from seed or by removing the small cormels growing around mature corms.

![Tulipa 'Monte Carlo']

Tulipa 'Monte Carlo'

Hardiness: *Zones 3-8, to 10 if chilled*

Type of bulb: *true bulb*

Flowering season: *spring*

Height: *6 to 28 inches*

Soil: *well-drained, sandy, fertile*

Light: *full sun*

Synonymous with spring to many gardeners, tulips' egg-shaped buds unfold into a profusion of forms ranging from inverted bells to flat saucers, stars, urns, deep cups, and lilylike shapes, sometimes with the petals reduced to mere ribbons. Petals may be smooth, curled, frilled, crisped, ruffled, flared, doubled, or waved. Tulips come in every color except true blue and are often striped, edged, flecked, flushed with contrasting color, or "flamed" in a zigzag variegated pattern. The hundreds of tulip species and thousands of hybrids are sorted by botanists into groups with similar origins, shapes, and bloom times. Species tulips, also called wild tulips or botanical tulips, generally have very early flowers on strong, sturdy stems, and are the parents of the taller hybrids, which bloom at various times throughout spring. The botanical *Kaufmanniana*, *Fosteriana*, and *Greigii* tulips merited their own divisions in the latest shuffling of botanical nomenclature. Low-growing species tulips can be grown in rock gardens or as edgings for beds or borders and may naturalize where conditions are right for their growth. Plant taller hybrids in informal groupings or formal patterns where they will produce blooms for several years before requiring renewal. Tulips can be forced for indoor bloom and make excellent cut flowers.

Selected species and varieties: Hybrids and species tulips are organized into 15 divisions used in the garden trade. *Division 1. Single early tulips:* Among the first to flower, in very early spring, on 6- to 14-inch stems with smooth petals in neat cups; 'Apricot Beauty' is salmon edged in apricot; 'Princess Irene', orange-splashed purple. *Division 2. Double early tulips:* Bowls of ruffled, doubled petals up to 4 inches across on 12-inch stems in early spring; 'Monte Carlo' is deep, clear yellow; 'Peach Blossom' has honey-scented soft rose petals edged with cream. *Division 3. Triumph tulips:* Satiny-smooth flowers in mid-

Tulipa 'Apricot Beauty'

spring on 18- to 24-inch stems; 'Attila' is pale purple-violet; 'New Design', cream flushed pink and apricot with leaves edged pinky cream. *Division 4. Darwin hybrid tulips:* Large, smooth-petaled ovals opening into flat cups up to 7 inches across in midspring on stems to 36 inches; 'Daydream' has yellow petals aging to apricot-flushed orange; 'Golden Parade', bright yellow petals edged in red; 'Ivory Floradale' is creamy ivory flecked with red; 'Parade', brilliant fiery red; 'Pink Impression', purplish pink. *Division 5. Single late tulips* [includes Cottage and Darwin tulips]: Distinctly rectangular flower cups, some with pointed petals, in late spring on stems to 30 inches; 'Blushing Beauty' is yellow to apricot-blushed rose; 'Georgette' has clusters of

butter yellow blooms with the edges aging to red; 'Halcro' is raspberry with a yellow base; 'Maureen', cool white; 'Menton', apricot pink; 'Mrs. J. T. Scheepers', pure yellow; 'Queen of the Night', deep maroon, almost black; 'Sweet Harmony', lemon yellow edged in

Tulipa 'Angelique'

white. *Division 6. Lily-flowering tulips:* Urn-shaped buds open in late spring into lilylike flowers with curved, pointed petals on 24-inch stems; 'Red Shine' is deep ruby red with blue center; 'White Triumphator', pure white. *Division 7. Fringed tulips:* Late-spring flowers with very finely fringed petals on 14- to 24-inch stems; 'Burgundy Lace' is deep wine; 'Fringed Elegance', yellow flecked with pink. *Division 8. Viridiflora green tulips:* Late-spring flowers with petals in varying degrees of green on 18-inch stems; 'Spring Green' is ivory white with the center of the petals slashed green. *Division 9. Rembrandt tulips:* Petal color is "broken," or variegated, with elaborately patterned stripes and blotches on 18- to 30-inch stems in midspring; 'Cordell Hull' is white streaked with red. *Division 10. Parrot tulips:* Tousled petals, exotically fringed, waved, crisped, and flared, on flowers blooming in late spring on stems to 24 inches; 'Flaming Parrot' is deep yellow flamed with crimson. *Division 11. Double late tulips* [also called *peony-flowered tulips*]: Bowls of doubled petals in late spring on 16- to 24-inch stems; 'Angelique' is deep pink shading to pale pink; 'Miranda', two shades of red with a yellow base. *Division 12. Kaufmanniana tulips:* Urn-shaped buds opening into large flowers with curved petals on stems under 12 inches in very early spring; 'Ancila' is soft rosy pink outside, white inside; 'Show Winner', deep scarlet. *Division 13. Fosteriana tulips:* Enormous blossoms in early spring on stems to 18 inches; 'Juan' is orange with a yellow base; 'Red Emperor', deep red. *Division 14. Greigii tulips:* Flowers on strong, 8- to 16-inch stems above attractively purple-mottled foliage; 'Czar Peter' is red rimmed with white; 'Red Riding Hood', deep red-orange with a black base. *Division 15. Species tulips:* T. bakeri 'Lilac Wonder'—rosy purple cups with yellow bases on 6-inch stems; Zones 5-9. *T. batalinii* 'Bright Gem'—yellow cups of pointed petals flushed orange, 6 inches tall; Zones 3-8. *T. clusiana* var. *chrysantha* [also called *T. chrysantha*] (golden lady tulip)—deep saucers, yellow inside, crimson edged with yellow outside, 12 inches tall; Zones 3-9. *T. dasystemon*

Tulipa dasystemon

(Kuen Lun tulip)—clusters of white flower stars tinged bronze and green, 4 inches tall; Zones 4-8. *T. linifolia* (slim-leaf tulip)—curled, pointed electric red petals and red-rimmed leaves, 6 inches tall; Zones 4-8. *T. pulchella* 'Violacea' (red crocus tulip)—tiny purple-red ovals tinged green at their bases, 3½ inches tall; Zones 5-8. *T. turkestanica*—clusters of white flower stars tinged violet, 5 inches tall; Zones 5-8.

Growing conditions and maintenance: Plant tulips in late fall, setting them at a depth equal to three times their diameter, or between 4 and 8 inches deep. Space according to bulb size; tulips can be thickly planted with no ill effect on bloom size, and close spacing enhances their impact. Plant up to 40 hybrid bulbs

per square yard or up to 60 smaller species bulbs per square yard. Note, however, that the famous variegation of Rembrandt tulips is caused by a virus that does not hurt them but can be harmful if spread to lilies and other tulips by aphids. Site Rembrandts far from susceptible plants. In Zones 9 and 10, tulips must be prechilled. It is preferable to buy them in that condition, but you can prechill them

Tulipa pulchella 'Violacea'

yourself by placing them in a vented paper bag in the refrigerator at 40° F for 9 to 12 weeks before setting them out; in modern frost-free refrigerators, however, you run the risk of drying them out. *T. bakeri* 'Lilac Wonder', *T. clusiana* var. *chrysantha*, and the hybrids 'Burgundy Lace', 'Flaming Parrot', 'Golden Parade', 'Halcro', 'Maureen', 'Menton', and 'Mrs. J. T. Scheepers' require no prechilling and may naturalize in warm zones. Allow foliage to ripen before mowing or removing it. Tulips tend to disappear over time; either treat them as annuals or dig and replant bulbs every 2 to 3 years as flowering diminishes. For indoor forcing, buy prechilled bulbs or refrigerate bulbs for several weeks, then plant up to eight bulbs 2 inches deep in a 6-inch pot. Keeping the soil mix damp, hold potted bulbs in a cool, dark spot at about 60° F for 10 to 12 weeks while roots form, then bring into a warm room between 65° and 70° F for bloom. Early single and double tulips will take 3 to 4 weeks to bloom; Darwins and other hybrid tulips, 6 to 9 weeks. Temperatures over 70° F will result in weak stems and poor bloom. Discard bulbs after forcing. Propagate tulips by removing bulb offsets, which will grow to blooming size in 2 to 3 years.

Urginea
(ur-GIN-ee-a)
URGINEA

Urginea maritima

Hardiness:	*tender or Zones 8-10*
Type of bulb:	*true bulb*
Flowering season:	*fall*
Height:	*3 to 5 feet*
Soil:	*dry, sandy*
Light:	*full sun*

Urgineas produce long spikes of up to 100 tiny flowers at the tips of tall stems that can be bent or twisted by the weight of the blossoms. The flower stalks appear in advance of a rosette of shiny, fleshy, narrow leaves. Plant urgineas at the back of beds and borders in areas that can provide dry summers while they are dormant. Elsewhere, plant them as pot specimens.

Selected species and varieties: *U. maritima* (sea onion, sea squill)—18-inch spikes of ½-inch white, yellow, or pink blossoms that open from bottom to top followed by 4-inch-wide leaves up to 18 inches long.

Growing conditions and maintenance: Plant sea onions in summer with the upper portion of the bulb out of the soil, spacing bulbs 12 to 18 inches apart. The bulb juice is irritating, and all parts of the plant are poisonous. North of Zone 9, pot bulbs in summer for fall bloom outdoors, then take foliage indoors to ripen. Propagate by removing bulb offsets in summer.

Vallota
(va-LO-ta)
GEORGE LILY

Vallota speciosa

Hardiness: *tender or Zones 10-11*

Type of bulb: *true bulb*

Flowering season: *summer to fall*

Height: *3 feet*

Soil: *well-drained, sandy, fertile*

Light: *full sun*

Vallota [also called *Cyrtanthus*] bears whorls of amaryllis-like blossoms with pointed petals forming deep trumpets around long, prominent stamens. Clusters of up to 10 flowers grow atop sturdy stems above clumps of straplike evergreen leaves. Vallotas can be used in beds and borders in very warm regions. Elsewhere they are cultivated as pot plants.

Selected species and varieties: *V. speciosa* [also called *Cyrtanthus elatus*] (Scarborough lily)—3-inch-wide deep scarlet, sometimes pink or white, flower funnels above 2-foot leaves.

Growing conditions and maintenance: Plant Scarborough lilies outdoors in Zones 10 and 11 in early spring, setting bulb tips at the soil line and spacing them 15 to 18 inches apart. For pot culture, allow one bulb per 6-inch pot and place bulbs only halfway into soil. Bulbs potted in spring will bloom in fall; soil should be kept damp during winter dormancy. Repot bulbs every 5 to 6 years, removing for propagation the small bulblets growing around the base of mature bulbs.

Veltheimia
(vel-TY-mee-a)
RED-HOT POKER

Veltheimia bracteata

Hardiness: *tender or Zones 10-11*

Type of bulb: *true bulb*

Flowering season: *late winter to spring*

Height: *15 to 20 inches*

Soil: *well-drained, sandy*

Light: *full sun*

Red-hot poker's oval clusters of up to 50 flower buds open from bottom to top into long, drooping funnels with curled lips. Clusters are carried on sturdy stems above attractive rosettes of glossy green leaves with wavy edges. Both leaves and stems are attractively mottled. Use red-hot poker outdoors in warm climates; grow as a pot plant elsewhere.

Selected species and varieties: *V. bracteata*—2-inch pink-red or pink-purple blossoms with green-and-white flecked lips above foliage and stems marbled green and purple.

Growing conditions and maintenance: Outdoors in Zones 10 and 11, plant red-hot poker bulbs 1 inch deep and 6 to 10 inches apart in fall. In pots, group several of the large, 6-inch bulbs together in large bulb pans for best effect. Plant them 4 to 6 inches apart with the top third of the bulb exposed and allow bulbs to dry off during summer dormancy. Propagate by removing bulb offsets after foliage withers.

Watsonia
(wot-SONE-ee-a)
BUGLE LILY

Watsonia 'Pink Opal'

Hardiness: *tender or Zones 8-10*

Type of bulb: *corm*

Flowering season: *spring or summer*

Height: *18 to 60 inches*

Soil: *well-drained*

Light: *full sun*

Bugle lily's simple flower funnels bloom around the tips of slightly arching stems above clumps of narrow, sword-shaped leaves. The spikes of blossoms which open from bottom to top are similar to gladiolus but are daintier and less formal. Bugle lilies will slowly form clumps in gardens in warm climates. Elsewhere, they can be grown as annuals. They make long-lasting cut flowers.

Selected species and varieties: *W.* hybrids—2- to 3-inch flowers in pastel shades; 'Bright Eyes' is powder pink; 'Dazzle', soft orange with a purple throat; 'Humilis' has pink flowers on 18-inch dwarf stems; 'Mrs. Bullard's White' is pure white; 'Pink Opal', bright pink; 'Rubra', dusty reddish purple.

Growing conditions and maintenance: Outdoors in Zones 8-10, plant bugle lily corms 3 inches deep and 6 to 9 inches apart in fall for spring blooms. Elsewhere, plant in spring for summer blooms, then lift in fall after foliage withers. Propagate from seed, although seedlings can be difficult to transplant, or by removing cormels.

Zantedeschia
(zan-tee-DES-ki-a)
CALLA LILY

Zantedeschia aethiopica

Hardiness: *tender or Zones 9-10*

Type of bulb: *rhizome*

Flowering season: *summer or fall*

Height: *2 to 3 feet*

Soil: *moist to well-drained*

Light: *full sun to partial shade*

Calla lily's gracefully curved and sculpted flowers have a cool, formal elegance few other blooms can match. Petal-like spathes curl into elongated trumpets with a flared lip pulled to a point. The waxy spathe curls around a colorful, sometimes fragrant, fingerlike spadix bearing the true flowers, which are tiny and inconspicuous. Up to 12 or more blossoms bloom at the same time amid broad, stalked, arrow-shaped leaves with wavy edges that are often heavily flecked and spotted with white for added interest. In warm zones, calla lilies are eye-catching specimens for beds or borders and will naturalize where conditions suit them. Elsewhere they are grown as annuals or as pot plants for patio or indoor use. Callas are prized as cut flowers.

Selected species and varieties: *Z. aethiopica* (common calla, giant white calla, arum lily, trumpet lily)—fragrant, snowy white flowers 10 inches long on 2-foot plants; 'Perle Von Stuttgart' is somewhat smaller than the species, with abundant blossoms. *Z. albomaculata* (spotted calla, black-throated calla)—

5-inch white flowers with purple throats on 2-foot plants. *Z. elliottiana* (golden calla, yellow calla)—6-inch golden yellow flowers, tinged greenish yellow on the outside, on 2½-foot plants. *Z. rehmannii* (red calla, pink calla)—3-inch pink flowers on 18- to 24-inch plants. *Z. hybrids*—'Black-Eyed Beauty' produces creamy white blossoms veined green, with a black throat or eye rimming the spadix; 'Black Magic' is yellow with a black eye; 'Cameo', salmon; 'Harvest Moon' is yellow with a red eye; 'Pink Persuasion', purple-pink; 'Solfatare' is a creamy pale yellow with a black eye.

Zantedeschia rehmannii

Growing conditions and maintenance: Outdoors in Zones 8-10, plant calla lilies in spring or fall, setting rhizomes 1 to 4 inches deep and spacing them 1 to 2 feet apart. Calla lilies tolerate boggy conditions and can be grown with their roots in water at the edges of ponds. North of Zone 8, start them indoors in early spring and transplant them outside after all danger of frost has passed for blooming in summer. Lift rhizomes in fall after foliage withers and store for winter. For pot culture, set growing tips of rhizomes at soil level and allow one root per 6-inch pot. Callas bloom about 2 months after planting. Golden calla lily can be propagated from seed. Propagate all calla lilies by dividing their rhizomes in spring or fall.

Zephyranthes
(ze-fi-RANTH-eez)
ZEPHYR LILY

Zephyranthes candida

Hardiness: *tender or Zones 8-10*

Type of bulb: *true bulb*

Flowering season: *spring, summer, or fall*

Height: *8 to 36 inches*

Soil: *moist, well-drained, rich*

Light: *full sun*

Zephyr lilies produce open stars of pointed petals surrounding a center of short, tiny stamens. The flowers face gaily upward on hollow stems above tufts of grassy leaves. They are mildly fragrant and sometimes open at night. The atamasco lily is excellent for naturalizing in borders or lawns, although its bulbs are poisonous. The other species need warm climates or may be grown as pot plants.

Selected species and varieties: *Z. atamasco* (atamasco lily)—3-inch white flowers tinged purple, blooming in early spring; Zones 7-10. *Z. candida* (westwindflower)—2-inch white flowers tinged rose in summer to fall; Zones 9-10. *Z. rosea* (Cuban zephyr-lily)—1-inch rose pink fall flowers; Zones 9-10.

Growing conditions and maintenance: Plant zephyr lilies 1 to 2 inches deep and 3 to 4 inches apart in spring. North of their hardiness range, plant them in spring and dig bulbs in fall after foliage dies back for winter storage. Keep stored bulbs barely damp. Propagate from seed or by removing bulb offsets.

Acknowledgments

The editors wish to thank the following individuals and institutions for their valuable assistance in the preparation of this volume: Geoff and Susan Cline, Los Angeles, Calif.; John Elsley, Wayside Gardens, Hodges, S.C.; Dr. August A. De Hertogh, College of Agriculture and Life Sciences, Department of Horticultural Sciences, North Carolina State University, Raleigh; Sally Ferguson, Netherlands FlowerBulb Information Center, Brooklyn; Carl Fischer, Noweta Gardens, St. Charles, Minn.; Bob and Dianna Gibson, B & D Lilies, Pleasant Valley, Wash.; Nicholas Gitts, Swan Island Dahlias, Canby, Ore.; Dr. Jack Hall, Horticultural Sciences, Virginia Polytechnic Institute and State University, Blacksburg; Becky Heath, The Daffodil Mart, Gloucester, Va.; Mr. and Mrs. Walter L. Hooker, Richmond; Internationaal Bloembollen Centrum, Hellegom, The Netherlands; Sherrie and Barry Jones, Alexandria, Va.; Bill Kennedy, Horticulturist, John Scheepers, Inc., Banton, Conn.; Sophie Langeveld, Horticulturist, Netherland Bulb Company, Easton, Pa.; Mr. and Mrs. Henry H. McVey III, Schley, Va.; LeRoy S. Nordhal, Silver Spring, Md.; Ray Struntz, Gaithersburg, Md.; Winky Woodriff, Fairyland Begonia Garden, McKinleyville, Calif.

Picture Credits

Bibliography

Books:

Bales, Suzanne Frutig. *Bulbs* (Burpee American Gardening series). New York: Prentice Hall Gardening, 1992.

Ball, Jeff, and Liz Ball: *Rodale's Flower Garden Problem Solver.* Emmaus, Pa.: Rodale Press, 1990. *Rodale's Landscape Problem Solver.* Emmaus, Pa.: Rodale Press, 1989.

Baumgardt, John Philip. *Bulbs for Summer Bloom.* New York: Hawthorn Books, 1970.

Brickell, Christopher (Ed.). *The American Horticultural Society Encyclopedia of Garden Plants.* New York: Macmillan, 1989.

Bryan, John E.: *Bulbs.* (2 vols.). Portland, Ore.: Timber Press, 1989. *John E. Bryan on Bulbs* (Burpee Expert Gardener series). New York: Macmillan, 1994.

Bryan, John E. (Ed.). *Bulbs* (Hearst Garden Guides). New York: Hearst Books, 1992.

Capon, Brian. *Botany for Gardeners.* Portland, Ore.: Timber Press, 1990.

Carr, Anna, et al. *Rodale's Chemical-Free Yard and Garden.* Emmaus, Pa.: Rodale Press, 1991.

Damp, Philip. *Dahlias.* Chester, Conn.: Globe Pequot Press, 1988.

De Hertogh, August A. *Spring Flowering Bulbs, 1986.* Translated by J. M. Visser. Raleigh: North Carolina State University, 1985.

De Hertogh, August, and Marcel Le Nard (Eds.). *The Physiology of Flower Bulbs.* Amsterdam, The Netherlands: Elsevier Science Publishers, 1993.

Doutt, Richard L. *Cape Bulbs.* Portland, Ore.: Timber Press, 1994.

Ellis, Quin. *A Bulb for All Seasons.* New York: Hearst Books, 1994.

Elwes, Henry John. *Lilies.* Compiled by Patrick M. Synge. New York: Universe Books, 1980.

Fox, Derek. *Growing Lilies.* London: Croom Helm, 1985.

Free, Montague. *Plant Propagation in Pictures.* Revised and edited by Marjorie J. Dietz. Garden City, N.Y.: Doubleday, 1979.

Garden Design Ideas (The Best of Fine Gardening). Newtown, Conn.: Taunton, 1994.

Gillanders, K. D., G. M. Paterson, and E. R. Rotherham. *Know Your Rock Garden Plants and Dwarf Bulbs.* Sidney, Australia: A. H. and A. W. Reed, 1973.

Glattstein, Judy. *The American Gardener's World of Bulbs.* Boston: Little, Brown, 1994.

Griffiths, Mark. *Index of Garden Plants.* Portland, Ore.: Timber Press, 1994.

Halliwell, Brian. *The Propagation of Alpine Plants and Dwarf Bulbs.* Portland, Ore.: Timber Press, 1992.

Hartmann, Hudson T., Dale E. Kester, and Fred T. Davies. *Plant Propagation Principles and Practices.* (5th ed.). Englewood Cliffs, N.J.: Prentice Hall, 1990.

Hobbs, Jack, and Terry Hatch. *Best Bulbs for Temperate Climates.* Portland, Ore.: Timber Press, 1994.

Hobhouse, Penelope. *Color in Your Garden.* Boston: Little, Brown, 1985.

Horton, Alvin, and James MacNair. *All about Bulbs.* San Ramon, Calif.: Ortho Books, 1986.

Ireys, Alice Recknagel. *Garden Designs* (Burpee American Gardening series). New York: Prentice Hall Gardening, 1991.

James, Theodore, Jr. (text), and Harry Haralambou (photography). *Flowering Bulbs Indoors and Out.* New York: Macmillan, 1991.

Jefferson-Brown, M. *A Plantsman's Guide to Lilies.* London: Ward Lock, 1989.

Liberty Hyde Bailey Hortorium. *Hortus Third.* New York: Macmillan, 1976.

Mackey, Betty, et al. *The Gardener's Home Companion.* New York: Macmillan, 1991.

Mathew, Brian: *Dwarf Bulbs.* New York: Arco, 1973. *The Larger Bulbs.* London: B. T. Batsford, 1978. *Lilies: A Romantic History with a Guide to Cultivation.* Edited by Geraldine Christy. Philadelphia: Running Press, 1993.

Mathew, Brian, and Philip Swindells. *The Complete Book of Bulbs, Corms, Tubers, and Rhizomes.* Pleasantville, N.Y.: Reader's Digest Association, 1994.

Olkowski, William, Sheila Daar, and Helga Olkowski. *Common-Sense Pest Control.* Newtown, Conn.: Taunton Press, 1991.

Phillips, Roger, and Martyn Rix. *The Random House Book of Bulbs.* Edited by Brian Mathew. New York: Random House, 1989.

Proctor, Rob: *The Indoor Potted Bulb.* New York: Simon and Schuster, 1993. *The Outdoor Potted Bulb.*

New York: Simon and Schuster, 1993.
Reader's Digest Illustrated Guide to Gardening. Pleasantville, N.Y.: Reader's Digest Association, 1978.
Reynolds, Marc, and William L. Meachem. *The Garden Bulbs of Spring.* New York: Funk and Wagnalls, 1967.
Rix, Martyn. *Growing Bulbs.* Portland, Ore.: Timber Press, 1983.
Rockwell, F. F., Esther C. Grayson, and Jan de Graaff. *The Complete Book of Lilies.* Garden City, N.Y.: Doubleday, 1961.
Schauenberg, Paul. *The Bulb Book.* New York: Frederick Warne, 1965.
Scott, George Harmon. *Bulbs: How to Select, Grow and Enjoy.* Tucson, Ariz.: HPBooks, 1982.
Simpson, Norman. *The Instant Guide to Healthy Indoor Bulbs and Annuals.* New York: Times Books, 1984.
Taylor's Guide to Bulbs. Boston: Houghton Mifflin, 1986.

Taylor's Guide to Garden Design. Boston: Houghton Mifflin, 1988.
Thompson, Mildred L., and Edward J. Thompson. *Begonias.* New York: Times Books, 1981.
Thompson, Peter: *Creative Propagation.* Portland, Ore.: Timber Press, 1992.
Propagator's Handbook. North Pomfret, Vt.: Trafalgar Square Publishing, 1993.
Toogood, Alan. *Propagation.* New York: Stein and Day, 1980.
Welling, Eleanor. *The Dahlia Primer.* Mayfield Heights, Ohio: Norawell Publishing, 1992.
Wilder, Louise Beebe. *Adventures with Hardy Bulbs.* New York: Macmillan, 1990 (reprint of 1936 edition).
Wilson, Jim. *Landscaping with Container Plants.* Boston: Houghton Mifflin, 1990.
Wyman, Donald. *Wyman's Gardening Encyclopedia.* New York: Macmillan, 1986.

Periodicals:
Bilderback, Diane. "Dahlias." *National Gardening,* March/April 1995.
Ferreniea, Viki. "Intimate Charm from Species Tulips." *Fine Gardening,* September/October 1994.
Fischer, Thomas. "Stars of Summer." *Horticulture,* August/September 1993.
Frese, Paul. "Paint Spring Pictures with Bulbs." *Flower and Garden,* September 1988.
"Gardener's World of Bulbs." *Plants and Gardens, Brooklyn Botanic Garden Record,* 1991.
Glattstein, Judy: "Little Bulbs Give Lots of Color." *Flower and Garden,* September 1987.
"Summer-Blooming Bulbs." *Flower and Garden,* April 1990.
Hayward, Gordon. "A Procession of Spring Bulbs and Ferns." *Horticulture,* March 1987.
Hensel, Margaret. "The Layered Look." *Horticulture,* May

1994.
Mattern, Vicki. "The First Colors of Spring." *Organic Gardening,* September/October 1991.
Miller, Harold. *Dahlias: A Monthly Guide.* Bellevue, Wash.: Puget Sound Dahlia Association, 1978.
Polk, Nancy K. "Rock Styles—Create a Striking Habitat for Alpine or Other Compact Plants in a Rock Garden." *Organic Gardening,* April 1990.
Reilly, Ann. *Landscaping with Bulbs.* (Storey Publishing Bulletin A-99). Pownal, Vt.: Storey Communications, 1987.
Ross, Marty, "Celebrate Species Tulips." *Flower and Garden,* October/November 1993.
Sheldon, Elizabeth. "Rock Gardening without a Rock Garden." *Horticulture,* April 1987.
Shreet, Joy Sharon. "Growing Hardy Cyclamen." *Fine Gardening,* September/October 1991.

Index

Other Publications:
THE NEW HOME REPAIR AND IMPROVEMENT
JOURNEY THROUGH THE MIND AND BODY
WEIGHT WATCHERS® SMART CHOICE RECIPE COLLECTION
TRUE CRIME
THE AMERICAN INDIANS
THE ART OF WOODWORKING
LOST CIVILIZATIONS
ECHOES OF GLORY
THE NEW FACE OF WAR
HOW THINGS WORK
WINGS OF WAR
CREATIVE EVERYDAY COOKING
COLLECTOR'S LIBRARY OF THE UNKNOWN
CLASSICS OF WORLD WAR II
TIME-LIFE LIBRARY OF CURIOUS AND UNUSUAL FACTS
AMERICAN COUNTRY
VOYAGE THROUGH THE UNIVERSE
THE THIRD REICH
MYSTERIES OF THE UNKNOWN
TIME FRAME
FIX IT YOURSELF
FITNESS, HEALTH & NUTRITION
SUCCESSFUL PARENTING
HEALTHY HOME COOKING
UNDERSTANDING COMPUTERS
LIBRARY OF NATIONS
THE ENCHANTED WORLD
THE KODAK LIBRARY OF CREATIVE PHOTOGRAPHY
GREAT MEALS IN MINUTES
THE CIVIL WAR
PLANET EARTH
COLLECTOR'S LIBRARY OF THE CIVIL WAR
THE EPIC OF FLIGHT
THE GOOD COOK
WORLD WAR II
THE OLD WEST

For information on and a full description of any of
the Time-Life Books series listed above, please call
1-800-621-7026 or write:
Reader Information
Time-Life Customer Service
P.O. Box C-32068
Richmond, Virginia 23261-2068

18.95

26,854-96 ✓

26,854-96 ✓